WHEN SUNFLOWERS BLOOMED RED

Kansas and the Rise of Socialism in America

R. ALTON LEE & STEVEN COX

University of Nebraska Press

LINCOLN

Portions of chapter 8 were previously published in "Drought and Depression on the Great Plains: The Kansas Transition from New Deal Work Relief to Old Age Pensions," *Heritage of the Great Plains* 34 (Spring–Summer 2006).

Publication of this volume was assisted by a grant from the Friends of the University of Nebraska Press.

Library of Congress Cataloging-in-Publication Data
Names: Lee, R. Alton, author. | Cox, Steven, 1958– author.
Title: When sunflowers bloomed red: Kansas and the rise of socialism in America / R. Alton Lee and Steven Cox.
Description: Lincoln: University of Nebraska Press, [2020] | Includes bibliographical references and index.
Identifiers: LCCN 2019019371
ISBN 9781496216236 (cloth)
ISBN 9781496219800 (epub)
ISBN 9781496219824 (pdf)
ISBN 9781496219817 (mobi)
Subjects: LCSH: Socialism—Kansas—History—20th century. | Kansas—Social conditions—20th century. | Kansas—Politics and government—1865–1950.
Classification: LCC HX91.K4 L44 2020 | DDC 320.53/109781—dc23
LC record available at https://lccn.loc.gov/2019019371

Set in Janson LT Pro by Mikala R. Kolander.

For Braden and his world

I hope he wants to read this book someday, not just because "Grandpa" dedicated it to him but because he will find it an interesting and important story.

R. ALTON LEE

CONTENTS

ILLUSTRATIONS

TABLES

ACKNOWLEDGMENTS

We are indebted to many people for assistance in researching this project. The Kansas History Center tops this list with its various collections and state newspapers on microfilm. The archivists—Teresa, Susan, Lin, Sarah—are a congenial, highly competent group that have been of great assistance over the years. Randy Roberts of Axe Library, at Pittsburg (Kansas) State University, provided his usual professional help on the Tri-State Socialists; Jeremy Drouin of the Kansas City (Missouri) Public Library helped with the library's clipping file; and Frank Nelson of the White City (Kansas) Public Library was efficient in facilitating interlibrary loans. We are especially indebted to William C. Pratt's essay "Historians and the Lost World of Kansas Radicalism." Following some of his suggestions and interpretations made this a better study than it would have been otherwise. Matthew Bokovoy of the University of Nebraska Press has been most supportive and professional through the production process.

ABBREVIATIONS

ADL	American Defense League
AWIA	American Workers Industrial Association
AWO	American Workers Organization
AWU	American Workers Union
CCC	Civilian Conservation Corps
CPI	Committee on Public Information
CPUSA	Communist Party USA
CWA	Civil Works Administration
EPIC	End Poverty in California
ERAA	Emergency Relief Appropriations Act
FERA	Federal Emergency Relief Administration
FSRA	Federal Surplus Relief Administration
FU	Farmers Union
GEB	General Executive Board
IWW	Industrial Workers of the World (Wobblies)
KAW	Kansas Allied Workers (later renamed Kansas Workers Alliance)
KERC	Kansas Emergency Relief Commission
KSHS	Kansas State Historical Society
NAM	National Association of Manufacturers
NEC	National Economic Committee
NPL	Nonpartisan League
NWA	National Women's Alliance
OWIU	Oil Workers Industrial Union
PWA	Public Works Administration
RA	Resettlement Administration

UMW   United Mine Workers

WAA   Workers Alliance of America

WFM   Western Federation of Miners

WNC   Women's National Committee

WPA   Works Progress Administration (later renamed Works
       Projects Administration)

YMCA   Young Men's Christian Association

WHEN SUNFLOWERS BLOOMED RED

INTRODUCTION

The extension of the process [of common ownership] until all the means
of production are brought under collective control, would realize the ideal,
exclusive ownership, . . . but the centralization must be extended so that
the collective ownership shall dominate and control all other ownership.

CHARLES H. VAIL, "Modern Socialism," *Worker's Chronicle*, February 13, 1913

Socialism, as used in this study, includes a broad spec-
trum ranging from the mild Fabians to the anarchists
of the nineteenth century to the radical Communists
of the twentieth. Kansas and the region had a mixed heritage of
agrarian radicalism. In the latter part of the nineteenth century
the Sunflower State was on the cutting edge of radical reforms,
using its powers to experiment with change. This strategy began
with the Alliance movement in the 1880s and continued with
the Populists in the 1890s. When the Populist Party collapsed
at the turn of the twentieth century, Socialists pressed for these
reforms for a decade and a half, until World War I produced a
deep-seated reaction and a split in the Socialist Party that lasted
for the remainder of the twentieth century, with sporadic out-
bursts of reform. As Fred Whitehead wrote, during this early
liberal period the state served as "a dramatic laboratory of social
experimentation, free thought, and wild political insurgency."[1]

In Government 101 we were taught the sophomoric definition of *socialism* as the government ownership and control of the
means of production and distribution. We later found out that

the notion of socialism was far more complicated. It was basically about love and care for the working class, agrarian and industrial.

Socialism has many versions and many supporters who played different roles in the Kansas movement. In that context it basically promoted the contention that the worker deserves the full value of his production through his labor. Capitalism was despised because, under this system, the capitalist exploits the worker's production by taking advantage of his labor.

The Marxian idea of class conflict imported from Europe was the ideal; this vision was adapted to different areas as American Socialists produced variations of the theme, but all would accept the concept that workers were exploited by capitalists and a system must be found to eliminate or at least mitigate this cruel process. In addition, most Socialists were pacifists because capitalists also exploited them by engaging in wars that were fought by laborers who lost goods and sometimes their lives in fighting these capitalist conflicts.

Socialists, as a rule, did not reject Christianity but anticipated the harmony and well-being of Christ's love once workers defeated the oppressive capitalist class and established public ownership and cooperative production. The Socialist Revolution, they believed, would result in the Kingdom of Christ. But first they must demolish capitalism. Regardless of which brand of Christianity, or atheism, the individual worker preferred, their common theme was to love thy neighbor. Once the revolution was accomplished, the freed workers would govern themselves through a coalition of equals chosen for the task.

The post–Civil War era saw the rise and spread of the Industrial Revolution in America, with its great benefits and great suffering for the workingman. Workers and farmers were placed at the mercy of the capitalist class, facing hazardous working conditions, low rates of pay, long hours, and no fringe benefits. Miners especially endured dangerous respiratory diseases, such as silicosis, as well as tunnel collapses and gas explosions. They faced the hazards of dealing with the company store, where they were forced to purchase necessities at exorbitant prices with the use of "clacker," or company money they received as pay. If they tried to strike to improve their conditions, Kansas miners also faced the probability of being replaced by black workers who migrated from the South after the war.

In Kansas industrial laborers were largely confined to the Tri-State Mining Region of the corners of southeastern Kansas, southwestern Missouri, and northeastern Oklahoma, areas with rich deposits of tin, lead, zinc, and low-grade coal. Mining was not an attractive occupation to Native Americans, so the Tri-State region attracted European miners from Great Britain, France, Italy, and the Balkan states.

Kansas workers first turned to unions to redress their grievances. Alexander Howat's District 14 of the United Mine Workers was a great success, with 100 percent membership. At the same time the Socialist movement was very attractive to downtrodden workers, both the American version espoused by Eugene V. Debs and the kind of socialism that these workers brought with them from Europe. This brand of political activity held workers in high esteem as socialism had as its key premise that we are our brother's keeper. The main goal of American socialism was to improve the workingman's lot in life through collective action.[2]

Socialism provided workers even more than this. To the young activist, socialism seemed to have not only goals but plans to achieve them that other political parties lacked. The "labor problem" sparked by the Industrial Revolution and the rise of big business arrived on the East Coast in 1877 and spread rapidly westward to Kansas with the railroad strike of that year. It gave rise to many reform movements, but the violence was finally suppressed with federal troops and in the process frightened the ruling capitalist class. These reform efforts were finally suppressed by federal troops and failed to unite workers, both rural and urban.

Soon after the Civil War ended, citizens of foreign birth flocked to the new state of Kansas, some directly from the homelands and others after originally moving to other parts of the United States. Heavily European, they took advantage of the land available, and ethnic communities arose as a result. In the late nineteenth century they lived in a state that was either Republican or Democrat, with only moderate opposition or competition from a third

party. The *American Nonconformist*, a radical paper and a major
voice for reform in Iowa, found a welcoming home in Kansas in
1886; it was published in Winfield for five years before moving
to Indiana. Its growth coincided with the rise of the Knights of
Labor, one of whose leaders, Christian Hoffman, a Kansan originally from Europe, became a key national figure in the Populist movement.[3]

For its first thirty years as a state, Kansas was mostly Republican. The population expanded in those early decades, and railways were built, crisscrossing the state. Industry spread into the
new state from the East. Kansans, who were at first agricultur-
ally minded, were becoming more industrialized. Farming had
provided a good living for many, but some farmers failed. Tax
issues, political graft, and agricultural problems resulted in disgruntled citizens. The economy suffered as taxes rose, ultimately
forcing many Kansans to look to alternative political groups or
parties to help them deal with the instability. Reforms were suggested, and political reform parties were created. From this rose
the Populist Party in Kansas.[4]

The Populist movement proved to be the next great protest
movement, but it, too, was unable to unite the working classes
politically. Many members of the Greenback-Labor Party and
the Knights of Labor joined with Prohibitionists, agrarian Democrats, and restive Republicans to form the People's, or Populist,
Party. When the Populist fusion with the regular Democrats fell
short of victory in 1896, the lack of "fishes and loaves," as Theodore Roosevelt expressed his loss in 1912, left the Populists without the political adhesive of patronage, and these malcontents
faced few acceptable political options. Many easily migrated to
socialism, which was gaining greater respectability by the turn of
the twentieth century under the aegis of the Progressive Reform
movement. Remnants of these various reform groups met in Indianapolis in 1901 and, singing the Marseillaise, formed the Socialist Party of America.[5]

During the Progressive movement (1890–1920) socialism
threatened to become a viable force in American political life.
With horror stories washing ashore about the radical theories and

activities of European Socialists, a majority of Americans feared this movement and tended to categorize its adherents as the caricatured bomb-throwing radicals who were intent on destroying the "American way of life." Most Kansans, who reflected middle-class values, joined this majority.[6]

The American Socialists were even more of an umbrella political party than most because they could never agree fully on a core set of beliefs. The socialism the German immigrants brought with them from Europe, that of the German political activist Ferdinand Lassalle, was popular in cities of the Eastern Seaboard and Chicago but never really found an audience on the conservative Great Plains. It seemed that every year Socialists were faced with issues that forced them to accept reconciliation or splinter into factionalism. Discord among adherents of socialism began in 1901, when Morris Hillquit, leader of New York Socialists, and Austrian-born Victor Berger of Milwaukee convinced Eugene V. Debs to form a coalition party. Debs acquiesced in this merger but soon joined William "Big Bill" Haywood to organize the Industrial Workers of the World (iww), or "Wobblies." When Debs found the iww to be unmanageable, in true Socialist fashion he joined the moderates, leaving Haywood with both his Western Federation of Miners (wfm) and the iww.[7]

From its beginnings in 1901, the Socialist Labor Party, led by newspaperman Daniel De Leon, refused to merge with the Socialist majority, a coalition of regional groups under Debs's leadership that often professed differing points of view. His group remained a doctrinaire segment of Marxist thinkers who anticipated the masses rising up to throw off their chains and establish by force the classless society of the future. This majority remained catholic in their national organization and sometimes had little in common beyond their red card membership. They insisted on pursuing a peaceful program to achieve their goals through the ballot box, forcing De Leon to withdraw from the movement in disgust. The members amended the Socialist constitution to bar anyone who advocated violence and in 1912 expelled Haywood and his wfm from the Socialist Party. Haywood subsequently became the leader of the iww, which used force to achieve its goals. The Fabian Socialists completely rejected the class struggle and its accompanying violence. The foreign-language federations constituted a splinter group that was essentially strong among the Finns of the Upper Midwest.[8]

Socialists everywhere insisted that capitalism was the root of almost all of society's evils. It produced periods of economic boom or bust, exploited workers, and resulted in poverty, hunger, and misery for the masses. Capitalists, they argued, were responsible for the world's wars and most of the ills of Western civilization. Socialists felt that Americans must abandon this evil system and institute one in which the people collectively owned the means of production and distribution. This revolution was inevitable: all that the workers needed to do was to rise up against their masters, throw off their chains, and establish the corporate commonwealth with all who produced society's goods. But Socialists differed mightily over the process of bringing about this utopia.[9]

Such an amalgamation often produced family fights when all could have pulled together. The American Federation of Labor (AFL) had the same goal as the Socialists, helping the working class, but the two groups were at odds. The De Leon faction wanted to organize industrial unions to compete with the AFL because it believed that skilled workers were abandoning the masses. Even liberal Socialists accused labor union leader Samuel Gompers of being too conservative and feared the right wing in their party would attempt to turn it into a labor party because Gompers remained nonpolitical. Debs even once referred to Gompers as "an old woman." There were other issues that caused friction between labor advocates and reformers. In the party elections of 1910 for membership on the Socialist Party's National Executive Committee (NEC), the conservatives won. Then the McNamara case the next year and the IWW strike in Lawrence, Kansas, in 1912 precipitated a crisis over the use of sabotage and violence as tactics.

According to historian John P. Diggins, Socialists continued to split over three political approaches: Ferdinand Lassalle, founder of the German Social Democratic Party, believed control of the government could be won politically through the ballot box, while Marxists insisted on political activity through organizing industrial unions; right-wing Socialists sought step-by-step changes, while their left-wing brethren envisioned an apocalyptic leap to success; and different groups continued to dispute how much violence, if any, was necessary to achieve their goals.[10]

Historian Gary R. Entz traces the evolution of the Workingmen's Cooperative Colony in Nemaha County, Kansas, settled by English colonists who were followers of Irish Chartist James Bronterre O'Brien. It lasted from 1869 to 1874, before disbanding. An early example of radicalism in the Great Plains, this colony demonstrates that the region was an attractive breeding ground for radical thought and activity less than a decade after Kansas achieved statehood. Some of its members would become involved in other forms of radicalism in the state several decades later. Entz also mentions Silkville and several other similar colonies that emerged in Kansas.[11]

There were several forms of Socialist settlements, including Owenism and Fourierism, attempted in early Kansas. British social reformer Robert Owen was a founder and proponent of utopian socialism, and French aristocrat Ernest Valenton de Boissière was an adherent of Fourierism, based on French intellectual Charles Fourier's belief that workers should be organized into self-reliant cooperatives. De Boissière tried an experiment in establishing a silk industry in the Sunflower State. In 1869 he bought thirty-six hundred acres in Franklin County in eastern Kansas and established the colony of Silkville. He constructed a "phalanstery" that would house some one hundred workers, a school, barns, and a blacksmith shop. He planted mulberry trees and began raising silkworms. His colony failed to prosper, however, as many of its immigrant workers were attracted by the prospect of a free homestead more than the project itself, and the French girls he brought over to reel the silk instead found a steady supply of local farmers for husbands and left the colony. De Boissière abandoned his colony in a little over a decade and returned to France.[12]

A Danish colony lasted an even shorter time. Louis Albert Francois Pio, a postal service employee, headed the Socialist Party in Denmark. In 1872 the bricklayers struck, and Pio called a protest meeting in support. The police arrested him for this "revolutionary threat," and he served three years in a Danish prison. Upon his release the police gave him a choice of exile or continued harassment. Denmark was suffering an economic downturn at the time, so he accepted foreign travel. He and eighteen followers, including some German Westphalians, homesteaded near Hays, Kansas. They agreed their homesteads would be held in common, but the colony they established suffered from the start from a lack of funds. The Danes and Germans were not compatible, and the women quarreled over preparation of the common meals. In six weeks the colony decided to sell out, giving each family $30 from the proceeds, and dispersed. Pio became a printer in Chicago, producing magazines and books on Scandinavia for American readers as well as other subjects.[13]

Early in 1885 a group of students at Washburn College in Topeka, Kansas, formed a study club to explore the principles of socialism. They became active and founded the Missouri Valley Division of the Workmen's Association in Topeka to circulate labor literature promoting social revolution. Their emblem, the Red Flag, signified the message Saint Paul preached on Mars Hill, that God "had made of all nations and that is the banner of one blood—the emblem of Fraternity." They established similar organizations in thirteen counties in Kansas, but the movement failed from a lack of continuous leadership.[14]

Major Republican and Democratic editors disliked populism and displayed their disfavor by refusing to capitalize the term *Populist* in their newspaper stories (much like some current Republicans refer to their opponents dismissively as the "democrat party"). These editors also despised socialism, and it appears they decided not to report Socialists' activities in hopes they would disappear. This paucity of coverage was not only a disservice to their readers but a severe blow to posterity because it created a vacuum for future researchers. One cannot rely on the *Kansas City Star*, the *Topeka Daily Capital*, or the *Wichita Eagle* for news accounts about socialism as one can for stories about populism or prohibition. The sagas of the IWW and the Nonpartisan League (NPL) were exceptions to this generalization. The labor of these migrants was so crucial for the significant wheat harvest in Kansas, especially after the outbreak of World War I, that the *Topeka Daily Capital* and area newspapers extended rather thorough coverage to their activities. In addition, conservatives feared the potential impact of the NPL on U.S. politics and wanted to keep abreast of the group's progress and setbacks.

Kansans played a key part in the growth of national radicalism, through the Populist and Socialist movements, led by individuals such as Governor Lorenzo Lewelling, G. C. Clemens, and Annie Diggs. Newspaperman Julius A. Wayland, a native Indianan, had moved to the state in the mid-1890s to run what would become the largest Socialist newspaper in the country. The Socialist politician and presidential candidate Eugene V. Debs, who was not a native Kansan, lived and worked in the state, particularly with Wayland, and would launch one presidential campaign from Girard.

This book is not a definitive history of socialism in Kansas. Given the paucity of sources, it is doubtful if a comprehensive story of the movement can be written. This study relied on newspaper accounts for much of its material, though copies of numerous short-lived Socialist newspapers in Kansas have been lost. For instance, the *Iola Cooperator* acquired a large press and agreed to print the *Changing Leader* of Chanute, the *Leavenworth Socialist*, the *Harvey County Socialist* of Newton, the *Linn County Socialist* of Pleasanton, the *Saline County Socialist* of Salina, and the *News and Views* of Sedan. None of these newspapers are in the collection of the Kansas State Historical Society. Perhaps copies exist in various attics across the state and will one day surface.

The Socialists were more disputatious than most political parties. Like their comrades everywhere, Kansas Socialists followed various paths toward achieving their goals as well as their own timetables. The Kansas weekly newspaper *Appeal to Reason* continued to stress the theme that the success of socialism was imminent. The workers, as soon as they were educated, would arise, unite, and seize control of the means of production and the distribution of goods, it professed, establishing the utopian world of the "cooperative commonwealth" of Populists' dreams. However, it never suggested any way to achieve this utopia. Historian David Shannon emphasizes the point that to understand the Socialist Party, "it is necessary to survey its regional parts, to put the spotlight on each of its centers of strength."[15] The purpose of this book is to survey one regional part.

Many of the Kansans discussed in this book followed one of the political patterns described here. From nineteenth-century radicalism, they joined the Populists and then the Socialists. Girard, Kansas, was the home of the major Socialist newspaper, Wayland's *Appeal to Reason*, and some of the important party members were Kansans who visited or lived in Girard, the county seat in Crawford County in southeastern Kansas. Some of these figures were blazing meteors in the constellation of American socialism; others were little known or obscure participants. We hope to tell their stories succinctly and accurately. They, like their Populist predecessors, ultimately succeeded in achieving most of their goals, and their interesting experiences are well worth recounting as they reveal a fascinating chapter of Kansas history.

Kansas Socialists enjoyed a more limited success than those in Oklahoma but followed the same principle of presenting their doctrine in terms familiar to the state's workers and farmers. They expressed the Republican ideals embodied in the "Declaration of Independence, the moral teachings of Jesus Christ, and the political theories of Karl Marx."[16]

Socialists in Kansas also had among their ranks one of the greatest publishers of his time. Emanuel Haldeman-Julius (1889–1951) took over the *Appeal to Reason* and established his printing plant in Girard. He ultimately published over five hundred million Little Blue Books on myriad subjects, including socialism and free thought, before his untimely death; he drowned in his swimming pool in 1951.[17]

Liberals in the midwestern states have consistently failed to unite protesting farmers and laborers into a cohesive political bloc, except for the Farmer-Labor Party in Minnesota. While Socialists and those who support the capitalistic system have almost exactly the same objectives of improving their lot in life or at least that of their children, capitalists have been more successful in convincing people to believe that their goals are at odds. And

American liberals have been unsuccessful in educating the masses to reject the ideal of so-called middle-class values, in contrast to European radicals, for whom clear class distinctions make it easier to appeal successfully to those class prejudices. Historically, it has been an uphill battle for American liberals and radicals to move their agendas forward and to make headway in challenging a capitalist society. The Socialists, in particular, viewed capitalism as the root of society's evils, despite the fact that there were some Socialists who were capitalists or would become capitalist in their thinking. The "capitalist Socialists" make a good starting point for this study.

1

THE CAPITALISTIC SOCIALIST

Emanuel Haldeman-Julius once wrote a story about Jack London. He quoted the great novelist as being more interested in his ranch and stallions than he was in writing about socialism. London hinted that he wrote for the money. It was completely acceptable for Socialists to exploit the capitalistic system and amass a fortune as long as they did not abuse employees and treated them as a Socialist should.[1]

Most Socialists differed from pure Marxists in wanting to bring about the reordering of society through peaceful means, via the ballot box. But they continued to split between "Big Bill" Haywood and his radicals versus the rich Socialists and members of the middle class who decried violence. Like the Populists, they saw the need to educate the masses to achieve this peaceful goal. Newspapers, such as the *Appeal to Reason*, were the principle vehicles to provide this instruction. Founded by Julius Augustus Wayland in 1895, this weekly became the leading Socialist newspaper in the world, with a circulation of 760,000 by 1913. Continued by Emanuel Haldeman-Julius after Wayland's death in 1912, its special editions reached perhaps four million readers, the largest circulation of any left-wing periodical in American history. Wayland consistently refused to involve his newspaper in the partisan battles of the Socialists while simultaneously pressing for their goals and growth.[2]

Wayland was born in Versailles, Indiana, and received only two years of public education. He was apprenticed in the newspaper industry and worked in his home area until he had suffi-

cient funds to purchase the *Versailles Gazette* and make it into a
highly partisan Republican journal. Not long after his 1877 marriage to Etta Bevan, a local girl, the young couple moved to Harrisonville, Missouri, a county seat thirty miles south of Kansas
City and twenty miles from the Kansas border. Etta had relatives
there, and Julius soon bought half-interest in the *Cass County Courier*. "Obviously," his biographer Elliott Shore claims, he "controlled more money now," apparently with money provided by
his wife's family. A confirmed Republican, Wayland published a
Democratic newspaper and soon was appointed postmaster by a
Republican president, Rutherford B. Hayes. Tensions developed
between Wayland and the local Democratic Party leaders over
newspaper policy. Soon Republican officials persuaded him to
leave the *Cass County Courier* and print a rival GOP paper called the
Cass County News. After three years, amid increasing local hostility, he sold out and moved the family back to Versailles, retaining
some real estate he had acquired during his time in Harrisonville.[3]

In 1882 Wayland migrated to Pueblo, Colorado, a boomtown
county seat on the mining frontier, where he established "Wayland's One Hoss Print Shop." While in Pueblo, William Bradford, an English cobbler, sparked Wayland's interest in socialism.
He introduced Wayland to Danish American Laurence Gronlund's 1884 book *The Cooperative Commonwealth*, to which he was
initiated into the Marxist theories of value, competition, overproduction, class relations, and the nature of the state. Wayland
described his complete conversion and immersion into socialism,
noting that he began by "incidentally" engaging in conversation
with Bradford, then "to be brief he 'landed' me good and hard.
He carefully nursed me into reading Carlyle, Ruskin, Gronlund,
and other works and I soon realized for the first time that I was
an ignoramus. I got interested and read rapidly. I saw new light
and found what I never knew existed. I closed up my real estate
business and devoted my whole energies to the work of trying to
get my neighbors to grasp the truths I had learned."

Wayland proved to be the typical convert who became more
dedicated to his "new-found" religion than the converter.[4] Wayland avidly absorbed the social theories of the British writer John

Ruskin, who was sufficiently famous to warrant his followers establishing Ruskin College in Trenton, Missouri. At this time Edward Bellamy's Socialistic novel, *Looking Backward*, was taking America by storm.[5] The local branch of New York–based Socialist-Labor Party of De Leon allied itself with Colorado Populists, and Wayland, too, joined the farm protest movement.[6]

Soon after returning to Indiana, Wayland published his first issue of the *Coming Nation*, a dedicated Socialist newspaper, in Greensburg in April 1893. During the next six months his paper, costing fifty cents annually and bereft of advertising, had reached his goal of a circulation of ten thousand and continued to climb. But Wayland paid a heavy price in advocating an unpopular political cause, and he and his family quickly became pariahs in Greensburg. Wayland was "a young man in a hurry" and decided he could greatly accelerate the movement by demonstrating what socialism really meant. He would literally create a cooperative commonwealth, a utopia he named Ruskin, in central Tennessee. The town would have the best schools, libraries, and parks, and the profits from the *Coming Nation* would support the commune until it was well established. It soon attracted both residents and industry. Settlers first paid their initiation fee with two hundred subscriptions to the newspaper, but this was later changed to $500 cash.

J. A. Wayland bought two thousand acres and deeded the land to the Ruskin Cooperative Association and sold the *Coming Nation* to the colony. Disagreements among the one hundred colonists could be expected, especially because they did not know each other before arriving in Ruskin. In any case extensive experience with the ensuing disputes forced Wayland to admit he was not a communitarian at heart, and in July 1895 he left the colony and moved to Kansas City, Missouri. Labor organizer Mary Harris "Mother" Jones found Wayland despondent when she visited him there. She and "three white-collar workers" convinced him to create a new newspaper, and one of them suggested the name *Appeal to Reason*. Taking its name from the revolutionary Tom Paine and his appeal to "common sense," the first issue debuted in Kansas City on August 31, 1895, with a printing of fifty thou-

sand copies. Mother Jones promised to get Wayland subscribers
and took copies of the first issue to Omaha, where she "gathered
several hundred subscriptions and the paper was launched." In
addition, Philadelphia social reformer Dr. Charles Fayette Taylor
"bought forty-seven hundred subscriptions" to give to physicians
throughout the nation. Wayland also utilized the country's bar-
bershops to advertise the new journal.[7] Meanwhile, the Ruskin
colony eventually failed, and the settlers united with a similar
settlement in Georgia.[8]

Unlike the *Coming Nation*, the *Appeal to Reason* was not a mon-
eymaker quickly for Wayland. With its lurid stories and radical
language, opposition wags referred to it as the "Squeal for Treason." During its first year it cost Wayland approximately $100 per
issue. He decided direct action was necessary to cut these costs.
He moved the newspaper to Girard, Kansas. The location was
not accidental. Girard is over one hundred miles south of Kansas City, in the first county west of Missouri near the Tri-State
region, known for its mining of coal, zinc, and lead. Many of the
residents were recent migrants from southeastern Europe who
brought their own brand of socialism from their home countries.
European-born political activist Laurence Gronlund noted that
Kansas was "ripe for Socialism." In fact, in 1893 Gronlund wrote
to Kansas Populist G. C. Clemens, expressing his interest in making Topeka the national headquarters of the Socialist movement
in America. Wayland explained that he "concluded to move to a
smaller place, buy a home, put in a printing plant and settle down
permanently . . . [in] Girard, Kansas, the prettiest little town I
found in three months hunting for a place to make my home."[9]

Late-nineteenth-century Girard was a rather typical small
county seat in Kansas. With a population of some two thousand
souls, it had its social stratifications with a few well-to-do citizens who dominated the social and economic life of the community. The large numbers of recent immigrants from southern and
eastern Europe who came to work in the coalfields and were scattered throughout the many mining camps of Crawford County
made it different from the counties to the north and west. With
the publication of the *Appeal to Reason*, Girard soon became the

mecca of the Socialist world, with leaders everywhere coming to pay homage to its publisher. Some decided to stay and live. Others could not bear to leave the East Coast for long, except for a short visit to the Wild West. A local Socialist newspaper two decades later described Girard:

> The greatest stroke of fortune that ever came its way was the establishment of the *Appeal to Reason* nearly 20 years ago. The *Appeal* has put Girard on the map of the world and there is scarcely a village or city in America where the residents have not heard of Girard and the paper which carried it to the farthermost corners of the entire world.
>
> The *Appeal* was small and insignificant when it first located in the county seat. A half-dozen employees were on its payroll and the people looked upon it with contempt and ridicule. No one dreamed of its becoming the world power it has. From its beginnings it grew and prospered until through its instrumentality Girard has a free mail delivery—the smallest town in the United States with that privilege. An appropriation has been made by Congress for the erection of a $75,500 post office building. The *Appeal* furnishes employment to from 60 to 100 people, among them a half hundred or more local girls. These girls have, according to the state factory inspector, better working conditions, shorter hours, and better pay than any other institution of its kind in the United States.
>
> Girard is also one of the first towns in the United States to elect a Socialist Mayor and [Crawford County] is the FIRST COUNTY to be captured by Socialists. Of course this was terrifying to some of the conservative people but even these have learned that Socialists are about like other people and are fully as competent and trustworthy as Republican and Democratic office holders.[10]

Wayland instituted what would later be branded Madison Avenue tactics of high-pressure methods to obtain new subscribers. He began listing new subscribers and the number of copies they purchased. He sponsored contests, awarding prizes to those sending in the highest number of subscribers. While he never solicited money to support the newspaper directly, he never hesitated to ask for donations so he could send copies to labor unions and to capitalist publishers.[11]

Appeal to Reason's circulation declined temporarily during the Spanish-American War but recovered rapidly afterward, and by the end of 1900 Wayland's aggressive new approach had 141,000 subscribers. On November 3 of that year he published a special edition, just before the presidential election, of 927,000 copies, establishing a single-issue total for a world's record of any edition up to that time. Eager to join the new trend of "muckraking" journalism, the *Appeal*, in 1904, commissioned then unknown writer Upton Sinclair to write "the Uncle Tom's Cabin of the wage slave," based on the recent meatpackers' strike in Chicago. A new convert to socialism, Sinclair spent several months in Chicago observing the plight of the workers, many of them immigrants. The novel that sprang from this experience—*The Jungle*—was first serialized in the *Appeal* in 1904, before being published in 1905 by Doubleday, Page & Company in a slightly shorter book edition.

Despite postal authority harassment and worse, in May 1910 subscriptions for the *Appeal to Reason* reached the 500,000 mark, and by 1913 it was the nation's leading Socialist newspaper, at 760,000, with special editions reaching 4 million readers. In 1912 Wayland moved the plant to its fourth, and largest, building in Girard. He was now the town's largest employer, with more than one hundred people working forty-seven hours weekly under ideal conditions. Wayland, a sound businessman, determined to have the latest and finest equipment. In emergencies his three-deck Goss press, which he claimed was worth $100,000, could print and fold 45,000 papers per hour, or 500,000 copies daily. This was barely adequate for the special editions. Other than the party itself, the *Appeal to Reason* was the most important Socialist institution in America. Especially during nonelection years, it provided "the excitement, vitality, and the continuity the socialist movement needed."[12] Its location in Girard, almost in the exact center of the country, made sending the paper via train in all directions an easy method of distribution, with a group of workers and subscribers Wayland labeled "the Appeal Army" assisting in soliciting new subscribers and sending issues as far as possible. There were other Socialist papers in the United States during the time, but the *Appeal* reached the largest number of readers. The

Party Builder in Chicago, the *New Age* in Buffalo, the *Advance* in San Francisco, the *St. Louis Labor*, and the *Minnesota Socialist* all competed with the *Appeal to Reason* but did not match the *Appeal's* subscription numbers.

Wayland agreed that his ownership of the paper seemed contrary to Socialist thinking, but after his bad experience with the *Coming Nation* in Ruskin, Tennessee, he was unable to find an alternative arrangement. The Socialist Party Constitution forbade it from having an official paper, so he could not donate it to the members. A collective ownership would threaten his concept of the purpose of the journal, and experience told him that democracy was no way to run a newspaper. This dilemma was not solved until after his workers struck the business and he reached a settlement with them.[13]

His greatest success in expanding the newspaper came with the "Appeal Army," a concept Wayland developed slowly but quite effectively. Instead of publishing the names of new subscribers, which consumed a lot of space, he printed names of Patriots, the Honor Roll, or hustlers of new readers. This concept grew over the next decade. If these hustlers could collect a group of subscribers receiving copies at the same address, they would enjoy a large discount. Some managed to make a living from the difference between the fifty-cent subscription rate and the group rate. In 1910 Wayland described his fifty-six thousand troops as the "Wonderful Army" and constantly praised their work. Wayland also raised additional funding by selling limited advertisements for poultry feed, fortune-telling, and patent medicines. He reiterated time and again that the Appeal Army made the *Appeal to Reason* the success that it became. The "Bundle Brigade" was an offshoot of this institution, its members receiving a bundle of five copies and dropping them in favorable spots.[14]

Wayland became a strong supporter and close friend of Eugene Victor Debs, Socialist candidate for the presidency from 1900 through 1920, except during the war election, when he declined the honor and Allan L. Benson was the Socialist nominee. Debs, a midwesterner from Indiana, like Wayland, was not a great theorist of socialism, but "he possessed the knack for winning over the doubting to the cooperative commonwealth." Very soon after founding the American Railway Union, Debs became involved in the Pullman Strike of 1894. Jailed by the Supreme Court for six months at Woodstock, Illinois, on the basis of the narrow interpretation that the strike he called had obstructed the flow of interstate commerce, Debs emerged from prison as a dedicated and popular Socialist. With the collapse of the Populist Party, he founded and led the Social Democracy movement and was a key leader in founding the American Socialist Party in 1901. Wayland, in the *Coming Nation*, celebrated Debs's release from the Woodstock jail in a special edition. Debs, in turn, congratulated Wayland on his *Appeal to Reason*, noting that "its friendly face appears everywhere. . . . More power to the *Appeal*."[15]

Public tolerance for Socialists to express their views before the turn of the century might best be illustrated with the experience of Debs in Topeka after the Pullman Strike. Later, when socialism appeared to be too radical, any speech by a Socialist in the capital city would have required police surveillance. However, in 1898 Debs was received at the capitol by the governor and state supreme court justices. The city police chief donated $5 toward Debs's expenses. All of them sat on the platform to hear Debs sing the praises of socialism. A reporter present observed that every man in the audience would have helped hang "any Federal Judge to a sour apple tree who would propose harm to the leader of the American Railway Union strike."[16]

For years the *Appeal to Reason* preached unionism, and its press workers eventually received the message and organized. When they did, they struck over the issue of Wayland hiring business manager W. F. Phelps and Wayland's brother-in-law C. D. Bevan. The publisher had previously announced that he would take no profits from the paper and that upon his death he would leave his printing plant to the Socialist movement. Phelps and Bevan objected to the denouncing of dividends, as they held stock in the company, and they fought the subsequent unionization. The staff demanded that the two recalcitrants be fired, and when Wayland refused, the workers struck. In thirty hours Wayland capitulated, with the compromise that his wife's brother could remain in his position and Wayland's son Jon would replace Phelps as business manager. Wayland was saddened by the episode because he could not give the paper to the Socialist Party and yet could not socialize the production and profits under the circumstances of conflict between the staff and his relatives.[17]

In the first issue of the *Appeal to Reason* Wayland expressed the principles of the "One Hoss Editor" that would guide the newspaper until World War I. Monopolies were changing the commercial aspect of the world and also, in the process, its social relations. In the struggle for supremacy, on the one hand, and for existence, on the other, neither the rich nor the poor had the time or inclination to think. The editor, therefore, would perform that function for them, pointing out "the tendencies of the times" and "to inspire hope of a fairer, more orderly system." "Private monopoly," Wayland warned, "is always oppressive, public monopoly always beneficial. This is the lesson. . . . Learn it, or perish as perished all the civilizations of the past." He also said on another occasion that it was "simply Ruskin turned into the language of the common people."[18]

Years later Wayland noted that he still received many inquiries about why he used the "one hoss" sobriquet. This was, he explained, "a plebeian appellation" that he had used when he opened a small printing shop in Pueblo, Colorado. Now he wrote to the laboring class, which is "not shocked at such expressions." Dull as this class is, he argued, any real reform to the capitalist system must come through its members. He would continue to lecture, explain, and "exhort them to better conditions" so the cooperative commonwealth would finally come about through their efforts. His biographer explains this philosophy of socialism as "blending its components into an established tradition of dissent and protest . . . as disparate as Thomas Jefferson, Andrew Jackson, and Abraham Lincoln with John Ruskin, Edward Bellamy, and Laurence Gronlund."[19]

J. A. Wayland was aware of the intellectual mood of his audience. He seemed to be at his best in writing to people of the Midwest who had attended the public schools, went to Protestant services, and belonged to one of the major parties. As Debs wrote him, "You have the faculty of reaching the common man." Wayland paid little attention to academic treatises on Socialist theory but reprinted heavily from Edward Bellamy's works and Henry Demarest Lloyd's *Wealth against Commonwealth*. He also used clippings from other reform or left-wing newspapers extensively and was generous to his readers in letting them "air their opinions."[20]

Socialists readily agreed that men are unequal: some are industrious, others are lazy; some are acquisitive, others are indifferent. They had no problem with a man becoming rich through his own efforts, but they insisted that employers treat employees as they would want to be treated themselves. They also argued that government should protect the weak from the oppressive and the strong and give all an equal opportunity. Government should, they determined, "level the playing field" in order to protect the workers.[21]

Wayland wrote on varied topics in the *Appeal to Reason*, always tying them to themes of socialism. He published an article by German American Socialist writer Ernest Untermann addressed to farmers, for instance, which noted that the difference between populism and socialism could be found in the platforms of the two parties. Populists demanded the abolition of national banks; issuance of legal tender notes; free and unlimited coinage of silver; prohibition of foreign ownership of land; a graduated income tax; public ownership of railroads, telephones, and telegraphs; direct election of the president, vice president, and senators; the eight-hour workday; and universal suffrage. "The interests of rural and urban labor are identical," Untermann concluded. Fundamentals of socialism included working-class conquest of political power; collective ownership of the means of production and distribution by working-class democracy; sexual equality; production for use, not profit; and producers to receive the products of their labor. Untermann, who later joined the Ruskin College faculty, insisted that Populists had sought to reform symptoms and not causes. The fundamental goal of both parties should be to "dethrone" capitalism and change the system of production. Wayland also noted that the United States had practiced a form of socialism for decades with its public school system, the U.S. Postal Service, libraries, state universities, and municipally owned utilities.[22]

The *Appeal to Reason* announced the report of the Homes Commission that President Theodore Roosevelt appointed to investigate family conditions in New York City. Many Republicans, who emphasized the importance of the family in American life, were eager to publicize the results of the investigation. In the category of prostitution, the committee investigated 2,000 women. It found that 402 were married; 71 had left their husbands for some reason; 103 had left their husbands because of "ill-usage"; their husbands had deserted 60 of them; 43 husbands had left them to live with other women; and other women had left home because of "non-support, drunkenness, infidelity." It discovered 294 widows who were forced into prostitution because they were destitute. Of the 2,000 women, 523 of them earned, on a weekly basis, $1; 336 made $2; 230 were in the $3 category; 127 earned $4; 68 fell in the $5 group; 21 made $6; 8 brought home $7; and 5 made $8. Only 2 earned over $20 weekly. This was "the situation under Capitalism," the editor explained. The U.S. Senate declared the report to be "unmailable" and told the Department of Justice to prosecute any person who circulated it. Wayland noted that Socialists were accused of breaking up homes and families through their advocacy of equal rights, and he was willing to risk his mailing privileges to print the report showing that poverty under capitalism was destroying the American family.[23]

The *Appeal to Reason* urged workers to vote for the cooperative commonwealth because "one strike there and for such an object will do you more good than a thousand strikes for a morsel of bread." The editor begged them to purge themselves "of superstition that there would be no capital if there were no Capitalists." This illusion led workers to go begging the capitalists for a job "in servitude," instead of searching within their own ranks. They must cease to believe that "there would be no land, no machinery, no industry, no exchange, if there were no monopolists; and no good management, no order, no society, if there were no corrupt legislators, no venal judges, no prostitutes of any sort."[24]

The *Appeal* sought to bridge gaps between socialism and Christianity. Some of its readers, though, attacked the churches for supporting capitalism. While the *Appeal* claimed to oppose only the pope and "Romanism," Wayland was decidedly anti-Catholic.[25]

Socialists were convinced that Jesus preached socialism. "The ethics of Socialism are identical with the ethics of Christianity," Wayland once observed in the *Appeal to Reason*, and he declared that "the first missionary work of Jesus and his followers was among the working class who heard him gladly. Jesus was crucified by the ruling classes because He was a labor agitator, arousing discontent among the poor. The early Christians practiced Communism and condemned private property until the wily Constantine corrupted the church. The Dark Ages began soon after Christianity became respectable and deserted the cause of the oppressed working class."[26]

On another occasion Debs told a reporter that Christ was an agitator who told the robbed and misruled and exploited and driven people to disobey their plunderers: "He denounced the profiteers, and it was for this that they nailed his quivering body to the cross and spiked it to the gates of Jerusalem, not because he told them to love one another. That was a harmless doctrine. But when he touched their profits and denounced them before their people He was then marked for crucifixion."[27]

Citizens in the nineteenth and twentieth centuries were expected to conform to American standards and values. Socialism, with its class-conscious basis and its threat, by numerous factions of the party, of violence, was thus viewed by many as contrary to the "American way of life." Wayland consistently argued to the contrary. He repeatedly insisted that socialism was, in fact, in complete keeping with the spirit of Jefferson and the American Revolutionary ideals.[28]

Wayland continued his speculation in real estate in various states and amassed considerable wealth in the process. He saw no contradiction between this enterprise and his fervent belief in and dedicated support of socialism. He admitted that gaining wealth was "nothing to be proud of." Apparently, he was not ashamed of it either. He once observed in the *Appeal to Reason* that "property which is for my individual, exclusive personal use . . . I ought to own alone. My right to it is as genuine and as sacred as my right to life," provided it was "not the result of the exploitation of the toil of others." He insisted that he was not alone in this thinking. He was convinced that the men who were doing the "best work" in socialism were "making money under the present social anarchy but are disgusted with it."[29]

The Wayland family lived the life of the upper-middle class in Girard, mingling with their neighbors and traveling about town in their carriage and team of black horses and, later, an early automobile. Their three-story mansion offered hospitality to visiting Socialist dignitaries, such as Mother Jones and Kate Richards O'Hare. Their house also hosted occasional parties for the young Waylands and their friends, who whiled away evenings drinking punch and playing whist and other card games.

Socialists in Girard met with the typical small-town agrarian hostility to radical ideas, but this resentment mellowed slightly as the two sides became acquainted. Elected by his peers, Emanuel Haldeman-Julius served as trustee for the public schools when his children attended them, and he participated actively in public affairs. Henry Vincent, son of the earlier editor of the Populist *Non-Conformist and Kansas Industrial Liberator* in Winfield, came to Girard in 1907 to work for the *Appeal to Reason*. Following the Socialist convention in 1908, Vincent and many of the leaders met in Girard to reminisce about their recent experiences. Henry noted that after Debs made his first campaign speech of the season in the Girard town square the previous week, the townspeople began responding more positively to socialism. Debs often stayed with the Vincent family when he visited Girard. Daughter Mary Vincent later recalled that her friends were drawn from Girard circles, not from immigrant families living nearby. Wayland contended that the success of the movement could be attributed to "men of substance" such as himself. He traveled to New Orleans at least once a year to enjoy his oysters and Creole food and on one occasion took his daughter Edith to Florida and then for a week in Havana, Cuba. He lived a rich social life in rural Girard and enjoyed his wealth.[30]

As the *Appeal to Reason* grew in circulation, Wayland required

editorial assistance from Fred Warren, a rising star in the Socialist movement from Rich Hill, Missouri, a mining town across the
Kansas line. He had previously served on the *Coming Nation* staff
in 1901 and attracted attention early on as a Socialist lecturer.
While he was "absolutely agin'" Warren's beliefs, the editor of
the local newspaper believed he had "made about the most rapid
strides before the public that have ever been made by any man
in the same length of time. He is about to crowd Debs off the
public platform." Warren soon became a key figure in the publication of the *Appeal to Reason*. Like his boss, Warren also pursued capitalist ventures.

Under the heading "Girard Capitalists Will Build Electric Line
to Camps," Wayland and Warren joined a company "of local capital" to build an electric railway from Girard to the coal camps.
Fred Warren was elected to the board of directors, J. A. Wayland
was made vice president, and a committee was chosen to survey a
line to the Crawford County mining towns of Dunkirk, Mulberry,
and Radley. The board of county commissioners gladly granted
the Girard Coal Belt Electric Railway Company a free right-of-
way for eleven and a half miles along county highways to the three
towns and two miles across the property of the Western Coal and
Mining Company. The grant limited the railway to fifteen feet
of the highways and stipulated that construction begin within a
year and the line to Dunkirk be completed within two years.[31]

Under Wayland's direction the *Appeal* "dispatched its own
Socialist organizers . . . sponsored study clubs . . . supplied literature . . . established a widespread Agitation League . . . and sent
copies of the *Appeal* to school teachers, union members, state and
federal legislators" as well as to newspaper editors throughout
the United States. It sent Debs, Fred Warren, and other Socialists on speaking tours, with the price of admission being a year's
subscription to the *Appeal*. It printed special editions for several
state Socialist organizations that were unable to print their own
newspaper. It flooded strike areas with supportive publicity and
opened its pages to accounts by strikers.[32]

As one source has noted, "No paper fused Socialism with Midwestern American values more effectively" than Wayland's Girard

newspaper. He, Fred Warren, Eugene Debs, and other editorial writers were born in the Midwest and were rooted in "quasi-Christian morality, home, family, and community," but they all agreed that only through socialism could these mores really be realized. Capitalism everywhere was subjecting these mores and values to stress and distortion. In order to attract new recruits to socialism, new meaning needed to be given to current values. In Wayland's writing the American traditions of protest and dissent were always evident, and his brand of socialism was the means to control the evil economic forces in society.[33] At any rate, it proved effective, as the *Appeal* grew to be the largest Socialist newspaper in the country.

J. A. Wayland eventually became an institution in Crawford County. Farmers came to town on Saturday night to do their shopping and sell their produce. Wayland would "gather up an armful of papers and pamphlets and walk around the square and put some piece of literature in every wagon and every buggy." On summer evenings he and members of his family would take a drive through the countryside, bringing along Socialist literature, and he would stop at houses and engage the occupants in conversation and leave some literature. He would encourage them to ask questions, and he answered them "all so kindly." He "hit them hard" but in a gentle way. He maintained patience when answering even the most absurd questions.[34]

Historian David Paul Nord made a study of the type of socialism the *Appeal* promoted and how it changed over the years. He contrasted two periods, 1901–12 and 1913–20. The first covers the years of Wayland and Warren, while Louis Kopelin and Emanuel Haldeman-Julius edited for the second period. The *Appeal* carried few stories on agriculture or popular democracy and a great deal of material on orthodox Socialist and economic theory. The early period carried more stories on trusts, monopolies, Wall Street, railroads, and big business. Wayland and Warren never advocated abolishing trusts but praised them as part of the "New Age" and recommended that the people control them. "The hurt is not because of the great aggregations of wealth," Wayland insisted, "but because of the private ownership of it."

Few of the stories of the early years treated the military and war, but this changed dramatically with the advent of World War I.[35]

The *Appeal to Reason* diligently reported foreign news, but this consisted mostly of foreign Socialist activities, progressive governments, and also despotic rulers. John Kenneth Turner, one of its staff assigned there as a reporter, covered the Mexican revolution. The newspaper also followed the Russian revolution but, as it progressed, continued to support the Bolshevik economic reforms although not the emerging repressive government.[36]

Wayland's newspaper particularly attacked the American court system, probably because the paper was often victimized by reactionary judges. The U.S. Post Office had the power to jeopardize the *Appeal*'s success with its various regulations. The newspaper needed its second-class postal rate for financial success. The postmaster general often withdrew this privilege temporarily over stories he or other government officials disliked or banned entirely from the mail some issues during the war that the office considered seditious. Federal judges invariably supported these decisions. Local postmasters who were superpatriots often ordered carriers not to deliver certain issues, causing a financial crisis for the editors. Judge Peter Grosscup of Chicago, the federal district judge who became famous in the Pullman Strike, or infamous in the eyes of Debs and union men, often was a target of the *Appeal*'s wrath. Warren wrote that the newspaper's "only interest in bringing to the broad light of day the Grosscup skeleton is to show you what kind of men are elevated to the bench where they wield a power despotic and autocratic and fraught with the gravest danger to the liberties of the American people."[37]

Many *Appeal* stories dealt with the social problems of "poverty, crime, child labor, prostitution, suicide, unhealthy working conditions, alcohol," all the results of capitalism, according to the paper. Wayland especially attacked the problem of "white slavery," and the *Appeal* was credited with creating "a vogue among the muckraking monthlies of New York." "It seems like a hideous nightmare of hell," he wrote, "and yet it is a fact of our everyday life under Capitalism." Later, when Wayland took his own life, it was because, as the *Appeal* expressed it, he was "hounded to his death by the relentless dogs of Capitalism." The conclusion was always the same: reform was futile, and ending private greed and private property was the only solution. Warren carried this theme even further, using fiction to attack the evil institution. The *Appeal* also often published stories of social activities of high society, such as lavish dinner balls for the rich or dinners for dogs while working people in the city were starving.[38]

The *Appeal* gave extensive coverage to Socialist activities and elections, which stemmed from Wayland's insistence that the ballot box was the best vehicle for political change. Debs's campaigns received wide publicity, as did municipal elections in which Socialists were candidates. While the paper often emphasized local elections as "practice for the real thing to come," workers were constantly advised to exercise their right to suffrage. The *Appeal* consistently addressed the theme of strong organization of the party but refrained from playing active roles in party politics or partisan debates and bickering.

The newspaper followed closely the great strikes and the prosecutions of Socialist and labor leaders. Debs, who often wrote for the *Appeal*, penned his famous "Arouse, Ye Slaves" over the "kidnapping" issue of the Western Federation of Miners leaders in Idaho. Most of the stories on organized labor were supportive, but the journal was critical of strikes that had no political foundation. Samuel Gompers and labor leader John Mitchell, who consorted with capitalists, were strongly criticized, and the *Appeal* eventually concluded that Socialist funds should support efforts to persuade people to vote for socialism rather than to support strikes.[39]

By 1910 Fred Warren was running the *Appeal to Reason*, leaving Wayland free to pursue his real estate interests. He signed a five-year contract with Warren for $25,000 yearly, a handsome sum at the time, and soon Warren was a leading and dedicated figure in Socialist circles, although a colleague once called him "a greedy Socialist." Warren was outraged at the injustice of kidnapping Big Bill Haywood, in lieu of the extradition process, for his trial for murdering former governor Frank Steunenberg of Idaho in 1906. He concocted a plot to demonstrate the class bias of the American judicial system. After the Supreme Court ruled the kidnapping constitutional, Warren offered a reward for the kidnapping of former governor of Kentucky William Taylor. Taylor had murdered his successor in cold blood, then fled to Pennsylvania and thence to Indiana, where these governors had refused to extradite him to Kentucky to stand trial. Warren sent the notice printed in red ink on the outside of envelopes. President Theodore Roosevelt was often savaged in the *Appeal to Reason* as "Rusvlt," and now his friend Taylor was being assaulted in print by the newspaper. There was no legislation specifically to prosecute for this proffered kidnapping or to deny the newspaper access to the U.S. Mail.

Roosevelt asked his attorney general, Charles J. Bonaparte, about this attack, and Bonaparte responded by indicting Warren for sending his reward offer through the U.S. Mail. Warren was harassed by pretrial delays and finally found guilty of intent "to bring the Supreme Court of the United States into ridicule and contempt." He concluded that the Roosevelt administration was trying to crush his newspaper with legal expenses, that the U.S. Post Office was burning copies rather than delivering them, and that "free speech and liberty of the press were at stake." Warren was sentenced to six months in prison and fined $1,500 plus costs. When the U.S. court of appeals affirmed his conviction, Debs wrote that "we must make hell howl when you go to jail and heaven smile when you emerge from it."[40] Believing he would have to serve his sentence in the Leavenworth federal prison, Warren launched an investigation of the prison facility with true stories of "brutality, sodomy, graft, and murder, complete with testimony from former inmates and prison guards." This exposure resulted in the firing of six prison officials and the retirement of warden Robert W. McClaughry. President William H. Taft issued an unsolicited pardon to Warren by canceling the prison term and lowering the fine to $100. Warren offered to pay the fine with *Appeal to Reason* subscription blanks, and that ended the affair.[41]

This legal episode had hardly ended when Harrison G. Otis and his virulently anti-union *Los Angeles Times* attacked the *Appeal to Reason*. In 1911 the McNamara brothers, James and John, and

Ortie McManigal, all members of the International Association of Bridge and Iron Workers, an American Federation of Labor (AFL) affiliate, were arrested and charged with dynamiting the *Los Angeles Times* building in 1910 and killing several people. Socialists quickly became involved in this crime when Job Harriman, Debs's running mate in 1900, became attorney for the accused. The *Appeal to Reason* automatically assumed the men were innocent and dispatched staff reporter George Schoaf to the city to unravel the mystery and the identity of the true bombers who had killed twenty people. Harrison Gray Otis, of course, blamed the union men.[42]

The case soon widened in scope beyond the lives of the McNamaras and McManigal. Newspapers used it to insist that trade unionists and Socialists believed in violence and advocated sabotage. The *Los Angeles Times* labeled the *Appeal to Reason* an "anarchist paper" that "appealed to the prejudices and the lurking criminality and the ignorance of its readers." Eventually, reporter Lincoln Steffens and attorney Clarence Darrow, working on the case at the behest of Eugene Debs, reached "a secret understanding with the prosecution," and the brothers pleaded guilty to the crime, to William J. Burns of the Burns Detective Agency. They were convicted and received a penalty lesser than death. This time the *Appeal to Reason* bet on the wrong horse and now had egg on its face. Otis and units of the federal government turned on the *Appeal* with a vengeance.[43]

Hostile federal agents haunted the streets of Girard, searching for negative stories, and repeatedly broke into the *Appeal* offices to search for evidence. Wayland had suffered personal loss—his second wife died from an automobile accident the previous year—and strain from this media assault quickly took its toll. Stories were soon fabricated about criminal tendencies of Wayland's ancestors, and he was publicly accused of seducing a fourteen-year-old orphan girl, then taking her to Missouri, where she was killed during an abortion. He discovered that, as a result, the federal government would charge him with violation of the Mann Act, the 1910 law against interstate transport of a female for immoral purposes. Wayland had suffered many attacks before, but this filth was too much for the melancholy fifty-eight-year-old, who had often been close to suicide. In November 1912 he put a gun in his mouth and ended his life.

Wayland's suicide did not end the *Appeal*'s troubles. Warren was indicted for sending "indecent, filthy, obscene, lewd, and lascivious printed matter" through the mail. He and the *Appeal* ultimately won their trial in 1913. Warren and the Wayland children successfully sued various journals for publishing the libelous stories, but in the end Warren was forced from the newspaper. Walter Wayland, son of J. A. Wayland, engaged Louis Kopelin as managing editor. The *Appeal* circulation reached over 750,000 in 1913, but subscriptions began to drag thereafter due to the effects of the Great War and poor editorial direction.[44]

Warren and the Wayland children engaged Socialist attorney Jacob "Jake" I. Sheppard to sue Andrew Allen Veatch, an Oklahoma state legislator and editor of the *Remonstrator*, an anti-Socialist publication, for libel and won. Faced with a settlement, Veatch persuaded the challengers to accept his personal apology instead. In February 1914 Veatch admitted that his story of how and why J. A. Wayland had died by suicide was without merit, and he retracted it. "A million people will look for retractions from other papers who copied the infamous report," Warren wrote, and "thousands in Crawford County will look for honest statements from some of our local press."[45] Socialist writer and editor Kate Richards, who married Frank O'Hare in the elegant Wayland home, eulogized Wayland upon his death:

> We shed no tears of grief; grief is for the naked lives of those who have made the world no better. For who are we to judge, or say that he has shirked his task or left some work undone? No eyes can count the seed that he has sown, the thoughts that he has planted in a million souls now covered deep beneath the mold of ignorance which will not spring into life until the snows have heaped upon his grave and the sun of springtime comes to reawake the sleeping world. Sleep on, our comrade; rest your weary mind and soul, sleep sweet and deep, and if in other realms the boon is granted that we may again take up our work, you will be with us and give us of your strength,

your patience and your loyalty to your fellow men. We bring not gold for flowers for your tomb, but with hearts that rejoice at your deliverance offer a comrade's tribute to lie above your breast—the red flag of brotherhood.[46]

Soon after Kopelin replaced Warren as *Appeal* editor, World War I began in Europe. Emanuel Julius arrived in Girard in 1915 from the *New York Call* to share the editorial duties at the *Appeal*. He soon married Marcet Haldeman, heiress to the local Girard bank and niece of Chicago social reformer Jane Addams. Acting upon Addams's suggestion, they hyphenated their names to Haldeman-Julius shortly after their marriage. When the United States joined the war in 1917, they changed the name of the newspaper to the *New Appeal* and joined the crusade. This betrayal enraged Debs and many Socialists, and the paper became a shell of its former self.[47]

Before her marriage Marcet Haldeman inherited control over her parents' bank in Girard, and her money financed the publication of the *New Appeal* for a while. It soon was losing so much money that Emanuel allowed it to expire and turned the printing plant into a large-scale publisher of the Little Blue Books series of American and European classics. These were 3½ x 5-inch paperback printings of "great books," which he originally sold for twenty-five cents, then ten cents, and later five cents. He made an international reputation and a good deal of money, ultimately publishing five hundred million copies of over two thousand titles. By 1929 his presses were capable of printing eighty thousand Little Blue Books every twenty-four hours, which led to his being referred to as "the Henry Ford of publishing." His purpose in publishing these classics was to educate. He hoped they would become "books of democracy" to help people throw off the shackles of tyranny.[48]

With the *Appeal to Reason* in Girard, the small town attracted or grew its share of Socialists, both in terms of visitors and those living there. One of the more interesting characters to be associated with Girard was Henry Laurens Call. Born in New York City in 1867, Call had studied mathematics and physics at Kansas

State College of Agriculture in Manhattan, Kansas, but became a lawyer and practiced in Topeka in the 1890s. He married Jessie Lewelling, daughter of Populist governor Lorenzo Lewelling, and was an active Republican until challenged by populism. He began a study to refute Populist ideas and became converted to the agrarian cause. He was well-known for his book *The Coming Revolution*, published in 1895.

Marcet Haldeman of Girard was Jessie's friend, and she described the Call romance in a letter to her family. Call made "ardent love" to Jessie when they both lived in Topeka. Then the couple parted for several years, but fate destined them for marriage, and they were finally united. The marriage was unsuccessful, though, which Marcet attributed to Call's sometimes harsh physicality, erratic behavior, and an obsession with séances, which were popular at the time. The more nervous Call became over his business ventures, the more demanding he became of Jessie. They became estranged, were divorced, and she took her life by poisoning in Chicago in April 1908. Henry later moved to New York to practice law and married Emma Johns, a noted concert pianist, well-known on the European tour. Both Calls converted to socialism, with Henry becoming famous on the party's lecture circuit. Emma wrote the music to accompany the words of *Appeal* writer Charles Lincoln Phifer's "Genial Gene." The *Appeal* published the music and lyrics in 1908, and it became Eugene Debs's campaign song. Just before he returned to Kansas, Call published *Justice*, in 1907.[49]

Henry Call and his new wife appeared on the doorstep of the *Appeal to Reason* office in Girard in April 1908 with blueprints and a proposal to build a passenger airplane. He promised to fly members of the *Appeal* staff to Chicago that summer to attend the Socialist National Convention. All they had to do was invest $2,500 in his airplane so he could acquire a factory to build it. Fred Warren, J. A. Wayland, Eugene Debs, John Vincent, and some of the staff immediately raised the money, and the project began building the first airplane in Kansas. The Wright Brothers had no formal training in physics, and Call believed their design, which they had successfully flown at Kitty Hawk, was "without scientific merit." Call had the scientific background from his studies at Manhattan, but his first model was an unbelievable contraption. He stressed "flight along the lines which nature had so successfully used in bird flight."

Call's overall design for his aircraft could be described as "amphibious." It "had the supporting surfaces . . . for flight, all the necessary parts for an automobile, and a passenger cabin designed as a boat." The craft was to be controlled by a system of rudders, one on top and one on each side of the cabin. It would be powered by two twenty-horse engines mounted at the front and each driving two steel propellers with four blades, one running forward, the other in reverse.[50]

Call wore fancy clothes, had a pleasant personality, and easily sold stock in his company to Girard businessmen. The *Appeal* advertised it and sold shares around the world. Soon the Aerial Navigation Company was capitalized at $2 million. In March 1909 the company established a machine shop to make its airplane parts and to repair wood and metal products. The original agreement with the *Appeal* staff called for secrecy until after a successful flight, but when Call foolishly began using the names of his Socialist investors, they withdrew their support.[51]

The Wright Brothers' aircraft required the pilot to shift his position and weight continually during flight, while Call designed his machine to distribute equilibrium mechanically. But he just could not get it to fly. The editor of a local newspaper, no fan of socialism, gleefully reported that "the bird remains firmly anchored to mother earth; in fact, it seems to be part of the earth." Call changed the propellers of the twin motors from four- to two-bladed spruce pine propellers driving forward, capable of one thousand revolutions per minute. When he tested them, mechanic H. W. Strubble did not expect its force and was sucked into a propeller and killed. Call designed a second aircraft, but upon testing it, a motor developed trouble, and it devastated the crankshaft on the first try, ruining a cylinder. Call decided his heavy engines were at fault, so he designed a workable aluminum rotary engine that his factory successfully built and sold to other aircraft builders. By Christmas 1909 he was experimenting with a one-man

aircraft. Observers noted that on tests "several times [it] showed
a tendency to lift from the ground," but still it would not fly. In
1911 Call continued designing new aircraft that refused to rise off
the ground. By that time his airplane factory, which was the first
west of the Mississippi River, was the third-largest aircraft plant
in the world. Airplane no. 15, using the French Berliot design,
finally had a successful flight on September 30, 1912. By that time
Call's company was bankrupt. The machine shop, though, was
a financial success during this period, repairing other wood and
metal products ranging from automobiles to mining machinery,
cash registers, pianos, locks, and roller skates. Call was killed in
1917 piloting one of his planes over the skies of Wyoming when
it crashed.[52]

Call's legacy did not die with him. One hot day in August
1927 a single-seat monoplane circled Girard during the county
fair. The pilot, Charles A. Lindbergh, having successfully completed his famous Atlantic Ocean crossing several months earlier,
cut his motor, glided over the fairgrounds, and dropped a metal
cylinder containing his congratulations on Call's efforts for the
town. He then disappeared over the western horizon on a cross-
country flight to the West Coast.[53]

Henry Laurens Call is just one of the many important, and col-
orful, characters who made a name for himself in Kansas. The state
had its share of Europeans who had come to the United States
and participated in the radical politics of the time. Christian Bal-
zac Hoffman was born in Switzerland and had come to America
with his parents, first to Wisconsin and then to central Kansas,
founding the town of Enterprise (near Abilene). Hoffman represented another type of capitalist who pursued a different path
in promoting his principles of socialism. Whereas J. A. Wayland
made his modest fortune in real estate and in developing into a
highly efficient publisher, the "millionaire Socialist" was involved
in various business enterprises with his family. After his father,
using savings from his work as a carpenter, built a flour mill on
Turkey Creek and established Enterprise, the Hoffmans quickly
became the social and economic leaders of the small town, and
the son found a pleasant environment in which to enjoy boyhood.

The family also dabbled in banking and real estate. The affluent young Republican boy was sent to Central Wesleyan College, a German Methodist school in Warrenton, Missouri, where he and his future bride, Catherine Hopkins, came under the influence of "a radical professor."[54]

Hoffman married his classmate and returned to Enterprise, where he entered the family business in 1877. His parents were concerned over his "eccentricities" but decided that with experience he would grow out of the peculiar ideas he had acquired in college. Beginning in 1875, he became involved in politics and, in his only term in the state legislature, introduced a bill to regulate railroad rates. For this the hometown folks branded him an "insurgent," and his lawmaking efforts did not please his parents. For a time Hoffman dabbled in publishing, forming a partnership in 1884 to publish the weekly *Anti-Monopolist*. He and his partner, W. H. T. Wakefield, were anti-monopolists who were concerned over the widening gulf between rich and poor, employee and employer. Powerful corporations were dominating and corrupting the government and using its power to promote monopolies. The young fellows should have discussed their politics more thoroughly, however, because it turned out that Hoffman wanted to continue his support of the GOP and Wakefield did not. This resulted in a parting of ways. As Hoffman became increasingly involved in the emerging Populist movement, he was gradually radicalized politically, which caused further estrangement from his rural community and family.[55]

Hoffman first ventured outside his father's flour mill to form a real estate company with A. S. Diggs (no relation to Kansas Populist, temperance leader, and poet Annie Diggs). They wrote a pamphlet describing the population, climate, and soils of Kansas to advertise their town of Enterprise. It listed the bargain real estate offerings they had for a lucky buyer. The company later expanded, becoming the American Land Company, which included two new partners. From this organization Hoffman was elected president of the new Bank of Enterprise and vice president of the First National Bank of Abilene. He was also active in a sawmill and a lumberyard.[56]

The Hoffmans, father and son, developed the most modern, efficient flour milling company west of Manhattan, home of Kansas State Agricultural College. Two of his children attended the college, where he served as regent from 1894 to 1901. He eventually became president of the Kansas Millers Mutual Insurance Company and the Kansas Harvester Company. The harvester company manufactured a header and thresher that, with two men and twelve horses, could cut, thresh, and bag thirty acres of wheat per day. Hoffman became "a leader and authority in the fields of winter heat and flour milling."[57]

Despite his business successes, young Hoffman gradually came to the conclusion that capitalism was "the individual and political expression of competition, of the principle of everyone for himself, and the devil take the hindmost. It stands for survival of the most cruel, the most brutal, the most cunning. That is why I cannot support it." Watching his area of Kansas being settled and the subsequent development of farm problems during the Populist era, Hoffman "saw the effects of capitalism upon a growing country . . . the rapid disappearance of 'chance' for the poor man." From this he concluded that the differences between the working class and the upper classes were irreconcilable and that socialism was the remedy to economic problems.[58]

When Hoffman made an investment in a colonizing company, the Sinaloa Company, in 1889, he began to study socialism seriously. He became president of the colony, with J. W. Lowell of New York City; an Herr Flursheim of Baden-Baden, Germany; C. F. Lindstrom of Topolobampo, Mexico; and John W. Breidenthal and G. C. Clemens as directors. The company publicized its activities through the *Integral Cooperator*, a small publication that Hoffman edited, and the Credit Foncier of New York City underwrote its financial aspects. The company bought two thousand acres of land in Sinaloa, Mexico, along the west coast, for a utopian colony. It advocated free land, free money, and free education. Workers were to be rewarded with the full fruits of their labor. The membership fee was $10, plus $25 for an improvement fund, $10 for the land fund, $55 for the transportation from Enterprise to Topolobampo, and $2 per hundredweight for freight to the colony. Between two and three hundred colonists left Enterprise with Hoffman in November 1890. Hoffman remained in Sinaloa until April 1891, when he returned to Kansas to organize other colonizing groups. He remained with the company until he and the president of the Credit Foncier were accused of being "great Capitalists" and making huge profits from the colony, and he withdrew.[59]

In 1894 Hoffman played an active role in bringing irrigation to central Kansas. He constructed an irrigation plant north of Enterprise, providing five miles of waterway to irrigate a two hundred–acre farm. A waterwheel of the flour mill operated the pump. At first he rented small plots to gardeners and later took over operation of the plant, with his son Ralph as the manager, and expanded its activities.[60]

In addition to these various pursuits, Hoffman became president of the Kansas Millers Association, and he and his father experimented with selling directly to foreign markets, especially shipping their best grade of flour to Paris. Expectations for this outlet failed to materialize when foreign millers began importing Kansas wheat and milling it at home. Hoffman insisted the problem lay in Kansas millers being charged a higher freight rate on flour for export than foreign millers paid on importing Kansas wheat. He was convinced that Kansans, railroads, and flour mills should be mutually concerned over this "great problem," but the Populists never addressed this issue directly. In 1894 Kansas chartered the Gulf & Interstate railroad to solve this problem, but the current depression doomed the concept.[61]

Hoffman joined the People's Party, and in 1895 he wrote an unpublished essay, "Populism—Its Future." In this essay he argued that the movement "proposes to abolish poverty" by preventing "the exploitation of the masses . . . by destroying rent and interest and the tribute levied by the monopoly of public utilities upon the industries of the people." The movement sought to free money "from the manipulations of private bankers and make it purely a medium of exchange and not a commodity." All public utilities would be nationalized "so that the profits that now go into the coffers of the few may be saved to the laborer." All this, he warned, would not be accomplished in a year or even a decade. It would take time to revolutionize society, views that he would later support as a Socialist with equal ardor.[62]

Following the disastrous defeat of fusion politics again in the election of 1900, Hoffman began exploring the feasibility of developing a new political party in Kansas. He canvassed a number of political friends and acquaintances about this need on the basis that the recent election exposed "a well-organized party with ample funds" being opposed by "a mob rather than a disciplined party." Hoffman was convinced it was time to develop a new Socialist Party that would force capitalists to pay corporate and income taxes for the common welfare and "lift the burden from the shoulder of the producer and place it where it belongs." The next year Debs and his followers would establish that party on the national level.[63]

Hoffman began studying Marx, Engels, Ruskin, Gronlund, and other collectivist writers seriously. His growing radicalism increasingly alienated him from the community and his family. In 1900 he ran for the state senate and did well, receiving 4,277 votes against his opponent, George Fullington, with 4,611. In 1903 he was elected general manager of the Farmers' Cooperative Shipping Association, and the following year he moved to its headquarters in Kansas City. It would handle grain, livestock, and other farm products, and all profits over 8 percent would be divided between patrons and employees. After he was charged with speculation and failure of the company to show a profit, the president asked him to resign, but he successfully challenged this decision. Charges were again brought against him, and this time he resigned, in 1905, but maintained that he had used his own funds in the speculation to which he admitted.

Hoffman also established the Banking Trust Company of Kansas City in 1904, but it failed in the Panic of 1907. The Hoffman family exchanged its stock with the successor organization for 7,860 acres of land in Wilson and Elk Counties. When Hoffman spoke in Kansas City in June 1910, he was described as "a millionaire miller." He owned forty grain elevators across the state that supplied his mills. When a listener accosted him for not practicing socialism, he responded with a laugh that he was "not living under a Socialist system." He supported socialism as a hard-nosed businessman who viewed the triumph of that program as inevitable. Six weeks later he was reported as having received a divorce on the grounds that his wife "refused to live with him" because of his commitment to the Socialist cause; they had "been separated for more than a year." All property rights were decided "outside the case."[64]

His divorce estranged his children in the process, and he retired at this point, turning over much of his property to his wife and children as a settlement. The same year he married Anne Ware of Kansas City. They moved to Chicago when he was appointed editor of the unsigned materials in the *Daily Socialist* in that city. This appointment came because of his previous newspaper experiences in Enterprise. At the same time he and his wife embarked on a lecture tour sponsored by the newspaper, visiting fifty places in eight states. Upon their return to the Windy City, he clashed with the other editor, J. Lewis Engdahl, over newspaper policy. Engdahl and the board of directors refused to allow him to publish an article critical of the Roman Catholic Church. In addition, he disagreed with newspaper policy over trade unions, believing that they did not deserve support as they were part of a capitalist plot and discriminated against unorganized workers.[65] Hoffman expanded his views on trade unions in his letter of resignation: "Trade unionism is not Socialism. The craft unions are the result of Capitalistic principle and practice, based on the idea of benefiting a part of the people at the expense of the rest. Trade unions attempt to defend their numbers not only against Capitalists, but against non-union workers as well, and since they cannot increase the number of jobs and employ all (only Socialism can do that), they are impotent to solve the economic problems." Union competition—or "labor slugging," as he called it—was merely fratricidal strife among the working class itself and was "economic determinism in its blindest, most ignorant and most brutal form."[66]

In 1914 Hoffman became involved in establishing the People's College in Fort Scott, Kansas. He was elected chairman of the governing body and later the college president and expected this work to occupy the remainder of his life. He had become acquainted with Eugene Debs while living in Chicago, and he successfully urged the great Socialist to become the college chancellor. The *Appeal to Reason* advertised the college through the summer of 1914, and classes began that fall. Again controversy followed Hoffman. When the Kansas Flour Mills Company, managed by his son Emmett Hoffman, became involved in a strike, some Kansas Socialists denounced Christian Hoffman because he owned stock in the company. Some of the college directors began pressuring him to resign because of the unfavorable publicity for the college. Hoffman defended himself by noting that his only association with the company was to draw dividends from it. His dislike of trade unions became evident because he charged the union with disseminating false information, but he was forced to resign his positions with the college.[67]

Just before the outbreak of war, Hoffman joined in a debate on the best process for abolishing capitalism. He argued that society had "advanced beyond the brute tactics of pagan ayes." Members of the modern "human family" used the peaceful means of "political combat" and that of education, not violence. Economic tactics were necessary for the working class to use in "direct industrial action," but the necessary appropriation of industry must be undertaken by political strength and action. Education, he declared, is "the supreme law of modern life," and through this would come political supremacy.[68]

Thenceforth Hoffman was active in Socialist politics only on the local level. He gave party speeches and wrote for the *Appeal to Reason*, especially urging Americans to remain aloof on the war in Europe. He insisted that it was not a revolution of the people against their oppressors but a war of "aristocracy" and should be denounced. Two weeks after a tiff with the *Headlight*, he was reported dead from "acute indigestion."[69]

Hoffman proffered a different type of socialism, making the point at one time that government ownership was not in itself socialism. He was certain that many non-Socialists did not understand the distinction of a capitalist government owning and operating a business for profit and a Socialist government owning and operating one "in the interest and benefit of the men" who worked for the company and the people who used its products. He rejected violence and believed his brand of socialism could be accomplished through the constitutional means of the ballot box.

While Hoffman made no great contributions to Socialist theory or the political success of the party, he continued promoting its welfare until his death. Debs believed his contributions to the cause required a personal memorial from him to be read at his funeral services, noting that Hoffman had made great personal sacrifices for the party and the common man. Hoffman's greatest handicap appeared to be his inability to decide definitely if he wanted to be a Socialist or a capitalist in his business relations with various Socialist projects.

These capitalists-turned-Socialists found southeastern Kansas, particularly the Crawford County seat of Girard, as a welcoming haven to live and promote Socialist ideals. That is not to say that all of Girard, or of southeastern Kansas, was Socialist or even strongly so. J. A. Wayland and Henry Laurens Call did bring excitement (and jobs) to Girard, but in the case of Wayland they also attracted fear and mistrust. The local immigrant mining community, spread throughout dozens of local small camps and communities with names like Red Onion, Breezy, Dog Town, Ringo, Walnut, Camp 50, Beulah, and Chicopee, was susceptible to conversion, if they were not already Socialists or union members. However, they did not have, nor would ever have, the wealth and perspective of a Wayland, Call, or Hoffman, Socialists who would live well in this region of few large towns. Pittsburg, twelve miles south of Girard, was the biggest in southeastern Kansas, with a population of fourteen thousand in the early twentieth century. Being Socialist in living and outlook was one thing, but in reality they lived a better life than the many struggling wage slaves of the mining and farming communities and might have easily passed for capitalists.

2

THE EMPATHETIC SOCIALIST

There were many types of Socialists that developed in Kansas. G. C. Clemens was an unusual one because of his personality. For many Socialists the party came first and people second. Not so for Gaspar Christopher Clemens, who was born in Xenia, Ohio, on April 23, 1849, son of a farmer and his wife, who were Methodists. His father traded the farm for a mercantile business, and the family soon fell on hard times. Clemens, who hated his given names and always referred to himself by his initials, G.C., was in effect on his own by age thirteen, not an unusual occurrence in the nineteenth century. He worked in a brickyard and as a cigar maker but still managed to receive a common school education. While teaching in the public schools he gave himself a good education in the classics, studied law, and in 1869 was admitted to the Ohio bar. The next year he arrived in Topeka to practice his craft, later saying he "stayed because he couldn't get away."[1]

Clemens presented a striking appearance—"once seen was never forgotten," as one contemporary expressed it. He bore an incredible resemblance to Samuel L. Clemens and never disabused anyone of their belief that he was related to the famous author, although he once remarked that "there is a party whose real name is the same as our own, but who, for some prudential reason perhaps, has for several years chosen to pass in the world under the alias" of Mark Twain. He was not annoyed that people often referred to him as "Topeka's Mark Twain," observing once, "We disown him, and want it distinctly understood that we are the only lunatic in this family."[2]

Clemens proved to be a remarkably good lawyer. He got off to an auspicious start when his bar exam in Ohio was described as "very brilliant and remarkable." He often was retained in cases in which defeat seemed certain, and he seemed to enjoy such contests, not for money but for the competition. In fact, Clemens never made much money because he regularly took cases from impoverished individuals or worked pro bono. As a result, he was constantly avoiding his landlord. One individual reported that "kindness of heart, overflowing sympathy, and a disposition to help the unfortunate were his dominant characteristics." He was a natural-born author and actor, and his eloquence in jury cases often brought verdicts "the law would not sustain."[3]

"If he had any conceits (and who has not)," another author wrote, "they were confined to the belief that he possessed extraordinary talents in literature and powers as a political revolutionist." Perhaps in an effort to emulate Mark Twain, Clemens published a weekly newspaper, the *Whim-Wham*, in which he gave expression to his eccentric and strongly held political views, with an occasional touch of humor. The paper lasted only one year because he had few advertisers and subscribers, with only some of his friends and political sympathizers to rely on. He soon reverted to his law practice in order to survive.

One of Clemens's early cases required his presence in federal court. It was a difficult trial, and he appeared before the judge with "a pile of books" designed to help him make an argument against a well-established legal principle that was "unchangeable." The judge gave him an hour to make his point, and "he attacked the proposition with all the vigor and force he could command." The judge remained unpersuaded but "was so impressed with the ingenious argument that he adjourned court and held the decision over until the next morning as a compliment to the young man's ability."[4]

Clemens enjoyed the difficult cases because they tested his intellectual mettle. In a case argued in circuit court before the future Supreme Court associate justice Samuel F. Miller, he attempted to confuse the judge with irrelevant points. When Judge Miller reminded him to keep within "the merits of the case," he responded, "If it please your honor, when the merits of the case are reached I lose all interest in it." One lawyer noted that Clemens was not a black-letter lawyer (one who will not move away from the literal meaning of the law) but, instead, relied upon his vast reading and great memory to carry him through difficult situations. The same writer believed him to be the best lawyer in the state on chancery jurisdiction, or the practice of equity. But those who knew him well regretted that he was "easily diverted from the work of the law to the exploitation of his peculiar political views." As a result, he fulfilled the maxim of American lawyer Rufus Choate about the fate of lawyers "who lived well, worked hard, and died poor":[5]

> Clemens was in straightened conditions much of his early years. As he said: I was poor. Alas, that is but too true. Your humble servant might have been frequently seen with an unseemly spot of mustard on his proboscis—the sole remnant of recently eaten free lunch—returning to his stately lodgings over an undertaker's shop, where the world, for all its sin and folly, was for a few brief hours, forgotten in balmy sleep, coveted and found upon the soft floor with chair and overcoat for a downy pillow. In those primitive Topeka days the subscriber's principal amusement was smoking a miserable pipe filled with still more miserable tobacco, in company with a few kindred Bohemians with kind hearts and empty pockets.

He readily admitted that he had "plunged into the whirlpool of vice and sin, then characteristic" of frontier Topeka.[6]

Clemens's inherent optimism made Kansas Prohibitionists an obvious target for his barbs. He had good words to say about "the fruit of the vine," especially in his younger, rakish days. On one occasion Governor John P. St. John, who also was the presidential nominee for the Prohibitionist ticket, was his object of scorn. In discussing the possible motives of Charles Guiteau for assassinating President James Garfield in 1881, Clemens observed that "the most probable theory is that he is insane, at least we are told that he talks and acts a great deal like his excellency, our Governor St. John."[7]

Clemens began his legal career as a conservative, but events convinced him to move leftward. First, he experienced financial problems. Topeka, the capital city, was growing, as was Kansas, and citizens there offered an immense opportunity to build a reputation. But at first it was a hardscrabble life. His motto, partly made in self-derision, was "Always get a retainer and get a refresher frequently." But many of his clients could not afford to pay him a retainer or even his fee. He had great sympathy for the poor and downtrodden and often took a case without fee if he believed the client had been a victim of the justice system and could not afford to pay.[8]

In addition, he had personal problems. He was becoming deaf by the time he reached forty. He also experienced some brushes with the police, citing the fact that the Kansas City, Missouri, police chief "once locked all outdoors against me," even refusing to allow him to speak in public places. He had adverse encounters with obstinate judges, leaving him with much empathy for those with similar experiences who had no training in the legal system. He called Governor John Leedy's attention to the use of women prisoners on the rock pile at the state prison at Lansing, and the governor immediately ordered an end to the practice. He became upset over a proposed reduction in faculty salaries at the state university and told the press that "when the cry shall be heard that we have driven learning from the state, and that accusation cannot be denied, I can but blush for my party and hang my head in silent shame."[9]

His encounter with the state troops, when he accepted an officer's commission, led him to study the militia law of Kansas, and he expressed his apprehension over the loose wording of the statute. Railroad workers, who were members of the Knights of Labor, struck the Jay Gould lines in 1885. The strikers then won their greatest victory in the nineteenth century with the active assistance of the Kansas governor, John Martin. Administration of the strike centered in Atchison, and railroad officials, hoping to lure the governor into sending state militia there, had both the sheriff of Atchison County and the mayor of the town wire the governor that a mob had taken control of the railroads. Governor Martin calmly had the reports investigated, concluded the strikers were right in their cause and peaceful in their actions, and declined to order out the militia. Furthermore, he persuaded the governor of Missouri not to summon his militia, and in the absence of soldiers and martial law, the strikers won a great victory.[10]

Clemens concluded that the state militia was expected to break strikes, and if it had been dispatched in this instance, the mayor and sheriff "would have crimsoned the streets with the blood of curious men, women, and children and provoked an insurrection that would have made that city a bloody field of battle." But he feared that the recent enactment of a new militia law carried this power "to a dangerous level." In case of insurrection or imminent danger thereof, the new statute authorized the commanding officer of a military unit to order out his men, "and when he has shot down everything in sight, he is to snatch up his pen and inform the Governor of what he has done." Any "hot spur of a militia captain could do this," and there was nothing to prevent a railroad company from arranging for workers to be awarded captain status on the militia companies. Clemens was convinced this violated the state constitution because it specified only the governor could call out the militia. His fears were realized, although Clemens neglected to call attention to it in the railroad strike in Emporia in 1878.[11]

As Clemens moved leftward in his political thinking, he began supporting unpopular reform causes, such as women's suffrage, mistreatment of Native Americans, and legal injustice. He became known as an empathetic defender of laborers against the oppression of the industrialist with the emergence of the "labor problem" in America. His allegiance became quite clear with his defense of the protestors in the Haymarket Square bombing in Chicago in 1886, in which eleven people died, including seven policemen.[12]

The eight-hour day became a major goal for workers in 1886, and on May Day, the traditional day of revolution in Europe, workers demonstrated nationwide for this objective. Proponents argued that the eight-hour day "would end the degradation of the endless workday: and, more importantly, would create more free time for self-education of the laborer to permit him to become a more efficient producer," ultimately, perhaps, instigating a cooperative system of production that would free producers from the wage system that stifled their potential. "Eight Hour Leagues" sprang up rapidly in cities, especially in Chicago, which had become the center of what many writers preferred to call "the center of anarchy in America."

These people were not anarchists in the strict sense of wanting to destroy government. They were left-wing Socialists with varying degrees of belief in the use of violence to abolish the capitalist system, but their opponents believed *anarchists* to be a useful appellation to apply to them. A century earlier the same advocates wore the label *patriots* or *rebels*, depending upon one's political orientation or attitude toward George III. In the late nineteenth century dynamite was employed commercially more often than in that earlier era. The media concluded that the pejorative term *anarchist* was descriptive of any radical who urged the use of violence to achieve ends, and the term soon became loosely applied to all "rebels" against the capitalist system. It should be noted that many of the radicals reveled in the term *anarchist* or *Communist* and encouraged its application to themselves. Interestingly, "radicals" often used their soapbox to read the Declaration of Independence publicly and shock conservatives who were ignorant of the "anarchistic" views it contained. Significantly, these so-called radicals contradicted the current economic theory that wages were inelastic, arguing that as productivity increased, capitalists could afford more dollars for wages and still maintain high profits.[13]

August Spies, a leading anarchist in Chicago, seemed to be everywhere as labor grew extremely restless in Chicago in the spring of 1886. He advised the activities of the strikers at International Harvester, the brewery workers pressing for a policy of union workers only, lumber pushers who were threatening to walk off the job, sewing girls who were striking periodically, and the city's labor force, which was in general turmoil. When Spies, a recent German immigrant, arrived in Chicago, he found work in upholstery, which served the large furniture industry in the metropolis. He also became a popular speaker for the labor movement. He spoke to a rally of strikers outside the International Harvester plant and, while he was orating, the whistle blew for the end of the shift for strikebreakers. The strikers rushed the factory gates and the scabs, and in the following melee, company police attacked them with clubs and guns and mortally wounded six men.[14]

That night several labor leaders met in the basement of a tavern owned by a Thomas Grief and laid plans for a protest meeting the following evening in Haymarket Square. Only two of the city's leading anarchists were present, George Engle, a toy maker from Germany, and Adolph Fischer, another German immigrant who worked as a printer. One of the leading Chicago anarchists, Albert Parsons, had not yet returned from Cincinnati, where he spoke to strikers there, bringing them news of the exciting events in Chicago and labor developments elsewhere. Those who attended the meeting in Grief's tavern planned a rally of supporters of the strikers and the eight-hour movement the following evening, on May 4, 1886, and plastered the city with posters announcing the event. The activities in Grief's tavern proved crucial in the subsequent trial of the Chicago anarchists. Louis Lingg, another German radical Socialist who was convinced that dynamite was the great equalizer in the death struggle with capitalists, brought several homemade bombs to the meeting. He was indifferent to the eight-hour movement but was pleased when several people accepted his bombs that night.

Some three thousand people assembled in Haymarket Square the following evening, on May 4. No one appeared to be in charge to begin the speaking. Spies opened the ceremonies by noting that it was called not to create drastic action but to protest the killing of six innocent men the previous day and to demonstrate support for the eight-hour day. When he spotted Parsons in the crowd, he called on him. Parsons spoke of his travels and the labor discontent he had witnessed and how the system must be changed. Mayor Carter Harrison listened to Parsons, then walked to the nearby police station to inform police inspector John Bonfield that the speakers were "tame" and he was going home.[15]

A cold wind began blowing in rain, and the crowd, following the mayor's lead, had largely dispersed. At that point a detachment of some three hundred police arrived from the nearby station, and after an English anarchist tried to incite the motley remnants of the crowd to violence, their captain ordered all assembled to disperse. Suddenly someone hurled a bomb into their midst, killing a policeman and injuring many others. The police opened fire on the people, and "wild carnage" followed, with seven policemen killed by their colleagues, or by someone, although a reliable witness said he saw no firing from the crowd; over seventy people were wounded.[16]

With the press printing the reports of Inspector Bonfield as if they were absolutely accurate, Chicago authorities and newspapers immediately blamed the anarchists for the murders. August Spies, Albert Parsons, Louis Lingg, Samuel Fisher, Johan Most, and three others were immediately arrested and brought to trial. Judge Joseph Gary sentenced seven of them to death, and one was given a prison term of one to fifteen years. Parsons had fled to a friend's sanctuary in Wisconsin but later returned and surrendered to authorities because he knew he was innocent. Most newspapers concluded that the trial had been fairly conducted and the defendants' sentences were justified. Their conclusions then were accepted by other newspapers across the nation. After William Dean Howells, Henry Demarest Lloyd, and Clarence Darrow petitioned the governor, John Altgeld commuted the death sentence of Samuel Fielden, Michael Schwab, and Oscar Neebe to life imprisonment, but four of the accused were executed, and Louis Lingg died by suicide. Altgeld, a liberal, examined the evidence and concluded that "a packed jury had been selected to convict" the anarchists and that "much of the evidence given at the trial was a pure fabrication." In addition, he said, Judge Gary "was either so prejudiced against the defendants or else so determined to win the applause of a certain class in the community that he could not and did not grant a fair trial." Altgeld also surmised that the bomb thrower had acted not in a conspiracy but "as an individual seeking revenge against a police force that had been beating and shooting unarmed working people." Conservative forces severely criticized the governor for this action, but he was heartily applauded by liberals. The identity of the bomb thrower was never discovered. Conservatives used this issue to fight trade unions, and it mortally wounded the Knights of Labor. The memory of the Haymarket martyrs endured into the twentieth century, observed every year on May Day, and November 10 was enshrined as a day to commemorate the hanging of the four with a visit to their memorial in Chicago's Waldheim Cemetery.[17]

Parsons had served during the Civil War at age fifteen in the Confederate Cavalry under command of an elder brother. Following hostilities, he returned to his home in East Texas and began a small newspaper in which, to the consternation of his friends, he advocated rights for blacks. He married a beautiful black woman named Lucy, and in 1874 they arrived in Chicago, where Parsons found a position in the printing trade. He soon became a sought-after speaker for labor causes.

Parsons undertook a lengthy speaking tour of the West in the summer of 1885, visiting Kansas, Missouri, and Nebraska. This tour apparently made a significant impression on Clemens. As he expressed it, Parsons brought the gospel of "Liberty, Equality, and Fraternity" to some twenty thousand laborers. His visit to Kansas was expedited by Socialist Charles A. Henrie (Parsons spelled it *Henry*) and Harry Vrooman. Vrooman had become attracted to socialism while a student at Washburn College. The Vrooman family were notorious Kansas radicals. Harry's older brother, Walter, who was a preacher, was also a member of the Socialist-Labor Party while preaching from a Congregationalist pulpit in Kansas City. The brothers and their father published a newspaper in the Knight chain and had an impact on a number of reforms in Kansas.[18]

For three weeks Parsons traveled through the three-state area during his 1885 speaking tour, going from Omaha to Kansas City to the Tri-State region farther south. In Ottawa, Kansas, a community one hundred miles north of the Tri-State, he spoke to three thousand "wage slaves" about the current "social order":

> It is our modern industrial system, with its world-wide markets, based on the institution of *private* property. It is the private ownership by a few members of society of the means of production and resources of life; such private ownership creating two classes—one the bourgeoi-

sie, or the propertied class, the other the proletariat, or property-less class. The propertied are thus made a privileged class who grow enormously wealthy by absorbing or confiscating the labor products of the propertyless, who become dependent hirelings of the proper-ties. . . . The American republic was proclaimed 109 years ago today, and its existence made possible because the men of that time were, comparatively speaking, economically free and equal. Their mate-rial and physical condition was such as to make the republic possible.

The Declaration of Independence that "all men are by nature cre-ated equal," are as much a truth but less an actuality to the people of the United States today as when our fathers proclaimed it. The men of that day possessed political freedom because they enjoyed eco-nomic liberty, and we, their descendants, are disfranchised, because we are disinherited—deprived of the means of life.[19]

Parsons's speeches in the Tri-Sate region "created a profound sensation and [were] the talk next day of every one in town." While there, he saw multitudes of unemployed men. He was invited twice to St. Joseph and to Kansas City and on two occa-sions to Topeka, where G. C. Clemens likely heard him. Parsons was a member of the Knights of Labor and addressed the local assembly in Topeka on the Fourth of July. Three days later he returned to the capital city, where he spoke for three hours from an express wagon in the middle of the street to an audience of just over 1,500 at the corner of Sixth and Kansas Avenue.[20]

The press in Kansas was noticeably indifferent to Parsons's speeches. The Ottawa, Pittsburg, and Topeka newspapers failed to report his presence, except for Topeka's *Commonwealth*, which referred to Parsons as "a street demagogue." The *Kansas Sun and Globe* (Kansas City MO) reported his speech in that city at some length. He addressed a large gathering on "Free Labor vs. Slave Labor." The editor noted Parsons was "a leading exponent of anarchical communism" and that his "arraignment of the pres-ent system . . . was very forceful, and, in the main, just." Parsons denounced the current trust movement, and the editor agreed that this trend "to drive out small dealers and manufacturers" was deplorable. But he disagreed with Parsons over the means to correct the capitalist system. "For the life of us," he said, "we cannot conceive how existing human nature could dispense with government." The anarchist insisted that "under a regime of communal property all men would deport themselves like angels." "The simple, incontrovertible fact," the editor concluded, is that "governments are a necessity" and, while "Mr. Parsons is doing a good educational work, . . . his measures of reform we must reject."[21]

Clemens would support most of Parsons's ideas by then, especially his denunciation of police gunning down unarmed workers and their families in the Haymarket Square incident. Clemens published a broadside in their defense. Calling it "A Common Sense View of the Anarchist Case," he addressed it to Governor Richard J. Oglesby of Illinois. Clemens quoted from the U.S. Supreme Court decision that "it is conceded that no one of the convicted defendants threw the bomb"—most were not even present when the "conspiracy" took place in Thomas Grief's tavern, but all were charged as accessories in the act. But to convict them of being accessories, Clemens insisted, authorities had to prove that they had advised the bomb thrower, a very obvious deduction, nor was any evidence presented that the unknown culprit had read any of the current anarchist literature. When calling for the Haymarket meeting, no one anticipated conflict there because the Chicago police had never attempted before to interfere with public meetings. Significantly, many of the defendants were not present when the meeting was planned, and no evidence was brought forward at the trial, obviously, to show that the bomb thrower had been present either because he remained unknown.[22]

Someone, though, was guilty of starting a riot besides the police. When officials ordered the crowd to disperse and they resisted (which was not proved), it was their duty to arrest them, "not to club them nor to shoot them." "Until arrest is resisted," Clemens asserted, "police are not authorized to act as a military force." The police in Haymarket Square acted illegally in using force on the unresisting people who were trying to go home. This, he concluded, was the purpose behind the Second Amendment: to bear arms to oppose such despotic acts. The Monday night "plan" to call a meeting the next day in Haymarket "was a lawful covenant of men." "To punish a man because we believe that because of the doctrine he holds he will commit a crime," according to Macaulay's *Essays*, "is persecution and is, in every case, 'foolish and wicked.'"[23]

Clemens also gave speeches during the summer in support of the condemned men and against strong-arm police tactics in Topeka. His subsequent broadside, titled "DAMNABLE! POLICE INFAMIES OF A SINGLE WEEK," discussed some dozen workers arrested "on suspicion" and sent to work on rock piles without trial for twenty-five days. He concluded with the demand for the abolition of the city police court and jail.[24]

"Revolution is inevitable," Clemens wrote of the recent national labor unrest, especially in the current railroad strikes. "The revolution must sweep over our land, be fought out. . . . The crisis is impending." Clemens was gaining a reputation for being a radical, and now, by defending the Haymarket actions of protesters, many began calling him the "Topeka Anarchist."[25]

Clemens certainly added to his reputation as a radical when he and David Obermeyer undertook to defend the ideas of Moses Harman, a teacher, minister, and journalist who lived in Kansas during the late 1800s. Harman published a periodical, *Lucifer, the Light Bearer*, in Topeka; it stressed free thought and sexual liberation. The state charged his daughter, Lillian Harman, and Edwin Walker with unlawful cohabitation because they performed their own wedding ceremony according to her family traditions. Clemens and Obermeyer defended Lillian Harman unsuccessfully in the state supreme court. They also defended her father, Moses, by arguing that if sending *Lucifer, the Light Bearer* through the U.S. mail was violating the obscenity laws, then so, too, would mailing the Bible and works by Shakespeare, Swift, and many other authors. The judge complimented them on their "ingenious argument" but ruled against them and sent Moses to prison.[26]

The great railroad strike of 1885 made obvious the state's lack of means for industrial arbitration. Governor John Martin sent a message to the state legislature stressing his experience in the unrest and his conclusion that this process was needed. The Knights of Labor expressed interest in cooperating, and without investigations or hearings, the courts immediately established such boards to arbitrate labor disputes. They were following the lead of several states that had established such boards, and many were urging a national one. The program proved worthless immediately as strikes broke out the following year again on the Gould railroads. Jay Gould and his team broke the strike without arbitration, and this labor loss began a significant decline in influence of the Knights of Labor.[27]

Three years later Clemens authored an essay on trade unions that revealed his deep empathy for the cause of labor and also that he was on the path to becoming a Socialist before he became a Populist. The millions of workers in the labor movement had experienced "suffering, self-denial, abuse imprisonment, and even death," he wrote. "Its goal is not just work. Workers want a decent living, which they get by working for wages. The ultimate aim is not just providing jobs but to allowing workers to live a decent life through paid work. Beyond living, they also want to achieve leisure to enjoy what wages would buy."[28]

The goal of workers in the Middle Ages was the nebulous "just wage," but in the nineteenth century that changed to workers earning a living wage. Employers should pay their workers what had been earned over and above what the employers should retain as their own. But here lies the nub of the problem: what pay should an employer receive? Clemens used the parable of the entrepreneur on the Missouri River who advertised for five hundred men during flood stage to catch driftwood on even shares. Scores of men responded and fished for driftwood for two or three days, giving the advertiser his half, which he hauled away at once. When the men finally realized what they had agreed to, they were too embarrassed to raise "a disturbance." If the earth belongs to a few, they should pay the workers a "just" wage because they are allowed to live here at the owner's sufferance. But if the earth and its natural resources belong to all people, as did the driftwood, Clemens insisted, then workers have the right to their earnings without sharing them with anyone. Therefore, "if we appeal to moral right, natural justice . . . we do away with wages altogether," he argued, because the mine belongs to all, the driftwood belongs to anyone who retrieves it, and each is enti-

tled to the fruits of his labor. The employer did nothing to create the mine because, Clemens explained, it "was put here by the
earth's Creator and belongs to no man or set of men, no matter
what the laws you have made say to the contrary. . . . This railroad, this factory, and this machine shop were made by weary
human hands from materials supplied by nature," and "not one
of you ever did a day's work on these things." This was the heart
of socialism. It was at this time that Clemens joined with other
reformers, including C. B. Hoffman, to invest in a utopian colony at Topolobampo, Mexico.[29]

As agrarian conditions worsened in the late nineteenth century,
especially for middle-class farmers who were deeply in debt for
farm machinery or land expansion, efforts to organize these dis-
contented workers accelerated. The farmers sought unity with
workers because the goal of both groups was the same. Workers pursued a living wage for their families, and agrarians sought
the full value of what they produced. Clemens, with his agrarian,
laboring class background, empathized with farm organizations
that were trying to ally with the Knights of Labor. It was natural for him to become involved in current political issues, and he
was especially aroused over the extent of poverty in this period
of overproduction. "Can it be supposed," he asked rhetorically,
"that a limited few of the human race can, with safety to themselves, lock up all nature's stores, and pile up human food to rot
while a starving world looks on?"[30]

These angry agrarians formed the People's, or Populist, Party
in 1890 and were an immediate political success in many areas.
In 1892 the Populists secured the election of their candidate for
governor, Lorenzo Lewelling, and, they thought, a Populist-
controlled legislature. When the Populists arrived in Topeka to
claim their legislative seats, they discovered they had outright
control over the upper house, but the Republicans held sixty-five
certificates of election, the Populists fifty-eight, with two Democrats in the lower house. A number of these candidates challenged the election of their opponents, and Clemens represented
several of the Populists in court. The resulting melee was appro-
priately labeled the "Legislative War."

Clemens wrote a pamphlet to assist the Populists in organizing the lower house. The secretary of state, Clemens argued, does not organize either body of the legislature; he merely presents to each house "a list of the members elected thereto." But first the members must be organized to receive the list, and this could not be accomplished until it was determined who had legally won each district. Merely holding a certificate of election is not "*prima facie* evidence of entitlement to a seat." Each claimant must decide for himself, and if disputed, he and "those who dispute with him must come to some agreement." Of the sixty-four Republicans, two had not been elected to their seats. These two, therefore, could not participate in organizing the house. Clemens urged all disputes be set aside until the house was organized, then let that body settle the dispute as the members of each house controlled their membership. "The scheming, unscrupulous European owners of Kansas corporations (the Santa Fe railroad)," Clemens said, are responsible for this chaos and Kansans should "draw the fangs of these reptiles." "A PEOPLE'S HOUSE OR NONE," he concluded.[31]

The Populists organized the Senate. When the Democrats joined Republicans in the House, the Populists barred them from the chamber. The Republicans battered down the door with a sledgehammer, and in the process Clemens and a National Guard private "sustained injuries and shed blood." The opposition press blamed Clemens and fellow Populist lawyers Frank Doster and W. C. Webb for the "war." The Republicans retained physical control over the house chamber by force, so the Populists met in another room in the capitol for the next thirty-one days. The issue was taken to the state supreme court, with Doster, Webb, and Clemens representing the Populists, and to the surprise of no one, the judges voted by party. The controlling Republican judges found for the Republicans.[32]

Clemens blasted the "unblushing mendacity" of the Republican justices, accusing them of reaching the "sham" decision before they had heard the case. He had to be careful, though, not to go too far because charges of the type leveled against two members of the court would do him "little good in a professional way." Given this background Governor Lewelling suffered through many controversies during his two years in office, and Clemens frequently represented the administration in court appearances, in which he fought hard.[33]

Over the next few years a number of factors coalesced to alienate Clemens from the Populist Party. He strongly opposed those Populists who insisted on fusing with the Democrats, who advocated free and unlimited coinage of silver at the ration of sixteen to one, and "Silver" Republicans in 1896 to support the William Jennings Bryan–Thomas Watson ticket. While this slate went down to defeat nationally, it captured all three branches of government in Kansas. Clemens's friend Republican William Johnson joined the two new Populist justices, Frank Doster and Stephen Allen, to appoint Clemens as the reporter for the state supreme court. It became his duty to prepare the decisions of that court and the court of appeals for the next two years. One historian noted that this work was "always well done, and he adopted some new features in indexing which many regarded as substantial improvements."[34]

The Populists lost the elections of 1898, and Clemens lost his position. He subsequently worried over fusion with Bryan and the Democrats, who continued to stress the issue of "free and unlimited coinage" of silver at the official ratio of sixteen to one. While he retained his original commitment to the Populists on gradual reform, many of them had begun to moderate their views under the pressure of fusion. He noted that "we can put silver back where it was in 1873, but we cannot put the world back there. And, in the world of today, with its gigantic trusts and combinations—none of which our proposed allies permit us to touch—would free silver restore the conditions of twenty-three years ago. What folly to even dream."[35]

"Alas, our party is no more," he lamented. "Designing men, followed by people foolish enough to believe that mere scheming can advance a noble cause[,] have left it a hopeless wreck." "What is this fusionist party?" he asked. The Democrats had not abandoned their party but, instead, had been building up their own political organization. "There is not a Populist among their committeemen," Clemens noted, but "there are many Democrats serving on Populist committees." The Populist state committee, he charged, "moves, lives, and has its being only in the sunshine of the Democratic State Committee's favor."[36]

After the Fusionist defeat in 1896, Clemens was ready for an organization of "true reform." He declared that "while the People's Party lived," he "steadfastly refused to join a Socialist Party, for the People's Party in Kansas was headed for outright Socialism." When the Fusionist movement killed the Populist Party, he began organizing the Socialist Party. "So numerous and urgent have become the requests from Populist comrades," he reported, that he was taking it upon himself to start a Socialist Party for the "true Populists" so they might find "a congenial home." "I must forsake the Fusionists or the Socialists," he announced, "it is no longer possible for them to remain together."[37]

In his "Appeal to True Populists" Clemens waxed eloquent on his insistence that fusion meant that the Populists would become a "single-issue" party. The Fusionist

> traitors to the holy cause of the people would have us abandon, as they have already abandoned, every aim of our party, in order that we may secure the accession of old party politicians, who, we are coolly informed, are too ignorant or too Capitalistic to endure even the mention of postal savings banks, the public ownership of public utilities, a national currency issue direct to the people with out the intervention of banks, the extinction of the monopoly of the earth, or the paring of the rather dangerous claws of the federal courts. About all these things we are to be silent, lest we hurt the feelings or shock the barbaric prejudices of our proposed Allies. And what mighty achievement is to justify this sacrifice of principle? We are to enable every owner of a silver mine to coin its product into silver dollars![38]

All this for people "many of whom do not even live nor hold citizenship in this country," he noted, in reference to foreign financiers.

As early as 1893, he was in communication with Laurence Gronlund, who viewed the political situation in Kansas as ripe for socialism. The great Socialist thinker had written an exploratory letter to several Kansans, and Clemens was the only one who responded positively. Gronlund decided to relocate his head-quarters to Topeka. He planned on being at Emporia for the upcoming Alliance meeting because he had been invited to have "a hearing" there to promote socialism. Because he planned on Topeka as his future headquarters, he asked Clemens to send him the names of "a dozen of the most progressive men and women in your city."[39]

Once he had committed to socialism, Clemens entered the fray with his usual energy and enthusiasm. He organized the Socialist Party at a meeting at the National Hotel in Topeka on April 21, 1897. F. E. Miller of DeSoto was elected state chairman, Clemens as state organizer and secretary, and G. A. Gordon of Cedar Junction as treasurer. These officers were to serve as the state committee when the central committee, composed of eight members, was not in session.[40] Shortly thereafter, Clemens appeared in Pittsburg to spread the message. He was described as "the most distinguished Social Democrat of Kansas, the apostle of social democracy in the state." He deplored the current divisions within socialism and wanted Socialists to unite and pursue "a vigorous . . . forcible plan of action." Further, he believed that Socialists could and should unite with other organizations to achieve the common good.[41]

The state's leading newspaper, the *Topeka Daily Capital*, announced in February 1898 that Debs and Edward Bellamy were planning on launching a new political party, the Social Democracy Party. A meeting was held in Debs's room in the New Markham hotel in Denver with James Hogarth, a one-time leader of the American Railway Union, and "a number of local radicals." The same journal announced the following month that this group planned on launching its first colonies in Kansas. In an interview Debs said that Kansas was "the most hopeful state in the union for furtherance of our work." He planned on coming to Kansas to speak, and Clemens would accompany him on his tour.[42]

In June 1898 the first state convention of Socialists met in Fort Scott to nominate candidates for state office and plan campaign strategies. The platform demanded a quick end to the Spanish-American War, an increase in military pay, a cut in officers' salaries, and issuance of paper money until legal tender was abolished. It included the radical plank that "all lands should be the property of the whole people to be held in common" and "the abolishing of gold and silver until legal tender can be abolished." In accordance with activist Etta Semple's demand, the convention went on record as opposing use of the Lord's Prayer in public schools. Mrs. Semple, an atheist, was nominated for state superintendent of schools.[43]

In 1900 Clemens wrote a pamphlet, *A Primer on Socialism*, in which he expressed his concept of the political and economic philosophy of the movement, to which he would dedicate the remainder of his life. He insisted that the sole purpose of socialism was "a practical plan to make possible a happy life." This required only to change the motive and management of the industries that provide for the maintenance and enjoyment of *physical* life. There was no need to change government; it would still be needed. Those who want to change governments are Communists, he declared. Socialists say that land, forests, quarries mines, mills, factories, railways, canals, steamships, telegraphs, telephones, waterworks, waterpower, electric plants, plants for distributing heat and light coal yards store, delivery wagons, and so on, belong to all, or at least they need to supply everyone with a good living. All would need to work to acquire a good living, but the present work could be halved by eliminating the profit factor. Every worker would receive an equal income throughout the community. "Government does not need to be made over; it need only to be used for proper purposes," Clemens wrote. Socialism, he added, "will provide a living for those who work for it, and will give all an opportunity to work, and there its mission will end."[44]

Clemens elaborated on this philosophy in an essay printed as part of the proceedings of the Second Annual Convention of the State Society of Labor and Industry entitled "Labor Legislation and How to Get It." The Fourteenth Amendment served as the basis for the bar against securing good labor legislation. The amendment was adopted to protect the newly freed slave in the Civil War. From then until the turn of the century, Clemens argued, judges interpreted the phrase on denial of "life, liberty, or property" to protect the capitalist class. Setting a limit on the workday, such as no more than eight hours, denied the worker the liberty of contracting for as many hours as he wished. This clause, in turn, protected the employer in using his property as he wished, without regulations, and for the state to force him to pay a minimum wage would deprive him of his property "without due process of law." Clemens refused to accept the idea that the Fourteenth Amendment intended to mean "in low cunning so to tie the hands of government as to prevent it from interfering with the establishment of a new and more galling slavery of both black and white," as judges were interpreting it. He wanted the old political economy "to make way for the Sermon on the Mount." He predicted that a new industrial system would rise and that "the Golden Rule will be human law that needs no sanction of prison or scaffold to gain its obedience."[45] Clemens lamented the fact that

> not all lawyers, not all judges, have fought in freedom's ranks. Many of them have ever been ready to help rivet more securely the fetters upon the limbs of the oppressed. Many, with their faces to the past, have not seen the approach of the future. Many have gazed with such prolonged rapture upon the splendors of sunset that they have caught no glimpse of the glory of dawn. Many have stood for old use, and blasphemed progress. Some of these have not blushed to support the proposition that government may protect the physical health of the citizen, but must be approvingly silent when, at the will of avarice, only such trifles as his mind and his soul are destroyed.[46]

Clemens believed that public opinion must be "educated to the plane where the science of human greed, otherwise known as political economy, ceases to be a guide to human conduct." Socialism provides the underlying principle for labor legislation, he concluded, and "on no other principle can it be maintained to be right." "Wearily," the nation's poor have been waiting for Christ's promise and His summons to "come unto me all ye who are weary and heavy laden, and I will give you rest."[47]

The Populists met in a state convention in the spring of 1899. There was no doubt from the beginning that the anti-Fusionists were in control. A motion was made immediately to name a full slate of candidates. Price Thomas, "a colored Populist," opposed this decision, arguing that "the only sensible thing to do is to fuse with the Democrats." Clemens quickly took the floor in opposition. The "famous wit and agitator" spent the next ten minutes "in the most scathing sarcasm," denouncing the fusion idea. The Democrats had already nominated their ticket. Clemens was "tired of the Populist Party with more than 100,000 votes in Kansas humbling itself before this dwarf with less than 30,000 votes." He concluded that if this convention "contemplated such action he would not be party to it."[48]

Clemens's speech created an enthusiastic buzz. Colonel Fred Close took the floor, stating that a group of Democrats who "had repented their action in excluding the Populists from their deliberations" was at the door, ready "to make overtures." Clemens again took the floor to describe the Democratic committee as "presumptuous," saying that for the Populists to receive them would be "degrading." He was fighting for "principle," not "merely a swapping of offices." The Democratic candidate for mayor was supposedly in favor of municipal ownership of a waterworks, but who was certain of this? Everyone at this convention was known to be in favor of municipal ownership, so why nominate an unknown for mayor? If they did, Clemens would "not disgrace my hand by dropping a ballot in the box" for him.[49]

The chair noted that the Democrats were willing to allow the Populists to name two candidates for the school board, one councilman, a justice of the peace, and a constable. "What magnanimity! What generosity!" exclaimed Clemens derisively. "Gentlemen, it is astounding. We were not prepared for such overtures." When the Democrats left empty-handed, the motion to name a city ticket passed without opposition, and Mr. Clemens won the nomination for mayor. Clemens by then was almost deaf and was unaware of the turn of events until a news reporter shouted in his ear, "You have been nominated for Mayor." When he protested, the conventioneers remained adamant. "Well," he said, accepting the inevitable, "if I am to fight this water company, I want a good city attorney." The convention then named Frank Herald, whom Clemens endorsed, for the office of attorney.[50] Clemens ran a vigorous campaign but was overwhelmed by Charles Drew, the favored candidate, who polled 4,624 votes to Clemens's 674. Dr. W. T. Taylor garnered 746 ballots. At this early stage no Socialist could hope to be elected mayor of Topeka.[51]

Such crushing defeat encouraged Fusion Populists to renew their fight in the August conventions. Separately, the Democrats and Populists agreed on a common ticket. Nominating R. B. Kepley for sheriff proved to be a divisive move because of the issue of enforcing prohibition. While the Populist platform called for "strict enforcement" of the laws, Sheriff Kepley was known for his tolerance of "Demon Rum." Immediately after the reading of the temperance plank, Clemens took the floor and, in a characteristic move, called the resolution "cowardly." "Why don't you say what you mean?" he demanded. "The resolution is infamous. You don't mean all laws [but one law—prohibition]." This was a play for the temperance vote, he declared, reminding the delegates that the People's Party demanded "state ownership on the liquor question."[52]

Clemens was ready to abandon the Populist Party for the Socialist Party he was organizing as a state organization. The Populist Party had died after fusion failed in 1896, and efforts to promote fusion failed in 1900, leaving the People's Party to be buried.[53]

This demise came at the zenith of the debate over expansionism during the Spanish-American War and the "pacification" of the Philippine Islands. Clemens, the empathetic Socialist, came down on the side of imperialism in the campaign of 1900. One might not expect that he would have taken this position given his previous career, but he connected it with his dominant goal of expanding education. "Where Capitalism goes," he explained, "education will go; discontent with Capitalism will go; Socialism will follow. . . . Expansionism is right, for it is creating historic development and hastening the end of misery in the world."[54]

In the summer of 1900 the Socialist Party chose Clemens as its candidate for governor of Kansas. The *Appeal to Reason* saw him as a "genuine Populist," more concerned about achieving "the great principles of the reform movement than about the success of those Populists who were campaigning for political office." These Populists were "never loyal to personalities," the newspaper added, and they "hanker after some new field of theory to conquer, and Socialism is becoming very attractive to them." In 1898 the Socialist candidate for governor received 625 votes. Clemens was "a man of intellectual attainments: and has shown "a good deal of activity." The *Appeal* predicted a better showing in 1900.[55]

Clemens traveled to Pittsburg to appeal to the miners of Cherokee and Crawford Counties, not for their vote but for "fair play." He insisted that he had been "slandered by a set of infamous scoundrels in your district." He had challenged accusers who were saying he was paid by the Republican Party to "meet him anywhere in the mining area." He had reserved the opera house in Pittsburg for October 4, and he invited the miners to come and "judge." His opponents were "confessed liars and there will be a packed house," he promised. William Stanley, a Republican governor who became the transition to the new emerging progressive leadership in the state, was unbeatable. Clemens, however, won a record 1,258 votes, a rather respectable showing for the second Socialist race for governor.[56]

Meanwhile, Clemens was pursuing his legal career and continuing to assert his version of social justice. He pioneered in Kansas in the struggle for civil rights. In 1879 the state legislature approved separating black and white children in elementary education in first-class cities. The Topeka school board segregated, and in 1903 William Reynolds tried to enroll his child in a white school. He was rebuffed and, through his lawyers Clemens and F. J. Lynch, sought a writ of mandamus to force the school board to comply with Kansas law requiring a "uniform system of common schools." "Common," the plaintiff argued, meant "all the people" regardless of race, color, religion, or social standing. The decision also violated the "uniform" requirement as it applied only to first-class cities. The counsel picked up on Justice John Marshall Harlan's dissenting opinion in *Plessy v. Ferguson* (1896) that the Constitution was "color blind." To no avail. The state supreme court sustained segregated schools until after the *Brown v. Topeka* decision in 1954.[57]

In 1899 Clemens defended the Populist regents of Kansas State Agricultural College against charges of corruption regarding an issue dating back several years. For some time Populists were convinced that the state college had been neglecting the teaching of "political economy." Led by Populist members, the regents of Kansas State Agricultural College in 1884 voted to institute a series of lectures on the subject. The resolution called for the lecturers to be "Nonpartisan," and they asked Thomas E. Well, lecturer for the Boston Union for Practical Progress, to fill the new position. The Republican press, always eager to criticize the "Pops," assumed Well would promote Populist ideas. An ardent exponent of academic freedom, Well was still angry over the decision by Wisconsin's Lawrence University to dismiss him in 1892 for "his alleged radicalism in economics." President George T. Fairchild of Kansas State was certain Well was teaching Socialistic economics. The regents, in turn, were convinced Fairchild was an "uncompromising" Republican with autocratic tendencies and had outlived his usefulness.

During the election of 1896 partisan hostility toward the college increased on both sides, and the new Fusion government cut operating costs and faculty salaries, added another regent, and extended regents' terms to four years. John Leedy, the Populist governor, appointed five new regents, including C. B. Hoffman, who introduced a resolution that in effect fired the faculty. When Republican president Fairchild resigned, they chose Thomas Well as the new chief executive. The regents promptly rehired the faculty members whom Well approved and also recruited new professors to complete the faculty list. The recruits included some radicals who had been terminated by their schools. Republicans won the elections of 1898, and the new legislature, unwilling to wait its turn to pack the board of regents, brought suit against C. B. Hoffman and another Populist regent for irregularities in managing college affairs. The new board of regents reduced the curriculum of the radical professors and canceled a commencement address by William Jennings Bryan.[58]

Clemens successfully argued for Hoffman that there could be no delay of action when a writ of ouster was issued because the investigation was incomplete. He won until the state supreme court could hear the regents' appeal, and their appeal hearing was advanced to November 10. Clemens lost this case when the Republican-dominated state supreme court found that the Populist regents had administered the college "to serve their own whims." One salary had been fixed $200 "in excess of that fixed by law," and they had illegally appropriated money for "a dining hall and bookstore (Socialistic schemes) without warrant of law."[59]

During Clemens's last years of legal practice, prohibition proved to be one of his main targets. Most of these cases concerned violations of the law, which indicated that he "sensed that John Barleycorn had far too often been made the scapegoat for the problems" produced by the emerging industrial society. It was the social system, he argued, not alcohol, that created the problems.[60]

In the spring of 1900 Clemens contacted a number of Kansans he believed might be Socialists or were candidates for the party. "Hundreds" of Populists had heard of his "transmigration to Socialism," he said, and asked him what they should read to understand his new politics. He answered their inquiries and sent another letter; many responded positively to his suggestion that the state Socialists needed a newspaper and some new money for support. He began collecting news of Socialist activities and planned to print a state Socialist newspaper. He also decided that "it should contain some other things" besides socialism so that people might be "deluded into reading it." Thus was born the *Western Socialist News*, a brief eight-page journal that, unfortunately, was doomed to be short-lived for lack of financial support.

Clemens used his special brand of humor to raise money to support his journal. If not enough people cared to contribute at the start, then this would indicate there was not enough demand to justify his time and labor to produce it. "Please consider that the hat has been passed," he wrote. If readers wanted the newspaper to continue, then they had to "cough up." "Lest my attempt to be classical may have obscured my meaning," Clemens declared, "permit me to repeat in more unambiguous terms: If I am to continue this publication, I want money, want it awful bad, and want it right away by the hatful." But the project, unfortunately, proved to be too costly, both in money and time, which was not forthcoming, and Clemens published only five issues.[61]

In the second issue Clemens included a short essay on socialism that is worth quoting in full:

> Socialism does not attack private property—the things one has for his own comfort or pleasure. You have a beautiful home? Keep it. You harm no body by that. . . . A farmer has a quarter section and tills it. He is harming nobody and if he prefers to work his farm for himself, which would be foolish, Socialism will permit him while it pities him. But a gentleman in England owns a thousand acres of Kansas land that he does not use and which he never expects to even see. What possible reason can he have for claiming that land but that he wishes to live off the labor of Kansas men who lend their tired backs and till it? Can a man need a railroad all for himself? Is a street railway a mere private convenience for some man who lives in the suburbs and must have some way to get to town? Does a man need a coal mine for the sole purpose of feeding his own furnace or grate? The object of the owners of all these socially necessary things is to make money to live off the labor of people who work.[62]

In the June issue Clemens referred to attacks on him in his capacity as candidate for governor. He quoted from a Fusionist editor of a Wichita newspaper: "Clemens as simply Citizen Clemens, is no more to me than I am to Clemens; But Candidate Clemens who declares he is running for Governor in the interest of the people, but in reality an assistant Republican, *needs some attention*. It is more than a right, it is a duty, to task a man who, claiming to be a friend to the people, is giving their enemies his ablest assistance *in keeping locked the gate of reform*." Clemens retorted that he would continue to "keep locked the gate of reform" by fighting fusion because that path "requires the most disgraceful and brazen trafficking in office." He was happy to know, too, that the Fusionists "have at last conceded that as a candidate for Governor" he needed some attention.[63]

In the September 1900 issue of his Socialist newspaper, Clemens circulated a story from the pro-Fusionist *Kansas City Times* that the Republican State Central Committee was pushing his candidacy for governor. The committee had been secretly circulating a petition for his candidacy to divert "a large anti-Republican vote" from John Breidenthal. The secret "was given away" by some who were asked to sign the petition. No one but Republicans were asked to sign. If this occurred, Clemens insisted, "it was done without our knowledge or consent." He concluded that the *Kansas City Times* "think[s] things seem to have got bowlegged."[64]

By this time Clemens felt he was spending too much time running for governor to continue publishing his newspaper. He was also tired of the tribulations of being secretary to the party. He wrote his comrade John D. Haskell of Abilene that he "was d—d tired of it all." Clemens wrote the national secretary, describing the Kansas plan of organization, but instead of properly replying directly to Clemens, the secretary sent a circular addressed to all Kansans. "Let them take their old organization," he wrote, "and do what they d—d please with it. I shall be around at official ballot time."[65]

Clemens ran for state district attorney in 1902 but lost to Republican C. C. Coleman by a vote of 158,256 to 4,408, but he was increasing his state vote. He then campaigned for one of three seats on the state supreme court in the election of 1904 and again increased his statewide vote. The winners captured over 190,000 votes, but Clemens and the other two who placed third together received 12,652. Thus, his total statewide vote rose from 1,258 in 1900 to over 12,000 ballots four years later.

This was his last campaign. He was plagued with pneumonia and, while at work in his office, died on October 6, 1906. At that point he had four prohibition cases pending before the U.S. Supreme Court, testing the constitutionality of the Kansas law. The Elks Lodge conducted his funeral services. The judicial branch shut down that day, and the members of the Kansas bar attended his farewell en masse.[66]

G. C. Clemens was a Socialist for the people. Not afraid to get involved with the more radical form of socialism, Clemens did exhibit empathy for the cause and for its supporters. His life was relatively short, but he accomplished much during his years, espe-cially in the courtroom representing many minority groups as he battled social injustice. He wasn't afraid to get out of the court-room and rub elbows with the people. Using humor to reach an audience, he showed compassion and empathy not always found in Socialists of the day.

3

THE FEMALE SOCIALISTS

The women's movement in the late nineteenth century helped shape the Socialist effort of the twentieth
century by creating women's clubs, rural temperance
societies, and agrarian reform movements resulting in populism.
Its early leaders identified women's right to labor and the subsequent need to establish their economic and political rights to
secure a coequal position with men. The Socialist Party itself
was male dominated, with women relegated to secondary tasks of
various auxiliary duties in the East. Farther west, males accorded
women more equality and more fair treatment.[1]

The "labor question" now included the issue of gender. National
leaders such as Frances Willard joined the Women's Christian
Temperance Union's (WCTU) work on prohibition, along with
woman's suffrage. Willard had read Edward Bellamy's *Looking Backward* on the advice of Laurence Gronlund, a novel that prompted
"hundreds of women" to promote the goals of socialism. It was
largely Willard's influence that widened the institution of which
she soon became the head, so that it represented something far
more than the mere liquor question. "It stands today for purity,
honesty and education as well as temperance" in what Willard
called "Christian Socialism or Christianity applied." In Kansas
the women's movement combined the forces of prohibition with
woman's suffrage, and September 1891 saw the founding of the
National Women's Alliance, with Annie Diggs as one of the original signers. Supporters, however, were greatly disappointed over

their failure to obtain inclusion of their program into the Populist Party agenda in 1892.[2]

"Our Little Annie," as Populists throughout the Great Plains affectionately referred to Annie Diggs, was born Annie Le Porte in London, Ontario, Canada, on February 22, 1848. Her father, Cornelius Le Porte, was of French descent, and her mother, Ann, was an American. The lawyer-father moved the family to New Jersey, and Annie was educated there by a governess, convent school, and public schools. Attractive, petite, barely five feet tall and weighing under one hundred pounds, she proved to have a biting tongue in the field of politics. She moved to Lawrence, Kansas, in 1873 and "took a position," as contemporaries expressed it, demonstrating pianos. She soon captured the heart of a postal worker, Alvin S. Diggs, the same year. They married and raised a boy and two girls. Being a mother and housewife consumed her time, especially when the children were small.[3]

Annie gradually eased into politics, first deciding that the university students in Lawrence were being ruined by "demon rum." On Election Day in 1877 she was assigned to provide lunch for "dry" poll workers but became caught up in the mood of the movement and found herself speaking that afternoon, advocating the temperance cause. This experience, plus the fact that many females at the time were beginning to make their mark in serving protest and improvement causes, led Diggs to become active in politics. "Politics just grew on me," she remembered later.[4]

A few years later Annie wrote a strong defense of the unusual antics of Carrie Nation, the hatchet-wielding opponent of saloons in "dry" Kansas. She considered Mrs. Nation "the most conspicuous person in the United States today" because "the evil attacked is of great magnitude, and . . . the method of her attack is so unprecedented and spectacular." Nation operated under the principle that saloons were illegal and thus were fair targets for her hatchet. From outward appearances "Mrs. Nation is just a wholesome, roly-poly, gray-haired grandmother," but then "presto change she discloses a totally diverse view; she is puritanical, unsparing in judgment, all without harshness of manner or asperity of temper." Part of this, Diggs concluded, was Nation's

constant quoting of biblical verses and her claims that she had
been appointed by God to wage her one-woman battle against
drinking. "There is in all this," Diggs added, "not one hint or
taint of insanity" because, as she put it, she was not "austere, narrow, or vindictive as was John Brown." Diggs expressed the hope
that with women empowered to vote in municipal elections in
1887, they might free Topeka from the saloons that were operating despite the law. She expected the women voters in Topeka
to meet "the solemn responsibility of seizing the opportunity and
solving the problem."[5]

Diggs eased into her active political life slowly. She filled the
Unitarian pulpit for a while, wrote pieces for the local newspaper, and was busy at home being a housewife and mother of
three. Agrarian woes in Kansas led to the Alliance movement,
and she began writing a column of Farmers' Alliance activities
for the *Lawrence Journal*. This led to her position as an associate
editor for the *Topeka Advocate*, the official vehicle for the Kansas
Alliance movement. In this outlet she "railed against the saloon
and capital punishment and for women's suffrage and Socialism." She described her boss and editor of the *Advocate*, Stephen
McLallin, as "demanding truth and accuracy" in publishing the
newspaper. Annie learned well the business of reporting from
this stern taskmaster.[6]

She also emerged gradually as a speaker for the developing
agrarian cause. A city girl uncertain of which end of the cow produced the milk, she was dedicated to helping desperate farmers,
and she could do this with her pen and, she soon discovered,
with her voice. In 1890 she attended the founding of an Alliance
unit in Downs, Kansas, as a reporter. Much to her surprise and
consternation, she was asked to speak. Using the themes of her
editorials, Annie was an immediate hit with the farmers. "Acci-
dentally, I found I could speak extemporarily," she later recalled,
"and never did anything else."[7] A contemporary described Annie
as a speaker:

> Imagine a little woman, slender, almost to frailty, barely five feet tall,
> and weighing only ninety-three pounds. Picture . . . a face on which

shines the light of zealous endeavor and enthusiastic championship of
a beloved cause; rather thin lips, an intelligent forehead from which
the hair, now fairly sprinkled with gray threads, is brushed back
pompadour-like; twinkling eyes that alternately squint almost shut,
then open wide as she expounds her favorite doctrines of socialism;
a trifle nervous, a soft voice and an occasional musical little laugh as
she talks, and you have a fair photograph.[8]

John J. Ingalls, Kansas's senior Republican senator, had made
bitter enemies over the years, but more important, farmers were
criticizing him harshly for his "do nothing" position in refusing
to face agrarian problems in Congress. A reporter from the *New
York World* asked him if "political ends justify the means," and
Ingalls responded that "the purification of politics is an irides-
cent dream. Government is force. Politics is a battle for supremacy. Parties are for the armies. The Decalogue and the golden
rule have no place in a political campaign." *Advocate* editor Stephen McLallin and other agrarian reformers decided it was time
to put Ingalls "out to pasture."[9]

Annie and Populist activist Mary Elizabeth Lease led the attack
to defeat Ingalls for reelection in 1890. Annie delivered a speech
in Jewell City that lasted from 4:00 p.m. until it was too dark to
continue. The two women carried the battle across the state and
successfully helped William Peffer unseat the Republican icon.
While they were as different as two people can be and thoroughly
disliked each other, Lease and Diggs worked well together for
the common cause. But they enjoyed differing lifestyles. While
Lease rested comfortably in a sleeping car on the campaign trail,
Diggs remained in the day coach, where she could talk to farmers, "smooth over the petty frictions that arose, and compromise
the different points that threatened party unity." The historian
of Kansas populism admitted that while she was inferior to Lease
"in spectacular crowd-pleasing attributes," Diggs's "charm was
an antidote to the Populists flamboyant and erratic element."[10]

Thenceforth Annie Diggs rose rapidly in the ranks of the Populist Party, founded in Kansas in the summer of 1890. She was
active at the Ocala, Florida, meeting in 1890 and later the follow-

ing year in Cincinnati to form the national People's Party. She was a delegate to the Omaha gathering in 1892 to select James B. Weaver as the party's presidential candidate and accompanied General Weaver on his campaign tour. "Using humor and pathos," she would turn aside the charges of "anarchist" hurled by her opponents and asked simply why "the Republican pledge— 'Protection of the American Laborer'—did not protect the workers from unemployment and sweatshops." She often attacked the "conspiracy of silence" by which workers everywhere, rural and urban, "were kept from a knowledge of their common situation and their need for concerted action." Why could not the farmer and the wage earner see their commonality and unite to achieve their common goals? She lambasted the policies of the two major political parties that resulted in unemployment and were responsible for the "famine-pinched, emaciated babies, sweltering and gasping in foul alleys, reeking with green slime, fetid with the stench of offal, horrible in vermin."[11]

Annie's influence on the Populist Party continued to expand. In July 1896 she served on the Populist National Committee, headed by Herman E. Taubeneck, and in May 1897 she was elected president of the Kansas Women's Free Silver League. She was an ardent supporter of woman's suffrage, giving the U.S. Congress the benefit of her views on suffrage in 1894, and in 1899 she was elected president of the Kansas Equal Suffrage Association. She took the arguments against women voting and turned them around: "Their physical peculiarities remove them from arduous contact with affairs," but this includes "only a small class of women"; "women are too good for politics and must not be contaminated with them," and yet "they are too untrustworthy and uninformed to be permitted to vote"; the "negro" was given the ballot for personal protection, and "women need the ballot for self-protection."[12]

Diggs played a key role in the debates over an equal suffrage amendment to the state constitution in the Populist Convention of 1894. She represented the positive side and Peter Elder, state House speaker, the negative in the final debate. The two had faced off on this issue in 1891. Diggs insisted that the question was important to men as well as women and not just for doubling the state suffrage. She brought cheers from the audience when she expressed the belief that "the vast majority of this convention means to stand by their own Populist women and give us their votes for this amendment." "Don't you want to have the leverage of having the gratitude of the women in this state?" she asked. "Don't you want to be able to say, to the Populist Party belongs the honor of not only submitting this amendment, but also of supporting it at the polls?" Elder had long opposed woman's suffrage, but "his rambling speech was no match for her downright reasoning," which "carried the day."[13]

Unlike most diehard Populists, Annie supported Fusion as she believed the Democratic Party had improved greatly since the first major Fusion ticket in 1896. She was adamantly opposed to imperialism in the Spanish-American War and wrote a poem, which was a paean to the Filipinos, called "Little Brown Brother." When asked her opinion about the election results that appeared to be a rebuke to Republican imperialism, she expressed her delight. Although the Republicans enjoyed gains in Kansas, "there were several communities that showed Fusion gains." This, she asserted, "was not played up in the Republican newspapers." She thought the times were unusually propitious for Republicans because the Kansas Twentieth Regiment had just returned home from the Philippine Islands and the GOP took advantage of their "fame and glory."[14]

When her employment with the state library terminated, Diggs became embroiled again in the political issue of Fusion. She found herself a Fusionist, at odds with Mary Elizabeth Lease, who vehemently rejected Fusion as a betrayal of Populist principles. Lease, in a speech in the state capital, accused Diggs of disloyalty to the cause. "Woman, you have lied," Diggs responded, to cheers from the audience, and she prepared a list of demands to take to the Democratic State Convention in Fort Scott in 1900. She insisted they accept public ownership of public utilities and the initiative and referendum as an initial condition of Fusion.[15]

"Petticoat Politics," Democratic leaders jeered at the demands, refusing association with a dry suffragette. The convention steamrolled the convention with planks that offered nothing to the Populists. "Suddenly it screeched to a shocking stop," when the delegates began responding to Diggs and her Fusionist demands. It turned out she was "the boss of the Fusionists in Kansas" and thus the boss of the Democrats as well. One reporter observed that "there was a three-ring political menagerie" in Fort Scott, "with one Annie Diggs as ringmaster." The *Kansas City Journal* declared that "she has more political sagacity than the whole bunch of past party leaders put together." The old leaders used dictatorial tactics, while she "leads by first finding out what the common people of her party want and then going to the front to help them get it." "She is the most influential member of the three (Democrat, Populist, Silver Republican) parties," claimed the *Topeka Daily Capital*.[16]

A disgruntled C. W. Fairchild of Kingman, however, chided Diggs for giving the post of attorney general to the Democrats in exchange for the nomination of David Martin for the state supreme court. Fairchild asserted that John Breidenthal, the Fusionist candidate for governor, telegraphed the Democratic meetings in Fort Scott not to "sacrifice the Attorney General in any circumstance," which was achieved over the long haul, though, it appears that Annie got the best of the bargain as many politicians would trade the office of attorney general for a seat on the supreme court.[17]

With the political death of populism, Diggs was free to promote other causes. She wrote the chapter on the woman's suffrage movement in Kansas for the Anthony-Harper edition of the *History of Woman Suffrage*. She wrote for newspapers, lectured, and gradually eased out of state politics and into broader social issues. She traveled to Europe to see economic problems from a different perspective. Out of this trip came two significant essays.

In 1903 *Cosmopolitan* published her story on the English village of Bourneville, founded by George Cadbury, an English Quaker and a member of the British Cadbury confection family. He used a "modest" inheritance to transfer his workers from the slums of Birmingham. He moved his cocoa factory five miles out of the city and built a modern residential area, donating the houses and grounds to successive boards of trust. The income from the project was spent on maintenance and public welfare for the project. Tenure for individuals in their cottages was perpetual, and their rents went into the trust fund. The project was based on the concept that "man may not live by bread alone; his birthright includes the right to play as well as work." The town included playgrounds for the children and for adults. The company employed two "professional instructors" in athletic sports. All girls employed in the factory were required to exercise daily in the gymnasium. Trained medical help was provided, and there was housing available for the aged, a factory orchestra, and various technical schools—a truly model company town for the working class.[18]

The following year Diggs wrote about Cadbury in the "Captain of Industry" section of *Cosmopolitan*. George Cadbury was a model modern businessman. To him it was not charity but good business practice to provide a healthy home atmosphere for his workers. He gathered his people every morning for a simple prayer and the exchange of kindly words. He was "a strong believer in organized labor" and gave both moral and financial aid to striking workers. He supported minister Joseph Chamberlain's drive to establish an old-age pension program. During the Boer War, Cadbury remained true to his Quaker upbringing and refused to bid on government contracts for military supplies, bringing on himself the opprobrium of being pro-Boer. When the *Daily News* suffered because of its anti-war stance, he assumed control of the newspaper and continued its policies, except for eliminating sports news because of its support of the national betting mania, popular with the working class. His ranking as a "captain of industry" combined the dual role of managing a significant commercial enterprise "and a mighty host working toward social amelioration."[19]

During her later years Diggs wrote *The Story of Jerry Simpson* and *Bedrock*. *Bedrock* was a seventy-page book to promote her ideas with the subtitle of "Education and Employment, the Foundation of the Republic." She hoped to promote the goals of the Social Center movement by promoting free public lectures and night school classes to assist workers in improving themselves.[20]

In 1912 Diggs moved to Detroit to live with her son and died there four years later of muscular dystrophy. She was buried in Lawrence, Kansas. She once admitted to a reporter that at heart she was "a Debs Socialist." "My idea of Socialism," she said, "is that theory of government which would have all industries and all enterprises, which widely concern the public convenience and the public morals, owned and operated by the public," a moderate vision of that expounded by Eugene V. Debs.[21]

Other women Socialists appeared on the plains of Kansas, with Girard producing its share of them, especially in attracting capable ones to help produce Socialist publications emanating from that town. Josephine Conger, born in Centralia, Missouri, loved literature at an early age, and the family sent her to college at nearby Columbia. She later learned the publishing business by working on her brother's country newspaper. Conger spent two years at Ruskin College, where she studied Ernest Untermann's translation of Marx's *Das Kapital*, among other subjects, and became a Socialist journalist. The *Appeal to Reason* described Ruskin College as "the American side of the Oxford Movement." Located in the small town of Trenton, Missouri, one hundred miles northeast of Kansas City, it had departments in Preparatory, Art, Music, Normal, Oratory, and Industrial, including a 1,500-acre farm, and twenty faculty members. A niece of J. A. Wayland, Conger's big break came when she moved to Girard to edit a woman's section at the *Appeal to Reason*. From this opportunity she became a leading Socialist woman editor.[22]

Conger's column hewed to the *Appeal's* homey and intimate touch to reach readers by publishing original poetry on womanhood, children, and the class struggle, and she followed the woman's suffrage movement closely. She viewed the Socialist platform as "the only possible emancipation of women and children from tyranny and superstition." In keeping with the tradition of the "Appeal Army"—Wayland's volunteers who helped distribute and sell the *Appeal to Reason*—she included a returnable coupon with the inscription "I am interested in Socialism and the Emancipation of Women," which readers could clip, sign, and return to the *Appeal* office. Conger continued to solicit personal messages, most of which, she reported, came from California and Kansas. Most respondents were older housewives, many on farms, who enjoyed occasional trips to town to learn and to agitate. Her columns thus reassured readers that they had soul mates in the common cause. She also offered the prize of an $1,100 Wing Piano to the woman who submitted the most subscribers to the *Appeal to Reason* within a certain period as part of Wayland's program to expand his subscriber list.[23]

The Socialist Party began to evolve in the first decade of the twentieth century, first to the change from local autonomy to an increasing reliance on the national office in Chicago and the new daily newspapers and pamphlets it produced. Second, in 1908 the National Executive Committee (NEC) directly addressed the "woman" issue by creating the Woman's National Committee (WNC). With the assistance of her husband, Japanese Socialist Kiichi Kaneko, Josephine Conger-Kaneko began publication of a new journal, *Socialist Woman*, to train women in socialism and to activate them. The new publication was basically an expanded continuation of her column for the *Appeal to Reason*. Under ideal conditions necessity and reason would foster men and women working side by side in all phases of the movement. But the male-dominated orientation of socialism and the absence of acknowledged equality of women in the party led Conger-Kaneko to emphasize the independent status of women in their efforts to achieve recognition rather than being taken for granted.[24]

Renaming the journal *Progressive Woman*, Conger-Kaneko struggled to continue publishing without support from paid advertising until 1912, when the *Appeal to Reason* began financial retrenchment and stopped publishing other periodicals. Wayland continued to print *Progressive Woman* on his presses, but Conger-Kaneko had to find some method of subsidization. Caroline Lowe, WNC correspondent, offered her assistance, but Lowe's successor withdrew the offer. Conger-Kaneko explored the alternative of changing the periodical's name to the old *Coming Nation*, but the WNC then declared it was no longer a women's publication. Conger-Kaneko surrendered and ceased publication.[25]

By 1914 Conger-Kaneko was frustrated with the party bickering over the woman issue. She wrote in the *Coming Nation* of the party's dilemma over a sponsored newspaper. In 1904 the national convention rejected the concept of a party press and turned down her uncle Wayland's offer of the *Appeal to Reason* to be the official publication. A decade later the party concluded it should own its own press because the privately owned journals had "stunted" the party's "intellectual growth." By this time World War I had begun, and like many American Socialists, Conger-Kaneko would oppose the war.[26]

May Wood Simons was a marked contrast to Conger-Kaneko in her opposition to having a separate woman's organization. Born May Wood in 1876 in Baraboo, Wisconsin, to a devout Presbyterian family, Simons planned to become a medical missionary. Saving money from her teaching position, she managed to attend Northwestern University. In 1897 she married Algie Simons, and they moved to Chicago, where they became Socialists. May Wood Simons sought success, both as a housewife and an intellectual companion to Algie and his work on the *International Socialism Review*, *Chicago Daily Socialist*, and the *Coming Nation*. Simons almost succeeded in winning election to the NEC in 1910 and served on the WNC as an exponent of woman's suffrage.[27]

Simons sought to develop her literary skills and earned another degree from the University of Chicago and a master's degree from Northwestern University. Her study, "Women and the Social Problem," was well received, and she became a leading authority on the woman question. Before the Industrial Revolution, she wrote, women were "producers for home consumption." With the introduction of machinery, though, women were "transformed" into producers for national consumption. Simons noted that the "home industries" had thus grown into "great business" units and women had "gone shoulder to shoulder with man into the great factory, shop, and even the mines." As a result, "capital exploits both alike and leaves to either but a scanty subsistence." Hence, there could be "no sex movement," but male and female alike must work for "economic freedom." Capitalism had destroyed all previous labor gender divisions, and the system "buys the labor power of men, woman or child without any distinction."[28]

Simons also lectured at the Intercollegiate Socialist Society, the National Socialist Lyceum Bureau, and later Ruskin College. She was filled with self-doubts and was conflicted between the pleasures of family life and working for Socialist purposes. She lost a baby during the early years of her marriage, suffered an emotional collapse, and became overly protective of her second child.[29]

Woman laborers, Simons believed, faced the same problems as men, and as men were "turning to the Socialist movement, far more reason has the working woman to look in this direction for the solution of her present conditions." At last, she realized, there existed a political party that welcomed women and even promoted equality, both economic and political, between the sexes. As a result, women were responding to this opportunity and were joining the Socialist Party, taking an integral part by being on committees, making their voices heard, and even public speaking on Socialist and equality issues.[30]

With her personal emphasis on family life, Simons believed Socialists would have little success in recruiting housewives, especially farm women, who were so isolated. While she could never resolve this inner conflict and remained adamant against separate organizations, Simons believed that the role of the WNC should be to eventually bring women into the regular Socialist movement. When the WNC failed in this endeavor, she was prepared to abandon the committee. She firmly believed that household life over the centuries had made women "physically weak, mentally narrow, and politically powerless." Thus, the party would be unable to recruit housewives successfully, and others should move into modern public roles.

The *Coming Nation* also began to suffer financially when the *Appeal to Reason* suspended its printing. What began as a parting of ways turned into a name-calling contest. Algie Simons eventually accused Fred Warren "of bad faith, of assassinating the paper, of being a greedy Capitalist, a traitor to the working class." Warren countered with "bad faith, of dishonesty, of misrepresentation." Then May Wood Simons moved the paper to Chicago, where it received support from the national headquarters until 1913, when Josephine Conger-Kaneko, after the death of

her husband, took it over.[31] Both May and Algie left the Socialist Party and supported American involvement in World War I.
For her the movement was finished.[32] She died in 1948.

Caroline Lowe was born in 1874 in Ontario, Canada, and
attended schools in Oscaloosa, Iowa, before moving to Kansas
City. She became a Socialist in 1903 and soon won acclaim for her
recruiting abilities in Kansas and Oklahoma. As a former schoolteacher in Kansas City, she began her party work by using contacts
she had made working for the Kansas City Teachers' Association.
She hustled the Tri-State region through schoolhouse meetings
in small towns in the area, selling subscriptions to party publications and distributing party applications. Lowe proved to be particularly successful in working the encampments in Oklahoma.[33]

Josephine Conger-Kaneko felt that the Kansas Socialists had
failed to do anything toward recruiting women to the Socialist
Party and, at her urging, sent Caroline Lowe into the field in September 1908. Lowe worked as a clerk in the district court office
in Pittsburg, Kansas, organizing in her spare time, and soon she
was recognized as being among the top recruiters. She began
spending her summer vacations in Oklahoma, visiting the various camps and gatherings. By 1914 she reported attendance there
at five hundred for each meeting, and in many places it "reached
several thousand." Leaders of the two major parties "came out in
force" to combat this success, but by the end of the second day
they would always "retire from the grounds heartsick and filled
with forebodings."[34]

She described typical encampment activities with C. D. S. Oakford and young son Paul, a celebrated Socialist prodigy, and "Comrade" T. L. Buie" being opening day speakers, and on the second
day Lowe spoke, as did H. G. Creel, reporter for the Socialist
newspaper *National Rip-Saw*. The third day saw "Comrades" Kate
and Frank O'Hare and Oklahoma Socialist H. H. Stallard. All
this, she said, pointed to a victory in Oklahoma "within the not
far distant future." Recognizing this potential, the party leaders
were trying to educate the members to "an understanding of the
duties and responsibilities" that would rest on them with eventual
victory. If only women could receive the franchise, she believed

"the 10,000 dues-paying membership would be almost doubled," as half the audience in these encampments were women.[35]

Because of Lowe's activities, a grand encampment was held in Pittsburg in September 1909. The first day's speakers included activist Walter Thomas Mills; on the second day Kate Richards O'Hare, Crawford County Socialist George Brewer, and Caroline Lowe addressed the crowd. On the third day O'Hare, Lowe, and Socialist-suffragette Lena Morrow Lewis appeared. The final day had a morning lecture by O'Hare in the morning, and a "Dr. Batlender," an Italian speaker from Pennsylvania, also spoke. Meanwhile, during these four days, "Comrade Emma Johns Call provided music that cannot be excelled in America." Tents rented for $2 and above, cots were provided for twenty-five cents, and despite the drought, "water would be free."[36]

In 1911 Lowe took over direction of the WNC as general correspondent and began producing recruiting pamphlets, which numbered some thirty leaflets by 1913. The WNC asked women to "band together . . . and carry our literature to the women in bondage everywhere." They responded by delivering over 1.5 million leaflets in 1913 alone. Many followed the practice of "petticoat pockets," which they sewed on the outside of their undergarments and filled with leaflets, a notebook, and a pencil to jot down names and addresses of potential members.[37]

By 1913 Lowe expressed the desire to return to Pittsburg and her recruiting work in the field, especially in nearby Labette County, Kansas. She subsequently reported four meetings at Chetopa. "Before the second night the whole town was talking Socialism, and by the third lecture the hall was packed and many standing," she would say. At the end of the next gathering the WNC organized a local of twenty-one members, ten of them women. With the war and the disintegration of the Socialist movement in Kansas after 1917, Lowe was admitted to the Kansas bar and practiced law in Girard until her death in 1933. Among other cases she joined the legal defense of the IWW in the aftermath of World War I.[38]

Lowe served on the defense team headed by Fred H. Moore in IWW trials in Seattle, Omaha, and Chicago, and at their conclusions they came to Wichita to defend the Kansas IWW. Among other activities Lowe testified before the House Judiciary Committee on its amnesty proposal, noting the role the oil companies played in convincing district attorney Robert McCluggage to make the initial arrests of the Wobblies primarily to protect their properties. The local press also played a role in pursuing "a systematic campaign of vilification" against the IWW. After months of litigation the IWW was desperate for defense funds, so Lowe traveled throughout southeastern Kansas to solicit money from her old friends, which proved to be an unsuccessful undertaking as they were largely unresponsive to the plight of left-wing Socialists. She proved particularly impressive during her part in the four-hour summation of the defense at the end of the Wichita trial. Although this was her first appearance before a jury, she made good use of her lecturing skills until the more experienced Fred Moore arrived and concluded the summation, but to no avail. The IWW members were convicted and languished in Leavenworth prison from 1919, until 1923, when President Calvin Coolidge commuted the sentences of political prisoners. For three years Lowe and other Wobbly attorneys fruitlessly fought the granting of a permanent injunction against IWW activities in Kansas. Lowe eventually joined the Callery Law Firm in Pittsburg, working there until she resigned in 1932, preceding her death from uterine cancer the following year.[39]

Most party members advocated their own particular brand of socialism, and this was true of Kate Richards O'Hare. Variously known as the "first lady of American Socialism," "the heart of the movement," "the voice of the voiceless," "the livewire of Socialism," and after 1917, "Red Kate," she was born Carrie Kathleen Richards near the small Kansas town of Minneapolis, in Ottawa County, most likely in 1876. The Richards family farmed, and Kate, one of five children, grew up on this Kansas frontier in a sod house. The children helped with the chores, attended the local schools, and enjoyed a convivial family life. In her young years Kate showed a penchant for mechanics. She later described her days of childhood as "wonderful," saying they "laid the foundation of my whole life." The family fit the model of the small but prosperous farmers who supported the Alliance movement and then the Populist Party, until 1887. That year's blizzards were followed by severe drought, and Andrew Richards lost his farm.[40]

Forced to move to the city, Andrew left the family and sought work in Kansas City, Kansas, finding employment in a foundry. Kate endured a traumatic experience with the poverty her family endured that year, until they joined her father and she could continue her elementary education and her interest in the family church, the Disciples of Christ (Cambellite). They lived in the West Bottoms, where Kate was exposed to a life of industrialism, poverty, and crime, quite different from her agrarian origins. She graduated from Central High School, completed a yearlong course at Pawnee City (Nebraska) Academy, and taught elementary school in rural Nebraska. The pay was a meager $30 monthly for bleak drudgery, and she returned to Kansas City after the term ended to become secretary for a machine shop her father had established. She also became involved in church work among alcoholics and women forced into prostitution by extreme poverty. She soon became aware of, and disillusioned with, some of her fellow parishioners, who employed child labor and rented property for brothels.[41]

Her innate interest in mechanical things, and support from her father, led Kate to become an apprentice in the machine shop. During her four-year apprenticeship she was relegated to the dirtiest, greasiest jobs because of her gender, but she persevered and became one of the few female members of the International Association of Machinists. She also read the currently popular *Progress and Poverty*, *Wealth vs. Commonwealth*, *Looking Backward*, and Ignatius Donnelly's *Caesar's Column*, absorbing their Socialist messages. She attended union meetings and debated politics, for which she was taunted because females were not expected to take part in "men's talk."[42]

One evening she attended a Cigar-Makers' International Union dance that proved to be a pivotal point in her life. Mother Jones spoke that night and introduced Kate to her concepts of socialism. Still active in the labor movement at age seventy, Mother Jones was a living legend among those who knew her. Kate talked to her and later described the night as "one of the mileposts in my life that I can easily locate." Later Kate wrote that "out of the blackness of the working class night, she flashed across our nation, a portent of the rising tide of revolution."

Kate later described her great epiphany in some detail. She was dancing with her boyfriend

> when another unionist rushed up to my partner and eagerly whispered "Mother Jones is in town, let's go get her and have her make us a speech." In an instant I was forgotten and without a word of apology my friend left me deserted on the dancing floor and bounded out of the room in search of Mother Jones. As my anger over my desertion cooled my curiosity to see the woman who could make my best beau forget me so completely grew. I wondered who "Mother Jones" was and if she were so very young and handsome and what she would speak about. Soon I found the boys scrambling up the stairs propelling between them a strange and striking female figure. Then I felt quite sure that the boys must have captured some quiet old Irish washwoman on her way home from a day of labor. The figure was rather short and dumpy, dressed in a rusty black gown. The hair was silver white and had been hastily screwed into a hard knot. The collar was askew and an old fashioned bonnet tipped rakishly over one ear. Panting for breath, a merry laugh belying the harsh words she used, she soundly berated the "byes" for dragging an old lady out of her snug bed at the unholy hour. . . . My friend said "Kate come and get acquainted. . . . This is Mother Jones. I wanted you to meet her; she can make you understand things I can't explain." . . . In that first moment of contact I knew why I had been forgotten by my friend at the mention of her name. Here was one woman in a million, a personality that was fire-tempered, a soul that had been purified in world travel, whose voice I would follow to the end of the road. Of her speech I have only a hazy memory. . . . I saw only the SOUL, a soul that glowed with eternal youth; a soul that age cannot wither and that time only strengthens; the soul of humanity that forges every [sic] onward up the road of Progress toward the goal of human brotherhood.
>
> In a moment I was the center of an excited group of men all talking at once and hurling unknown phrases at me until my brain

was whirling. I escaped by promising to "come down to the office tomorrow and get some books." The next day I hunted up the office and was assailed by more perplexing phrases, and finally escaped, loaded down with Socialist classics enough to give a college professor mental indigestion. At last, down at the very bottom of the pile, I found a well-worn dog-eared little book that I could not only read but understand, but to my heart-breaking disappointment it did not even mention Socialism. It was the *Communist Manifesto*, and I could not understand what relation it could be to what I was looking for.

I carried the books back and humbly admitted my inability to understand them or grasp the philosophy they presented. As the men who gave me the books explained and expostulated in vain, a long, lean, hungry-looking individual unfolded from behind a battered desk in the corner and joined the group. . . . . The hungry-looking individual was J. A. Wayland and the dingy office the birthplace of the "Appeal to Reason." At last I woke up in a new world, with new viewpoints, and a new outlook. Mother Jones had left a mark on my life which will never be erased, she had given me the inspiration I needed to spur me into action just as she has done for thousands of others.[43]

J. A. Wayland led Kate through the classics of Marx, Engels, Gronlund, and Bellamy, and she joined the Socialist Party in 1901. That fall she moved to Girard to attend the International School of Social Economy taught by Walter Thomas Mills. She took classes in "economic history, cooperative movements, trade unionism, parliamentary procedure, and elocution." She also fell in love with a fellow student, Frank O'Hare, and they were married on New Year's Day 1902. The wedding took place in Girard, at the sumptuous Victorian mansion of J. A. Wayland, with Walter Thomas Mills officiating.[44]

The young married couple spent their working honeymoon by "barnstorming" the eastern United States, organizing Socialist locals in the coal mining regions of Pennsylvania with Mother Jones, and Kate surveyed industrial conditions in New York. While in New York City, she served on the editorial staff of *Wilshire's Magazine* and lectured to Socialists and industrial unions. Disguising herself in overalls, she collected data on sweatshops and published an essay on the exploitation of women in low-paying jobs and the efforts to organize them. After six months of this work, the O'Hares returned to Kansas City, where their first child was born in 1903.[45]

They settled in Kansas City, Kansas, where Frank worked as a party organizer and Kate wrote a column for the second *Coming Nation*, resurrected by Wayland and edited now by Fred Warren. Kate was given her own column, the first permanent one by a Socialist woman, in which she could develop her own arguments and recruit readers. Calling it "The Women Folks" and later "Our Women's Column," she appealed to her readers in their traditional role as mother and housewife in the same terms she was pursuing her own functions as Frank's helpmate and mother to his children. She asked women to become Socialists by appealing to their "tenderness, mother love, and patriotism." This phase of their life lasted only briefly.[46]

In 1904 the family moved to Oklahoma, where they spent the next five years farming and organizing for the party. A daughter was born there in 1905, and three years later twin boys arrived whom they named Eugene and Victor after their good friend Debs. Kate's father missed his daughter, and he and her mother joined them there, buying a half-section of farmland. When German American Socialist and writer Oscar Ameringer arrived in 1907, they joined forces, organizing summer encampments to recruit agrarian members to the party. It was in connection with this work that Kate established a lasting friendship with Caroline Lowe. She also built a reputation in this work second only to Eugene V. Debs as a "scintillating spellbinder."[47]

Following Frank's nervous breakdown from overwork in 1909, the O'Hare family moved back to Kansas City, Kansas. In 1910 Kate led the Kansas delegation to the Social National Congress in Chicago and became the first woman to run for a seat in the U.S. House of Representatives from Kansas, four years before women received the right to vote in the state. This was in the populous Second District surrounding Kansas City. In this era of pre–woman's suffrage she ran ahead of her ticket by polling 5 percent of the vote. She was especially strong in the working-class wards of Kansas City and the Tri-State region. Following this defeat she toured through the auspices of the lecture bureau of the *Appeal to Reason* until 1911, ranging from the Great Plains in the spring to the Southwest in the summer, the Midwest in the fall to the South in the winter months. Such a hectic schedule and arduous daily traveling were extremely difficult on her four children but also draining on Kate's strength.[48]

In 1911 Kate and family moved to St. Louis. The president of the Order of Railway Conductors arranged a speaking tour for her along the Rock Island lines, and when it ended in St. Louis, he introduced her to Phil Wagner, publisher of the *National Rip-Saw*, a popular Socialist weekly. Dick Maple, its founder, had suffered a stroke, and Wagner needed a competent editor. She and Frank took over the newspaper, with Kate as editor and Frank as circulation manager in charge of publicity. As Kate's speaking popularity rose, Frank also arranged her lecture tours. They invited Eugene Debs to join them, writing for the paper and working with Kate on the lecture tour. A subscription of fifty cents yearly to the *Rip-Saw* became the price of admission to Kate and Debs's lectures, and the circulation soon rose to 500,000.

Kate's style of editing followed that of the *Appeal to Reason*, and it became "a powerful influence" among the rank-and-file Socialists and later the "antiwar advocates."[49]

As Kate rose in prominence in Socialist circles, she was elected to high party office. In 1911 she held a seat on the Women's National Committee and also on the prestigious National Executive Committee. In 1913 the party chose her over New York's Morris Hillquit to represent it at the London convention of the Second International Workingmen's Association, the only woman to hold this status. The delegates elected her international secretary. Afterward Wisconsin Socialist and politician Victor Berger wrote Hillquit, "As for your friend, Kate Richards O'Hare, making the American Socialist Party ridiculous at the sessions of the International Bureau—why of course she will make it ridiculous," and they sought unsuccessfully to secure the election of Berger. Kate's success in organizing farmers on the Great Plains led the famous Socialist Jean Jaures to invite her to come to France and

advise French leaders on how to organize their peasantry. Kate
had to decline this invitation, but it is questionable how effective her approach would have been with French farmers. In 1916
she ran for the vice presidency of the United States, with Allan
Benson of New York as the likely Socialist presidential candidate, but was defeated by George Kirkpatrick of New Jersey in
a party referendum.[50]

Kate always considered herself a commonsense Socialist rather
than a scientific or "pure" one. She was militant but not an arm-
chair Socialist or an original thinker. But she was intimately knowl-
edgeable about conditions on the farm, factory, mine, and family,
and her views, writings, and speeches "were based on empirical
data and sociological investigations." She was prepared to abandon Marxist theory when it flew in the face of reality. She was
noticeably capable of adjusting the language in her speeches to
the locality and the type of audience she addressed. Kate readily listened to, and learned from, the vast numbers of people
she met on the lecture circuit. She was willing to provide compensation for property that would be taken during the coming
revolution. While she disagreed sharply with the urbane and intellectual Morris Hillquit and the "bossism" of Victor Berger, she
"admired the proletarian achievements of Milwaukee's Socialist administration." Kate endorsed the AFL's industrial unionism
but denounced Samuel Gompers's political conservatism. She
rejected violence and played an active role in expelling the IWW
from the party after 1912.[51]

Kate had a high-pitched, squeaky voice that Frank constantly
tried to moderate. It was not until after she recorded her voice at
the fair in St. Louis that she truly realized her problem, and the
two of them resolved it. Women's issues became one of Kate's
most persistent topics, both as a writer and as a speaker. For her
the capitalist system was the root of the woman problem. Long
hours in the factory, unsanitary working conditions, and inadequate wages all forced women to seek marriage as an escape
route. But marriage often proved to be no sanctuary, as their
husbands also faced adverse conditions. Men and women therefore formed loveless marriages, and the divorce rate during this

period noticeably rose. It was a deplorable cycle that Kate decried because work could be quite rewarding but, instead, had became a curse to workers. She participated in the hearings of the Missouri Senatorial Minimum Wage Commission. They found the average wage of St. Louis factory women to be $5.50 weekly. In her famous piece "Wimmin Ain't Got No Kick" she wrote that, first of all, they were baby-making machines; second, they were a source of cheap factory labor; and finally, they filled the ranks of prostitution.[52]

In the early 1890s Kate began to study prostitution in her days as a Crittenden Mission worker in Kansas City. She wrote angrily of the 720,000 known prostitutes in the nation and the one in six who died annually and ended up in a potter's field. In discussing prostitution and venereal disease, Kate regarded white slavery as the worst of capitalism's evils. This was not merely the work of vice rings who drugged the girls and sold them into the system but also of police departments and various other parts of government that formed "an informal conspiracy of illicit support" for white slavery rings. Socialism, she believed, would enhance woman's place in society as well as that of men. Machinery would serve the people: they could work four hours daily and have time to enjoy the fruits of their labor. Economic independence would drastically alter inequality in the institution of marriage. One of Kate's major goals to improve women's lives was expanding the scope of their education.[53]

Kate also was dedicated to the woman's suffrage movement. In the election of 1912 some one million citizens cast their vote for socialism, she wrote, and "possibly another million more men and women would have done so except for the fact that they were disenfranchised." Socialist thought, she observed, "has permeated every institution today and is shaping the thought and action of the race." The arrival of universal suffrage would mean the establishment of the cooperative commonwealth and the cleansing of society's institutions. While the home was "the logical location of womanly activity," at present "everything used in the home is produced . . . in the factory." Man's realm is "in harvesting the elements, conquering nature and creating and directing the machinery of production and distribution." Men could not do the thinking for women, and Kate O'Hare demanded equal suffrage as both gender and class rights.[54]

People, especially the clergy, were prone to blame the evils in life on God. Schoolhouse fires that claimed young lives as well as slaughter on the battlefields were met with the response "It is God's will." When Socialists demanded fireproof schoolhouses, the public branded them "impious, irreligious and atheistic." When Socialists blamed the horrors of war on capitalist greed, the more religious branded them heretics. When Socialists preached that prostitution and venereal disease were the result of "economic slavery," the clergy countered that they were merely "obscene, vile and licentious" because "God wills it so!" It was much easier, Kate asserted, to blame God for everything than to "give God a square deal and rebuild society in a decent, sane, humane manner."[55]

As Mari Jo Buhle notes, "Of the Midwestern leadership O'Hare most easily acclimated herself to a new campaign for sexual emancipation." Yet even here her support for family limitation was tentative. Birth control agitation fell to the younger and more formally educated women in the Socialist movement. Margaret Sanger, a trained nurse, became a leader in family planning in the United States. Her explicit addresses and publications on sex education, birth control, and hygiene often landed her in jail, especially after 1912, when she began a weekly series on the topics. Kate supported these concepts because of her belief that marriage in capitalism tended to destroy the family. Birth control must be practiced to provide options for poor people. Abortion should be available both to save the mother's life and to offer a solution to the problem of "sub-normal" infants. But she also feared the "rising tide of infanticide" in this period of race improvement through eugenics and decided against distributing Sanger's literature.[56]

One of Kate's favorite devices was to challenge any Democratic or Republican politician or lawyer in the audience to share the stage with her. She offered them $100 to debate her statement that the wealthy owned local public officials. "You fellows are smart," she taunted, "while I am only a woman with not enough sense to vote. Why don't you come on?" No one ever recorded that her challenge was accepted. In a speech in Coffeyville, Kansas, she told her audience how the Republican platform of 1908 was written. The platform committee, she claimed, was enjoying cigars and "liquid refreshments" in a hotel parlor when "a dapper little gentleman" took out a piece of paper that was pasted to a blank sheet and it was accepted as the party platform. The "printed slip bore the imprint of a printing office in New York just back of the Standard Oil office on Wall Street." Kate offered the podium to anyone who cared to disprove her statement. No one responded, and afterward an angry local Republican demanded to know why one of his bosses had kept silent. The politician responded: "I did not deny the statement because I could not. It was true. I don't know where she got the information but she got it straight, and if you want to know, that is just how our platform was written."[57]

The prospect of America entering World War I devastated the Socialist Party everywhere as its members opposed any capitalist war. In America in April 1917 it posed a difficult choice between party and country. This decision was easy for Kate O'Hare. For over two years she had been demanding that Congress exercise its powers to bring a halt to the war in Europe. She and Frank composed a three-act anti-war play that was performed throughout the country. Kate denounced those defectors who insisted they were Americans first and Socialists second, labeling it "perspective cant" and insisting she was "a Socialist, a labor unionist, and a follower of the Prince of Peace FIRST; and an American second." A convention was called for April 7, 1917, in St. Louis, one day after the American declaration of war, and Kate was one of the three delegates from St. Louis. The conference elected a committee of thirteen to formulate recommendations, and Kate won more votes than any of the other twelve. She presided over the committee meetings and played a key role in its recommendation to denounce American involvement in the war. The convention received a telegram from Debs urging resistance to the war, and members accepted the committee report, which also urged opposition to conscription, food exports and war taxes, and any encroachments on the Bill of Rights or labor activities.[58]

President Woodrow Wilson appointed George Creel to head the Committee on Public Information to sell the war to the American people as a "Great Crusade" and to promote his ideas for the postwar peace on the international level. Congress enacted the Espionage Act in June 1917 and the Sedition Act in May 1918 to provide severe penalties for aiding the enemy or obstructing recruitment of the military forces and prohibiting the use of the mail for treasonous or seditious materials. The sedition law prohibited in broad, nebulous terminology any "disloyal, profane, scurrilous, or abusive language" about the government, the Constitution, the flag, or the military and naval forces. These laws were aimed directly at the Socialists and pacifists.

Despite this two-pronged attack on freedom of speech and the propaganda efforts of the Creel Committee, which created a frenzy of patriotism, Kate O'Hare set out to cross the country with speeches opposing the war. She delivered over seventy addresses during this trip, "always in the presence of a representative of the U.S. Department of Justice," and at no time during her address did she urge opposition to the draft or any illegal activities. She made her seventy-sixth address at Bowman, North Dakota, on July 17, 1917. At this time the Nonpartisan League (NPL), founded by A. C. Townley and supported by Walter Thomas Mills, was highly popular in sections of North Dakota. An offshoot of socialism, the league was making serious inroads into the two major political parties and was to play a role in Kate's fate in Bowman. Some members of the group who invited her to their town also were Nonpartisan Leaguers, including postmistress Lillian Totten, who asked O'Hare to her house for tea after the two-hour lecture. Totten was feuding at the time with the previous postmaster, a Republican.[59]

Bowman was a small town of eight hundred, serving the adjoining farming community in the southwestern corner of the state. Kate later described it as "a little, sordid wind-blown, sun-blasted, frost-scarred town." There was no Department of Justice official present at her address, and unfortunately, there was no transcript or recording made of the speech. As nearly as she could recall, she presented her usual opposition to the capitalist war, saying that union workers and farmers had little to gain from a war that made millionaires of munitions makers and that the problems of the poor would remain unresolved, no matter who won the war.[60]

After O'Hare left Bowman, an unidentified person wrote North Dakota senator Porter James McCumber a letter that he had reprinted in the *Congressional Record*. The informant stated that Kate had said women who did not resist the war "were no better than brood sows" and their sons would become "fertilizer" in Europe. At the same time naval recruiter M. S. Byrne heard her speech and reported to his superior that it "tended to discourage enlistments" and encouraged "resisting the draft." She was arrested when she arrived at Devil's Lake and was taken to Fargo for arraignment on charges of "sedition and near treasonable statements." In the trial that followed, the press stuck the label "Red Kate" on her.[61]

James Phelan, a banker-politician at Bowman who violently opposed the Nonpartisan League, testified before the grand jury that Kate's speech interfered with enlistments and recruitment. The trial opened in Bismarck with headlines blaring, "Mothers of Soldiers Brood Sows; Sammies Fit Only for Fertilizer, Said Mrs. O'Hare." U.S. attorney M. A. Hildreth paraded twelve witnesses before the jury of businessmen to testify that the headlines were accurate. V. R. Lovell, Kate's attorney, cross-examined them and established a series of variations of their remarks and that the witnesses were part of the Phelan political machine. Witnesses could only report from memory what they thought they had heard. On the stand Kate, too, could not recall her exact remarks but was positive she would never use such terminology in addressing women and their soldier-sons. She was certain she had delivered her standard anti-war speech. Judge Martin J. Wade, a Roman Catholic, was on record for previous anti-Socialist remarks and his disapproval of women taking part in public life. He advised the jury that the Constitution did not protect freedom of speech against violations of congressional law and that in time of war the nation must mobilize troops and had the right to protect itself against those who would interfere with this activity. The jury deliberated briefly and returned a unanimous verdict of guilty.[62]

Wade promised to pass sentence in one week. Kate asked for a new trial based on denial of her First Amendment freedoms, which he had done. Wade then permitted her to speak. She called attention to the fact that federal authorities had listened to her previous speeches on that trip and found nothing seditious in them. Then she said:

> It seems to me one of those strange grotesque things that can only be the outcome of the hysteria that is sweeping over the world today, that a judge on the bench, and a jury in the box, and a prosecuting attorney, should attempt to usurp the prerogative of God Almighty, and look down into the heart of a human being and decide what motives slumber there. There is no charge that if my intent or my motive was criminal, that that intent ever flowered, or ever was put into action—only the charge that in my heart there was an intent, and on that same charge of an intent so securely buried in a human heart that no result and no effect came from it, I went to trial.

Judge Wade was less cautious when he observed that the war could only be won with an adequate number of soldiers with the fighting spirit and funding. Congress therefore had every right to reach out and take hold of the people who are trying to kill the spirit of the American people. O'Hare, he insisted, had never said anything "about this good old United States; that she never expressed pride in its power, in its justice or its rights; that she never paid tribute to the American flag." "Every day that she is at liberty," he insisted, "she is a menace to the government"; he gave her the comparatively long sentence of five years in prison.[63]

O'Hare and Debs immediately campaigned to raise funds for her appeal but to no avail. In March 1919 the U.S. Supreme Court denied her a hearing. Accompanied by her longtime friend *Appeal* writer Grace Brewer, she reported to the Missouri State Penitentiary in Jefferson City. Eugene Debs would follow her to prison the next year for delivering a speech in which he called World War I the "supreme curse of Capitalism."

The prison Kate entered was ancient, outdated, and lacked all the reforms currently being promoted to improve the nation's penal system. It imposed the nineteenth-century rule of silence and used the convict labor system, illegal under Missouri law, and the concept of making money off of the inmates' labor rather than endeavoring to reform and redeem them to return to society. The women were housed in a separate part of the penitentiary. Kate O'Hare was put to work for five and a half days a week, nine hours daily, on an ancient sewing machine, hemming fifty-five blue denim jumpers daily, for which Missouri received fifty cents each and the state gave Kate fifty cents monthly. If the women failed to complete their work, they took it to their cells and finished it that evening. Women could scarcely endure this labor for two years before being assigned lighter labors. The building was the oldest in the compound, cold in the winter and stiflingly hot in the summer. Kate found the food intolerable, and it had to be eaten in silence. She had to share the same bathroom facilities with syphilitic women. On Monday and Tuesday evenings and on Sunday mornings, following required chapel, inmates were permitted an hour or so for socializing. Kate became good friends with fellow inmate and anarchist Emma Goldman during these periods.[64]

In 1920 Kate's name was presented to the party for the vice presidential nomination, which she lost to Seymour Stedman, a Chicago lawyer, probably because members thought one of their two candidates should not be in prison and unable to campaign effectively. As Oscar Ameringer suggested: "A lawyer is the only man whom the Socialist Party can nominate at this time. He knows just what to say and say it well and keep out of jail at the same time." Various groups, meanwhile, were raising money for Kate's appeals. She was bitter toward the national office, both for its notification that there would be no assistance in that direction because there were no funds but also for its neglect in sending her routine materials that all members automatically received while she was in prison. She suffered from a heatstroke and was denied medical attention until she collapsed at her machine. She never asked for a pardon because that would be an admission of guilt, but she sought commutation. Finally, on May 2, 1920, after she had served fourteen months, President Woodrow Wilson commuted her sentence.[65]

During her incarceration the American Socialists met in Chicago and splintered into three separate antagonistic groups: the Communist Labor Party, the Communist Party (CPUSA), and the Socialist Party, which had become a skeleton of its former self. Now bereft of her two-decade long vocation, Kate devoted the remainder of her life to prison reform along with speaking engagements to raise money for Debs's freedom. Twin Falls and Pocatello, Idaho, were on her itinerary, and neither town was particularly welcoming to her. She announced she would speak on "crime and criminals" in Twin Falls. American Legionnaires opposed her appearance, but she refused to cancel because she had "a constitutional right" to speak. The city council, however, heard that she planned to include some political remarks in her address and passed an ordinance forbidding public speeches without its consent. Her hosts completed arrangements for her to speak, but late in the afternoon of the scheduled day, ten people in three cars appeared at her host's house and kidnapped her. Twelve hours later one of the automobiles ran out of gas, and another had tire trouble in Montello, Nevada. Taking advantage of these diversions, Kate escaped and telegraphed Governor David Davis for protection, which he declined. The local sheriff found nine of her abductors in a Montello restaurant but refused to arrest them without proper warrants. Idaho officials declined subsequently to identify the culprits. The affair dragged on until Kate returned home to Girard without satisfaction.[66]

Kate's request to speak in Madison, Wisconsin, created a significant political hassle over free speech in the university-capital city. This was part of an ongoing feud over university control of outside speakers. The university president declined use of a campus hall, so her sponsors acquired a site on state government property. Local newspapers steered their articles more to sell papers than to attempt any means of expressing opinions or to minimize angry reactions. Among other topics the two newspapers rehashed the "brood sow" remark Kate allegedly made in Bowman, North Dakota, in 1917. Kate lectured to a huge crowd on prison reform. When a student in the audience began questioning her in a hostile manner, the crowd, which had been antagonistic at the beginning, "hooted him down." But the town and gown conflict remained after she left. During this visit Kate became acquainted with Thomas R. Amlie, a budding young Wisconsin politician who was involved in the incident.[67]

Kate's attack on Missouri's illegal convict labor system aroused the support of organized labor, and an "unusual" partnership of a joint committee of the United Garment Workers of America and the Union-Made Garment Manufacturers Association joined her crusade, with Kate as its "directing publicist." Her reform literature then reached over one thousand publications, and she was "actually driving prison sweatshops out of existence." This terrible practice involved forty-two states, 6 percent of the nation's prison population, and $43 million annually in America's consumer markets. The O'Hares tried to get the AFL involved in this effort, but during the 1920s the union was on the defensive against employers pursuing the "American Plan," adverse court decisions, and a rapidly declining membership, and it never played the role it should have in this campaign. It did, though, circulate Kate's articles through its news bureau.[68]

Kate's "Children's Crusade" made spectacular headlines with its program to send the children of political prisoners to Washington DC to appeal for the release of their fathers. Even her dentist, who was no militant, offered a donation to help fund the trip. The departure from St. Louis was caught on film as well as stops in a dozen cities along the route. At each pause rallies and demonstrations raised awareness and contributions, and the national media covered the event. Debs, out of prison, met the group in Terre Haute, but in Indianapolis, national headquarters of the American Legion, no demonstrations were permitted. When they reached the nation's capital, they were refused, as expected, a meeting with President Warren Harding, which Kate used to good effect in her writings. The previous year the president had commuted the sentences of half the political prisoners, including that of Eugene Debs.[69]

The term in prison and Kate's hectic pace in her new crusades proved too much for their marriage, and she and Frank divorced in 1928. Both of them remarried later that year, curiously on the same day. Kate married Charles C. Cunningham, a California engineer and businessman, with Walter Thomas Mills again presiding.

Socialist and writer Upton Sinclair led the End Poverty in California (EPIC) movement, then ran for governor in the Democratic primary election in 1934 and won. Kate left her comfortable home to work for his election. She had known Sinclair for thirty years and welcomed his efforts to unite diverse liberal groups. She worked with old colleagues during the campaign and used her connections with labor groups to good effect. Despite her exhilaration in doing battle again, Sinclair lost the race. When his Republican opponent charged that Sinclair would "Russianize" the Golden State and the old Left labeled him "a Socialist Fascist," Sinclair abandoned the movement. Kate continued with it, serving as chair of the Executive Committee and headed its education department, but as EPIC foundered without proper leadership to replace Sinclair, she tendered her resignation in late 1935.[70]

In 1937 O'Hare joined the staff of Thomas R. Amlie's Washington office for a year. He represented Wisconsin in the House of Representatives and was an important member of the liberal Upper Midwest coalition. In his youth he was an organizer for the Nonpartisan League, and as a congressman, he attempted to establish a national third party coalition of liberals during the Great Depression. Kate's presence in this campaign was useful to Amlie, and she enjoyed the work and was comfortable being around this power center. She became especially enthused over his work on a farm tenancy program, writing feature articles about it for some one hundred newspapers supporting his efforts.[71]

When Amlie was defeated in the primary race for U.S. senator, Kate returned to California. A few months later Governor Culbert Olson appointed a new director of penology, who hired Kate as his assistant. Food riots in the prison at San Quentin and fears of official reprisals prompted her to write the governor about her concerns. Within a few months he had appointed a new board of directors, which instituted reforms by banning cruel punishments and improving food and hygienic conditions, many of which were due to Kate's influence. She applauded the establishment of a minimum security prison at Chico but was in retirement at the time. In 1943 Governor Earl Warren invited her to sit in on the sessions of the State Crime Commission, and she attended her last one in late 1947. She died on January 10, 1948.[72]

Women in Kansas made their impact on the national scene. Their activities carried them out of the state and into other areas of the country, where they developed associations with other radicals, Communists, suffragists, labor leaders, and Socialists. On the national scene women such as Ella Reeve Bloor, Elizabeth Gurley Flynn, Mother Jones, Rose Pastor Stokes, and Frances Willard may have made more impact, but Josephine Conger, Annie Diggs, Caroline Lowe, Kate Richards O'Hare, and May Wood Simons all did significant work in Kansas, which in the grander scope played a major part in the national scene of radicalism. Nevertheless, they managed to still fill the expected role of women of the era—they were wives and mothers, all the while fighting for women's rights and the vote. The right to vote was slow in coming, despite women becoming more politically involved. They persevered, adding their voices to the rocky political and social causes sweeping the country.

While these women achieved limited success in their writing and recruitment, another group was beginning to surface. The miners of the Tri-State region of extreme southeastern Kansas achieved a moderate political success in counties where their numbers were concentrated. In Cherokee and Crawford Counties they managed to elect local officers and a limited number of county officials, which was important for boosting morale.

4

THE MINING SOCIALISTS

A different type of socialism, meanwhile, was emerging in the southeastern Kansas mining region. This version was adapted to the poor, working-class people of the area. Mining was a dangerous and uncertain occupation that American settlers to the region found undesirable. Those willing to work in the mines were primarily first- and second-generation immigrants from the British Isles. Mine operators later were forced to recruit many of their workers from countries of southeastern Europe and the American South. The 1880 census revealed that Cherokee and Crawford Counties had about two thousand foreign-born inhabitants, and a decade later this number had jumped to five thousand. These workers developed a distinct type of socialism, a European brand that evolved to suit their local mining culture.[1] Because of the influx of southeastern European workers, by the early 1900s the region had earned the nickname the "Little Balkans."

Employment in the mines was neither popular nor lucrative. Work was slack or nonexistent in the summers, and in the winters it meant seldom seeing one's children or the sun. Deadly gases often caused explosions and cave-ins. Many accidents resulted from falling rock, mostly from the roofs of tunnels. Children were abused by the European style of fathers taking them into the mines at an early age. Employers exploited workers by selling them their blasting powder as well as food and clothing for their families at outrageous prices at the local company store. Often the workers were paid in scrip, also referred to as "clacker," that could be spent only in the company store, with its inflated prices. If the miners became too demanding during a strike, the company imported black workers from the South as strikebreakers. Life was little better at the surface, where company houses were rented at premium prices. Socialist reporter May Wood Simons investigated miners' housing and announced that floors were often bare and the wives and children barefoot. She noted that "coal soot has blackened the walls and ceilings that never knew paint nor varnish. Or ragged paper flutters from the walls. Rough pine floors with yawning cracks, worn knobby over projected knots," she continued, "discourage cleanliness in the best of housewives among these miners. Through the broken roof and frail sides the rains ruin the few possessions of the miner's family and drip down on his wretched bed." The roads had no sidewalks, trees, or grass. Children often missed school on washdays because they had to go naked until their one set of clothes dried. The polluted drinking water resulted in 20 percent of the population being sick with typhoid fever at any given time. A schoolboy once began an essay on cows with the observation that "the meat of a cow is called soupbone."[2]

Legislative reformers enacted regulations that were erratically enforced by officials who respected the prerogatives of capitalists. Gradually, though, conditions improved, especially during the Populist Era and the Progressive movement that followed the farm revolt of the late 1800s. In one of the unusual periods in American history, the Populists sought unity with the wage earners to promote their common goals. When the Populists gained control of the Kansas government in the last decade of the nineteenth century, they proposed legislation to improve the working conditions of miners. A commissioner of labor and mining inspectors had been established earlier. Now the Populists enacted workers' compensation laws, abolition of child labor, statutes controlling the working conditions and hours of women and older children, abolition of the blacklist, establishment of small claims courts to give poor workers a means of redress and justice, the enactment of the eight-hour day for government employees, and control over convict labor. Many of these laws received only

sporadic enforcement for years, but they were a beginning, waiting to be enforced.[3]

It was one thing to enact protective legislation but another
matter to get it enforced. In 1911 Leon Benson, a Socialist from
Pittsburg, was elected state mining inspector. He soon discovered numerous violations of the mining laws. When one mine
supervisor refused to obey the regulations, Benson secured a warrant for his arrest. Much to the inspector's surprise, neither the
superintendent nor the county attorney appeared in court at the
designated time or sent a reason for their absence, and the judge
acquiesced in their inaction. A reporter discovered widespread
disregard for laws regulating mine safety inspections because state
attorney general F. S. Jackson had ruled that mining was not a
dangerous occupation in terms of the regulatory statutes. The
journalist then listed the results of ignoring the regulations as
costing a life per day—or seventy-seven accidents between July
1 and October 23, 1911.[4]

The miners desperately needed help, and in November 1898
the new president of the United Mine Workers of America (UMW),
John Mitchell, ordered his union to begin organizing the Tri-
State region. This resulted eventually in the establishment of
District 14 for the Tri-State, one of the most active units of the
UMW, especially after the members elected Alexander McWhirter
Howat as their president. The first president, George Richard-
son, had no interest in the political leanings of Socialist miners in
Crawford County, and they were searching for more aggressive
leadership. They found it in Howat, whom they elected in 1906.[5]

A ruggedly handsome, blond, blue-eyed Scotsman, Howat was
born in Glasgow. He migrated with his parents to Illinois, where
he obtained a job as a breaker boy in a coal mine (the worker
who separated the impurities of the busted-up coal by hand) and
grew up with John Mitchell, who thought highly of him. He later
worked his way back to Scotland, where he labored as a breaker
boy for a year, before returning to America. He was also a prize-
fighter until he was so badly beaten in Kansas City one night that
the sympathetic audience took up a collection; he used the money
to travel to the Tri-State region to seek work as a coal miner. He

soon gained a reputation for his ready profanity and for being a good miner, a hard drinker, "an especially bad person to engage in an argument . . . and a handy fist-fighter."[6]

Howat traveled widely. He was chosen to represent the UMW at the International Mining Congress in Vienna, Austria, in 1908 and again was a delegate to the same Congress in Hamburg in 1921. In 1918 President Woodrow Wilson appointed him—along with Charles Edward Russell of Washington DC, former editor of the *Appeal to Reason* Louis Kopelin, newspaperman A. M. Simmons of Milwaukee, and John Spargo of Old Bennington, Vermont—to address workers in Europe in an effort to build their morale. They reported their experiences to the president when they returned to America.[7]

There was another side to Alexander Howat that was seldom seen in public. He and his wife, Agnes, were fond of children but were unable to conceive one. A favorite niece described her uncle as "the kindest person I ever knew. . . . My mother told me she had seen him give the coat off his back when he saw a man walking downtown who had none. Many times he signed notes for friends. He was an eloquent speaker and had a very commanding appearance and manner. He loved to tease and had a twinkle in his eyes." Howat's vice president, August Dorchy, verified Howat's less than frugal spending and gifting habits. Despite his never being able to acquire much wealth, he was known for lending a few dollars to anyone who was down on his luck. Mother Jones, hard-bitten veteran of many labor wars, said she "never saw a man who, as a leader, had the complete love of his men as Howat did."[8]

Alexander Howat was a Socialist, as were many of his mining followers in the Tri-Sate region. Eugene Debs was popular in these coal counties, and in 1914 the District 14 convention called for a Socialist government "as the strong right arm of labor." Howat was absolutely fearless, a natural-born leader, and his men would follow him anywhere, especially regarding coal and Socialist activities. Known as the "czar of the Kansas coal fields," his district had 100 percent membership, was the most powerful union in Kansas, and was the best organized west of Illinois. He would later challenge John L. Lewis for leadership of the UMW and would lose only through a questionable court interpretation in 1930.[9]

Socialism had a particularly powerful appeal to Howat's miners. Not only was their leader born in a foreign country, as many of them were, but there was the added factor of their social and economic status. They were part of the "new" immigration from southeastern Europe, compared to the "old" immigration of previous decades from northwestern Europe. The old immigration had melded into American society rather quickly and thoroughly compared to the difficulty of the newcomers, whose language roots and cultural mores were quite different from the "homogenized" Americans. Use of alcohol was a case in point.

Kansas had been dry since 1880, when voters approved the prohibition amendment to their constitution. The mining counties, however, always had a supply of "deep shaft," as their moonshine liquor was labeled, and try as they might, Kansas authorities were never able to "dry out" these counties. Walter Roscoe Stubbs, Republican governor from 1909 to 1913, during the rapid rise of the Socialist Party among miners in Crawford County, was especially diligent in trying to dry out these dangerous political opponents with their radical philosophy that was fueled by "Demon Rum." In 1910 he threatened to send in the state militia to assist Sheriff E. J. Merriweather if he did not enforce prohibition more thoroughly. When Stubbs became governor, the county had 150 open saloons. He closed them down, but there were reported "numerous leaks in the lid," and Stubbs was determined to seal them. John Marshall, principal deputy from the state attorney general's office, who actually did the closings, had better knowledge of the situation. He realistically believed that it would require two years' effort to eliminate liquor being "secretly sold in the backs of old buildings, in sheds and out of the way places." State officials never completely dried out Crawford County.[10]

The state faced similar problems in Cherokee County, immediately south of Crawford County. Governor Stubbs requested the resignation of county attorney A. L. Majors for his lack of diligence in enforcing the liquor laws in his county. District Judge E.

E. Sapp "failed to accept the same" until he could appoint attorney Charles Stephens after "an ouster suit" was begun against Majors.[11]

Also of significance, the recent immigrants were lowest on the social and economic ladder in Kansas and, as such, were more attracted to socialism because of its appeal to the poor and "downtrodden." These miners were clannish and possessed "a social inferiority complex," and the class conflict ideas of socialism tended to reinforce their prejudices.[12]

More important, approximately 70 percent of the miners in Crawford County pursued "the personal political philosophy of their leaders . . . in spite of the basically political orientation of the pressure group politics" of the UMW. They never really accepted the Socialist intellectuals, but they idealized Debs, Mother Jones, and Alexander Howat. In addition, according to one expert on the subject of politics and miners, Howat followed the "schizophrenic philosophy" of speaking at Socialist rallies and urging miners to join the union but at the same time "would not subordinate the immediate economic and political needs of the miners to the long-range economic goals and Marxist ideology" of the Socialist Party.[13]

State party chairman G. C. Clemens reported in 1900 that the Cherokee County mining camps were "ablaze with Socialist enthusiasm." And, he added, the mining camps of Crawford County were as well. He predicted the Socialist ticket in 1900 would receive twice as many votes there alone as the entire state ticket in 1898. He was not "indulging in ordinary political speculation" when he insisted that if the elections were held "now before any further missionary work," the party should receive over fifteen hundred votes in those two counties.[14]

Philip Henry Callery, a Socialist, was District 14's legal counsel, and Howat kept him busy with his challenges to the constitutionality of the Kansas Industrial Court throughout the 1920s. Callery's father, who had migrated from Ireland, died in 1880, the year of his son's birth in Carthage, Missouri. Philip and his older siblings had to help their mother in extracting a living from the family farm, so he received little formal education. In 1903 he graduated from the International School of Social Economy in

Girard. He married Ida Rello Haymond of Durant, Oklahoma, in
1909 and in 1913 became secretary to George R. Lunn of Sche-
nectady, the first Socialist mayor in New York state. While in this
position, Callery took correspondence courses from the LaSalle
University of Law. When he moved to Kansas, he was admitted to the bar of the state supreme court and the U.S. Supreme
Court. Callery became a leading orator and lyceum lecturer for
the Socialists and had the honor of nominating Eugene Debs
for the presidency in 1908. Callery was particularly noted for
his Irish wit and his "keen understanding and mastery of the art
of oratory."[15]

Debs described Callery as "one of the most brilliant and promising young men on the American platform today." The *Chicago
Examiner* labeled his nominating speech in 1908 as "one of the
greatest . . . ever delivered before a Socialist body in America . . .
a speech during which men and women wept." The auditorium
was packed, and for two hours Callery captivated the audience
with tales of sacrifice and departed heroes to the cause, bringing tears to the eyes of many. In 1915 Callery established the law
firm of Callery and Callery in Pittsburg, which became the official counsel for UMW District 14.[16]

His wife, Ida, had a politically active Populist father who incul-
cated this interest in his daughter. Born in Kansas, in 1906 she
received a teaching certificate from Bacone College in Muskogee,
Oklahoma, and taught in a federal Indian school in Wetumpka,
Oklahoma. In 1908 she was elected state secretary of the Oklahoma Socialist Party and from 1911 to 1914 served in the same
capacity in Arkansas, where she solidified her reputation as a
"skilled grassroots organizer." She continued her legal studies
in 1914 in the People's College in Fort Scott, with which Philip
Callery was associated, and attended the University of Oklahoma
Law School. She was admitted to the Kansas bar and joined her
husband in the law firm of Callery and Callery.[17]

Women "constituted an estimated twenty-five to thirty-five percent" of the Socialist Party membership in the trans-Mississippi
South. Ida Callery contributed significantly to this membership
statistic with her dynamic leadership and stump oratory. She was

not an original thinker or a prolific writer, but she excelled in the art of organizing red card members, both male and female. In her recruiting efforts she stressed grassroots participation and the dictum "Organize, organize, and then organize." She utilized picnics, ice cream socials, and county fairs in her recruiting and introduced the Oklahoma encampment meetings to Arkansas. In the law firm of Callery and Callery she stressed strict application of the Federal Employers Liability Act by coal companies and offered help to workers pro bono. She worked with Socialist trade union leaders, such as Alexander Howat of District 14, Fred Holt of District 21, and G. E. Mikel of the Arkansas Federation of Labor. On April 17, 1917, Ida died prematurely in Pittsburg of peritonitis, shortly before her thirtieth birthday.[18]

The local Socialist newspaper lamented her death, which ended a career that was "just beginning to attain its most bountiful fruition." After she arrived, Callery and Callery became known as a hospitable law office for the poor. "No one in distress was ever turned away or received coldly by the Callerys," an editor insisted, "always their tales of tribulation were listened to with genuine sympathetic attention, their needs administered to and their rights looked after regardless of whether there was a legitimate earned fee to be gained or not." The local court adjourned, and the Kansas bar turned out en masse for her funeral.[19]

Howat kept Callery busy with his legal escapades against the Court of Industrial Relations. Established in 1920, it forbade unilateral action by either side in the collective bargaining process and even eliminated the democratic principle of negotiating a collective bargaining agreement. It was, instead, an industrial court of three members who would determine all collective bargaining issues unilaterally. As one critic noted, Governor Henry Allen seemed determined "to legislate labor-management behavior just as the Kansas prohibitionists had already legislated drinking customs."[20]

Howat described Governor Allen as "one of the worst enemies organized labor ever had," and he was determined to test the law until the courts dismantled it. The issue was drawn with the Mishmash case in 1918. Carl Mishmash was employed in a mine as a boy and at a boy's wage, and when he turned nineteen, he requested a man's pay, agreeable to the union contract. The company declined to act, and the squabble continued for three years, until Howat's miners finally called a strike to force the owner to comply with the contract. The Industrial Court approved the raise and back pay through the district court clerk and ordered Howat to call off the strike. He responded that the money must be paid through the mine office or the strike would continue. He refused to recognize the Industrial Court jurisdiction and was sentenced for contempt of court. John L. Lewis, seeking an excuse to curtail the growing independence of Howat, suspended District 14 for defiance of union laws and named new officers.[21]

Frank P. Walsh was President Woodrow Wilson's appointee to chair the Industrial Commission to investigate national industrial strife, with Callery representing Howat in court. District court judge A. J. Curran of Crawford County presided over these trials, and when Socialist Charles Cordray ran against him for election to his position, the Socialist miners turned out in numbers; Cordray received as many primary votes as the Democrat and Republican candidates combined. This frightened the major party leaders, and they joined forces to reelect Curran and to make certain that a Socialist never again won office in the county. At this point the state brought criminal charges against Howat, and he was convicted and sentenced to six months in prison. While in jail, Howat called a strike against a mine company whose foreman gave his own son a job over the protests of a man with more seniority. Howat was again charged with contempt of court, convicted, and sentenced to prison, making this his third conviction running simultaneously. The day he began serving his sentence in the Columbus, Kansas, jail, his men declared a public holiday and struck in protest.

The U.S. Supreme Court sustained Howat's convictions but gave him his victory in another case. Workers of the Wolff Packing Company of Topeka submitted their grievances to the Industrial Court, which prescribed a new wage. The company refused to accept the court decision and appealed to the Supreme Court. In 1923 Chief Justice William Howard Taft sustained the workers and, in his decision, devastated the foundation of the Industrial Court. He declared that only three categories of business—utilities, public services, and those where natural law did not operate—to be "clothed in the public interest." The Industrial Court had been given jurisdiction in all labor-management cases because the legislature declared all of them to be "in the public interest," and the court held that it was insufficient for the state merely to declare it so. It was a great victory for Alexander Howat in the short run, a setback for public regulation, but over time a more liberal court would reinterpret the definition of *public interest* and the reach of state regulation.[22]

With the leadership of Alex Howat and Eugene Debs and the influential *Appeal to Reason* at their doorstep, Tri-State miners continued to develop their own brand of socialism, despite the conservative political emphasis of their national union leaders and the bombardment of UMW literature. The Socialists were less successful in the northern part of the coal mining region. The *Osage City Free Press* never mentioned Socialist activities in Osage County, and the *Weir City Journal* rarely had anything to report, almost as though the editor hoped that by not mentioning social-ism, it would disappear. He did report Debs's first visit to that city almost reluctantly. Debs drew large numbers at the opera house for his speech in the afternoon and another large audience that evening in the new Hargiss Building. The editor considered the nation's leading Socialist to be "an excellent talker of the mag-netic order" who explained his philosophy clearly and concisely. Debs could "draw some pretty word pictures while exhorting his theoretical ideas of socialism, and while there is not much of a clinching nature in his argument, one likes to hear him talk." This was Cherokee County, at the southern end of the Tri-State region. Socialists were most successful in the middle county of Crawford, where Girard is the county seat.[23]

Lack of religious restraints provided one of the reasons for success in the mining areas. Immigrants from southeast Europe were generally of Roman Catholic or occasionally Greek Ortho-dox background. Whatever their preference in the old country, in the Tri-State region they were so poor that they had no extra money to contribute to church collections and thus "were left alone by both priest and preacher." Political beliefs varied from priest to priest and preacher to minister, but the Roman Catholic Church fought "godless" socialism strenuously. Socialist leaders, in turn, were anti-clerical and generally anti-Catholic. As a result, social life in the mining camps centered around the union hall rather than the nonexistent church, and their natural leaders— the union officials—could spread their political ideas without competition from the pulpit.[24]

Because labor was such a large part of their lives, the political factor became an important concern. The Socialists tended to look out for the miners' interests better than average Republicans or Democrats. It was easier for Socialists to recruit miners, as they tended to be more pro-worker than either major party. Socialism drew a heavy following in the Tri-State region and had no shortage of influential and ambitious members within its ranks.

Although located between the coalfields and Fort Scott, Girard continued to be a center of Socialist activity because the party leadership either lived there or visited frequently. As early as 1897, R. D. Oliver, editor of the *Walnut Advance*, addressed a Socialist association at Fort Scott, condemning the competitive system and advocating a Socialist form of government as a replacement. If the Populists and Democrats supported this view, a Girard editor warned, "they had better retrace their steps instead of going headlong toward a precipice." With the failure of populism shortly after this time, many who were inclined toward it became Socialists. Before 1897 the Populists had worried about the emerging Socialists. One editor reported that the Populists were afraid they "would develop into a separate political party and destroy the Populist organization." The Populists, of course, destroyed themselves with Fusion in 1896.[25]

One year later Fort Scott hosted the first state convention of the Socialist-Labor Party. Delegates to the meeting nominated candidates for governor, secretary of state, and congressman at large. R. D. Oliver and M. V. Tibbs of Girard and James H. Roberts of Pittsburg were chosen as members of the State Central Committee. Oliver, a good speaker, called it "a historic day in

the annals of Kansas and will be read with pride by our children."
Now that Oliver "has affiliated himself with the Socialist-Labor
party," a Republican editor queried, "what will the Demo-Pops
do for campaign orators?"[26]

In 1899 the *Appeal to Reason* asked Socialists to subscribe to fifteen thousand copies to be sent to newspaper editors throughout
the country to "educate" them. The editor of the *Girard News*
considered it abominable that Republican congressman E. R.
Ridgley of the Kansas Third District was the first to subscribe
to the fund. "How humiliating it must be," the editor lamented,
"for many who voted for him." While Ridgley empathized with
the Socialists, he also was hedging his bets.[27]

Critics of socialism abounded. When the Ruskin Colony failed
in Tennessee, a writer for *Gunton's Magazine*, a New York economics serial, concluded it was because of laziness. The colonists
were overly dependent financially on the *Appeal to Reason*, and
when the newspaper lost its appeal to readers during economic
prosperity, their members joined the Duke Colony in Georgia.
It was then renamed the Ruskin Commonwealth. The people
became "careless in habits and slovenly in dress, and the children ran wild. There was an un-resisted tendency toward indo-
lence . . . and the colony failed because the industrious and skillful
could not make headway against the indolent, the unskilled, and
the improvident." Those who wanted socialism to look ridiculous, and there were many, read these stories of fiasco avidly.[28]

Some observers believed that the rival factionalism between
Daniel De Leon's followers and the Socialist-Labor groups
accounted for the recent national success of the party. In 1900
the Socialist vote (Debs) for the presidency was 97,000, but four
years later it was 420,000. The boost came from the rivalry between
the two factions, the *New York Sun* concluded, because it came
"chiefly in a few states"—New York, Pennsylvania, Ohio, Illinois, Massachusetts, Connecticut, and Washington—where there
was intense competition. The party suffered meager support in
rural areas throughout the United States. The rise in the popularity of Socialist-Labor groups, the editor insisted, came almost
exclusively from "naturalized citizens," and having few recruits

among "native born Americans," the growth of the two factions was dependent on foreign immigration.[29]

Some writers expressed an opposing view that "the surprising growth of the party" came from former Populist support following the demise of that Agrarian Party. In 1902 there were five farmers and one each of physician, railroad worker, miner, barber, printer, and carpenter as Socialists running for Crawford County offices. The preponderance of farmers suggests that they probably were former Populists who joined the Socialist movement. In the election of 1904 the Socialist vote saw an increase among Populist farming communities. This included the states of Kansas, California, Nebraska, and Iowa. In Kansas, it was noted, Debs polled more votes than Tom Watson, the Populist candidate for the presidency.[30]

To add to their attraction and advertising, the *Appeal to Reason* Socialists in Girard purchased a wagon with a large gong. A Girard editor compared it to the "Black Marias," or patrol wagons used in large municipalities. On its maiden trip they drove it through the streets of Girard announcing an evening concert. That evening a number of men and women sang Socialist songs, a "Mrs. Lockwood" gave a recitation, and "Mr. Lockwood delivered an illustrated Socialist speech." The editor admitted, "The melody was all right, and the recitation well delivered." He derided the speech, though, as "an appeal to class prejudice."[31]

The ardently Republican *Pittsburg Headlight* happily reported that the Socialist rally in Girard Friday night "was such a small affair that very few knew it." There were a disappointing number of voters present, and during the speech of W. C. Benton, candidate for county attorney and the main attraction, the audience began leaving en masse, which resulted in the meeting ending prematurely with no further speakers.[32]

Two years later, in 1904, Socialist candidates for state office managed to pick up over three hundred votes in the county. When the Socialist state convention was held in Wichita in 1904, the Girard editor proudly pointed out that the candidate for state auditor, George D. Brewer, came from Girard, as did Allen W. Ricker, delegate to the national convention. Because of the large increase in the vote for Eugene Debs for the presidency, Debs predicted that his party would replace the Democrats in the near future. The real contest in 1908, he predicted, would be between the Republicans and the Socialists. The *St. Louis Globe Democrat* believed this prediction to be "absurd." The weakness of Alton B. Parker and his party accounted for the Socialist surge in 1904, the St. Louis newspaper concluded, and socialism was "not creating any alarm in the ranks of the Republican Party."[33]

Any public display of the Socialist red flag was certain to bring reprisals, or at least immediate attention. There was "a riotous demonstration" in Frontenac, a suburb north of Pittsburg, "when a band of armed men marched to the Labelle shaft and closed it, headed by a man carrying a red flag." Amid community condemnation Mayor John Beitzinger promised that this would not happen again and promptly swore in forty "of the best men in Frontenac," including leading members of the mining union, who were tasked with preventing any more red flags appearing in town.[34]

A serious incident occurred in Girard on a Sunday afternoon in 1908 that highlighted the potentially explosive relationship of socialism with the surrounding rural community. The *Girard Press*, whose Republican editor detested socialism, reported the affair from his viewpoint. His opinion was influenced by Marvin Brown having attacked his paper a few weeks earlier in his rival newspaper, the *Independent News*, on the union label proposition "and hit the churches a slap as well."[35]

On that Sunday, Bruce Rogers, Socialist candidate for county attorney and head of the book department of the *Appeal to Reason*, circulated a petition to request that the local committee secure a speaker for the Fourth of July celebration. He wanted the committee to invite Eugene Debs to deliver the speech. First of all, the editor noted, Rogers knew that Debs could not accept this invitation as he had already committed himself to speak that day at Coalgate, Oklahoma, and the Girard committee had thus secured another speaker. Second, "Rogers' desire to cause trouble in his normal condition was not helped any by the liquor which he managed to keep comfortably full of."

On the duly appointed holiday, Rogers "was insolent and insulting," denigrating the second-choice speaker and describing the holiday as a "Republican picnic." Rogers's brother-in-law celebrated the holiday by raising "the red flag of anarchy" at his home for the sole purpose of inciting a commotion. He "knew it would not further the cause of Socialism," the editor claimed, "and he courted trouble when he hung up his treasonable bunting" on this holiday. Sheriff J. E. Walsh, city marshal A. W. Barker, and night watchman George W. Brown marched to Rogers's home to ask him "to remove the obnoxious pennant." Rogers was not at home, so the officers "promptly removed the rag."

The following day, the Sabbath, again "with a little too much liquor aboard," Rogers met George Brown and "abused him with profane language." He promised to hoist another red flag and said that if anyone attempted to remove it again, "he would shoot him like a dog." When Rogers later appeared with a large red flag and carried it around the town square, he was "armed and intoxicated." When he arrived in front of a restaurant, two men, Gib Brown and Woody Sawyer, accosted Rogers, took the flag from him, and set it on fire. Rogers struck out at a bystander, who "knocked him out." Deputy Sheriff Merriweather arrested Rogers, relieved him of his weapon, and took him to jail to await trial.

Friends of Rogers defended his actions on the grounds that he was drunk and thus not responsible, and as a result, Rogers was dealt with "in a lenient manner." The *Press* editor noted that it was "a man's privilege in this country to cherish any religious or political belief that he sees fit, but he must not overstep the boundaries of the law." Socialists violated the law when they displayed "the red flag of treason," he insisted.[36]

When World War I erupted and Socialists opposed the United States' involvement in it, or any war, the editor of the Pittsburg *Worker's Chronicle* undertook an explanation of the red flag to counter the current public belief that it was a symbol of "anarchy, riot, and bloodshed." Ceres, goddess of agriculture, and Minerva, protectress of laboring men and women, wore crimson vestments, the editor noted. The early Christians, therefore, who were of proletarian origins, favored the red flag as "the historic banner of persecuted labor." Laboring classes always displayed the red flag as the emblem of peace. The red flag had evolved into an international symbol of brotherhood, the solidarity of labor and its struggles. To Socialists the blood of all nations is red, as is the blood shed to promote the causes of labor. The red flag was an international symbol and was not intended to replace the flag of any nation.[37]

The Crawford County Socialists made rapid gains at the ballot box in the first decade of the twentieth century. They were running candidates for office even before the political collapse of the Populists, and in 1898 G. A. Callahan, running for associate justice of the state supreme court (judges ran for their office at this time) picked up eighty-one votes, while the candidates for governor and lieutenant governor garnered ninety-one votes each. Other Socialists that year averaged tallies in the mid-eighties. They received nearly the same support in 1900.[38]

In 1902 there were only 205 Socialist votes for Kansas governor. John Dowd, running for county clerk on the Socialist ticket in 1904, optimistically predicted a Socialist vote of "fully 2,000" in that election, while "others more conservative, thought perhaps 1,000 maximum." Dowd based his estimate on the fact that "every Socialist is in real earnest" and so they should "poll 100 percent of our vote." With Debs heading the national ticket in 1904, Granville Lowther picked up 1,144 votes as the candidate for state auditor, and those running for the secretary of state, treasurer, and their district representative all had about the same number of supporters. Debs and candidates campaigning for state office increased their votes by only 100 in 1908.[39]

After 1908 political activities by Socialists accelerated as they felt a quickening of their political potential. A conference of Socialist women met in Girard in June 1909. Mrs. Emma Johns Call graced it with music "that never fails to please with her renditions of both classical and popular airs," and Caroline Lowe, state organizer for women, opened the meeting. The following morning Grace Bower read a paper on Socialist literature, and that afternoon the women listened to papers on child labor, white slavery, and women's work abroad. Following committee reports, the conference adopted resolutions supporting the suffrage movement, condemning the federal court decision in the Fred Warren case (in which the *Appeal* editor was convicted for sending threatening material through the mail), condemning the white slave traffic and child labor, and endorsing the magazine the *Progressive Woman*.[40]

Three months later a newspaper reported the Socialists "had a full house at their meeting with Mrs. Call again providing the music. George Hibner, the Socialist candidate for governor the previous year, delivered the main lecture. Although he was a resident of Girard, it was his first public lecture in the city because he was out on the lecture circuit "most of the time, only recently having completed a tour extending to the coast." Later that month the Socialists held a four-day encampment in Pittsburg. Speeches were delivered by, among others, Caroline Lowe, Rolla Houghton, Kate Richards O'Hare, 1908 nominee for governor George Hibner, and Eugene Debs.[41]

Socialists again presented a full ticket in 1910. In this off-year election voter participation in the gubernatorial election was down. S. M. Stallard ran against incumbent Walter Stubbs for governor and received 739 votes to Stubbs's 4,020. Mrs. Harry Vincent campaigned for superintendent of public instruction in the race, and former labor commissioner Leon Benson was the candidate for the Third District congressional seat. Amazingly, Mrs. Vincent tallied 2,068 votes, and Benson, who was very popular in the coal mining counties, received 2,067 votes.[42]

The Republican-dominated legislature enacted a poll tax in 1911 to curtail voting by Socialists. This tax was stoutly resisted throughout the state, and Jacob I. Sheppard made an issue of it "on behalf of the malcontents" in the Tri-State region. The city commissioners ordered the arrest of anyone who defied the law, while the Socialist mayor of Girard, H. P. Houghton, opposed the tax. Chanute citizens were "disgruntled" over the law, and in Hutchinson the Anti-Poll Tax League was formed and retained Sheppard as its counsel until the tax was declared unconstitutional.

The Republican Party suffered a divisive split in 1912, with Theodore Roosevelt forming the Progressive Party when he failed to prevent William Howard Taft from receiving the Republican nomination. This move guaranteed the Democratic candidate, Woodrow Wilson, would win in the Electoral College, although Wilson received only 40 percent of the popular vote. Eugene Debs was approaching the pinnacle of his political career. His popular vote of 87,814 in 1900 increased to 402,000 four years later and to 430,000 in 1908. This vote more than doubled in 1912, to 900,000. Socialists swept all the offices in Crawford County in 1912, although a half-dozen of these contests were later challenged in court.[43]

When newly elected state senator Fred Stanton arrived in Topeka to take his seat, the Senate voted twenty-eight to ten not to seat him in what the *Appeal to Reason* called "the boldest attempt to steal an office in the State of Kansas." Attorneys for his opponent, Republican Ebenezer Porter, the incumbent of some dozen years, produced evidence that numbers of voters illegally crossed over from Missouri in the election and "scores of aliens" were allowed to vote after declaring their intention to become naturalized. He gathered stories that one voting place was "moved bodily to a Socialist hall," that "intoxicating liquors" were sold near another voting booth, and that "voters took the official ballots home with them and there received aid in marking them for Stanton." Stanton denied "most of the evidence" and insisted that he had won legally, but the election committee determined that Porter should have a plurality of four hundred votes. A majority of senators agreed with this recommendation, and he was given the seat. According to historian Stanley A. Vining, one committeeman described Stanton as "a dirty, uncouth sort of person and the state Senate just did not want that type of man in its membership."[44]

Actually, in this election five house Democrats moved to the upper chamber. As a result, the state senate contained twenty Democrats, nineteen Republicans, and one Socialist. To maintain control of this body, the Republicans needed to replace Stanton with Porter so there would be a twenty-twenty division and then Republican lieutenant governor Sheffield Ingalls could cast the deciding votes in case of a tie.[45]

Following the election of 1912, Peter Collins, a union man on the lecture circuit, challenged Eugene Debs to a debate. Collins was labeled a "fighting type of orator who backed his attack with quotes from Socialists." He offered to meet Debs anywhere and would pay him $500 for the opportunity. "The big Socialist leaders in this country today are not members of the laboring classes," he asserted. "They are millionaires for the most part, who are grafters, [Graham Phelps] Stokes, [Joseph Medill] Paterson, and all the rest. They are in Socialism for what they can get out of it, and they are getting it too." Collins considered trade unionism as "a great constructive movement" in the field of labor.[46]

In August 1912, just before the elections, the *Labor Herald* and the *Daily News* joined forces under the banner of the *Labor Herald*. It would continue to speak for the Kansas State Federation of Labor but would be printed in the *News* offices and would have a greater press capacity, including a large Webb printing press capable of turning out sixteen thousand copies of an eight-page paper per hour. The editors hoped to continue business advertising directed toward the common laborer and his family. The newspaper would become a Socialist organ in November 1913 as the *Worker's Chronicle*, and much more news of Socialist activities would become available for Pittsburg, Crawford County, and the Tri-State region. At the time editor George Brewer promised that it would "be conducted as a bona fide uncompromising Socialist County Newspaper" and the news in Crawford County and vicinity would be "gathered and interpreted from the viewpoint of labor's interests."[47]

Eugene Debs spoke before a large Pittsburg picnic crowd in late September. A group of 4,000 gathered to hear him, with 1,500 arriving by train. A band concert in the morning was followed by a nine-block procession to Lincoln Park, where Jake Sheppard spoke after Chairman C. H. Cordray called the meeting to order. George Brewer and Allen W. Ricker, Socialist nominees for state congressman and senator, respectively, addressed the gathering. Then Debs spoke, followed by May Wood Simons. Debs's thesis was that Theodore Roosevelt, the Progressive, or Bull Moose, candidate for president, was appealing for labor's support, but Debs insisted the voters judge Roosevelt by his record, not what he said. Both as governor of New York and as president, he had a bad labor record, including denouncing the Western Federation of Miners officials who were illegally kidnapped in Colorado and taken to Idaho to be tried for the 1905 murder of Idaho governor Frank Steunenburg. Five years earlier Roosevelt had described Debs as an "undesirable citizen," and now during the campaign he referred to him as "Brother Debs." The audience "applauded vociferously" as Debs denounced the former president.[48]

The election results in 1912 were ominous to the two major parties. Socialists won the county ticket in Crawford by nearly six hundred votes. Democratic county chairman Frank Comisky noted that the Bull Moosers voted for the national slate of Roosevelt, Republicans for Walter Stubbs for U.S. senator, and Arthur Capper for governor and "then jumped over and voted solidly for the Socialist ticket."[49]

The rock-ribbed Republican *Daily Headlight* called it a "close contest" in Cherokee County. The Democrats and Republicans ran "neck and neck" for state and county offices. The Socialists did not win any of them but ran strong in township races and elected Socialist Ben Wilson in the northern legislative district by a thousand votes. Otherwise, the Democrats took all other offices except two won by Republicans. The national split between Taftites and Bull Moosers hurt the party everywhere.[50]

After the Socialists made this strong showing at the polls, political activities grew nastier, at least according to the Socialists, who were on the receiving end of the nasty. A month following the election, Reverend Dr. L. M. Potts of the First Methodist Church in Pittsburg attacked the "Godless" Socialists in three successive Sunday evening services. Potts informed his congregation that socialism would destroy the fear of God in the minds of its followers and devastate the American home and that communism would eventually annihilate civilization. *Appeal* editor Allen W. Ricker answered Potts's charges before a large audience in the local auditorium. He called the attack "cowardly," and to Potts's charge that August Bebel's 1910 book, *Woman and Socialism*, was "salacious literature" and a defense of free love, he quoted the highly respected Jane Addams, who called it "Bebel's Great Book." Ricker, a religious man, insisted that socialism was indeed not communism, but Potts apparently did not know the difference between the two "-isms." Ricker concluded by challenging Potts to study the works of Karl Marx for a month and submit to a public examination on socialism. The *Appeal to Reason* would pay him the handsome sum of $50 "for his trouble." The reverend doctor never responded.[51]

Before the election of 1914, it was charged that "some Socialist politicians" sent a card to Protestants in Girard saying: "Will good Protestants permit the turning over of Girard to the Catholic Church? All the corrupt city governments in the United States are dominated by Catholics. If [Henry] Sauer should be elected, he and [J. E.] Walsh, both staunch Catholics, would be a majority of the city commission. Use your vote before it is too late."

Someone was playing dirty tricks. The Republican *Girard Press* insisted that Sauer was not a Catholic and that Walsh, although a Catholic, was a convert who was raised a Presbyterian. Grace Brewer, a close friend of Kate O'Hare; Maybell Hewett, of the city campaign committee for the Socialists; E. N. Richardson; and S. G. Salisbury signed a circular "denying responsibility for the card." No one came forward to claim authorship.[52]

Grace Brewer's husband, George, announced that the decision had been made to launch a Socialist county newspaper. This was necessary, he said, "not only as a means of defense and offense against the unscrupulous political enemies who have misrepresented and scurrilously assailed the Socialist movement of this community, but for the enlightenment of the people generally on matters of industrial and political importance." Brewer added that the news of the vicinity would be "gathered and interpreted from the viewpoint of labor's interest."[53]

Eugene Debs waxed enthusiastic over the new journal and George Brewer, its editor. Debs claimed he knew Brewer "almost as his wife knows him." The two had "traveled together month after month, ate and slept and planned and worked and dreamed together, and I came to know him as a younger brother and to love and trust him as if he were my own kith and kin." Brewer was the right editor for the *Worker's Chronicle*, and the county needed it because there would be "a fierce fight on the part of the cohorts of Capitalism" to defeat the Socialists for political office. Debs told the workers that they "sorely needed" the newspaper and they should "get to work at once with all the energy and enthusiasm they can muster, and roll up a circulation which, like a tidal wave, shall sweep the *Chronicle* into a position of commanding prestige and power."[54]

The *Worker's Chronicle* announced two months later that the Crawford County Socialists would present a series of plays and their themes would apply "to local conditions." Socialist politician Ethel Whitehead presented plans at the state Socialist convention in Hutchinson to depict Socialist doctrine in the form of plays using local talent. She was writing the first play and would use young people in the area as actors. She had successfully produced such a play in Los Angeles and, if successful in the Tri-State region, would take it out on the road, appealing primarily to young people "in more remote areas and the mining camps." In this connection the Young Socialist League made major efforts to promote socialism with picnics and various social gatherings directed at the younger set.[55]

By February 1913 Girard Mayor Houghton had "made so good" in his office, as did so many other local Socialist officials, that the Democrats and the Republicans decided they must join forces in order to defeat the "radicals" in the next election. The *Girard Press* warned the leaders of the two major parties what they must do in the next election to oust the interlopers. The *Worker's Chronicle* welcomed "with joy the merging of Capitalist forces" because the working class was "all powerful if they will stick together." The Socialist newspaper saw this coming merger as a "straw in the wind" and found it a natural development. Every political party that supports the capitalist system "must necessarily get into the same wagon to fight Socialism."[56]

Mayor Houghton was renominated unanimously a year later to run for his office. His opposition conceded he had performed well in his first term and had "pushed through more reforms than any other Mayor since the city's incorporation," but he was a Socialist, and election of any member of that party was considered a "disgrace" to any city. When "Hiz Honor" asked if the town merchants considered it a disgrace for the Socialist miners to come to Girard to buy from them, the answer was, "No, the trade of the miners is earnestly courted." The Girard merchants denigrated the statement "reported to have been made by one of the leading ministers" that "the miners are a disgrace to any town and Girard would be better off without a single one of them particularly when they are Socialists."[57]

In these elections of 1913, John D. Turkington won the office of Crawford County sheriff. The state's attorney general and "old party politicians" attempted to oust him from office. "A brilliant argument" by attorney Jake Sheppard persuaded the state supreme court to overrule the motions to suspend Turkington from office during the procedure and one "to quash certain depositions containing testimony detrimental to the old party officials" who had instigated the plot. These officials were so certain of victory that they "began fighting among themselves for the jobs in the sheriff's office. Much to their dismay, Turkington retained his post.[58]

The Socialists began work immediately after November 1912 to sustain their gains, meeting Sundays and workdays throughout the county. The "foreign miners" of the area were reported to have joined the Socialist Party "by the hundreds and were voted in the same numbers by the Socialists." "The Republicans saved a few county officials," it was reported, "but the Democrats came out a poor third in the race." In 1914 three tickets were again presented, but the campaign and results would come out quite differently than in 1912.[59]

The forces of opposition gathered in Girard in March 1914 to plan their course of action. The Socialist newspaper headlined the meeting "Socialists Were Not Invited," noting the Democrats, Republicans, Bull Moosers, Prohibitionists, and anyone opposed to the radicals had attended. They were composed of lawyers, merchants, bankers, politicians "and their wives" but only a few Socialist workers. "A lifetime city worker, a broken-down politician and retired capitalist," a real estate agent, an insurance man, and Henry Sauer were nominated for office to represent the "so-called better classes." Sauer, the editor noted, was not "primarily a Girard man" but basically conducted his business in Pittsburg, his hometown. Although Pittsburg and Girard had seen twenty years of "bitter and unabating" struggle for the miners' business, they were finally united against a common foe.[60]

At the same time, the editor reported on the county gathering of the Socialists. It was a rowdy meeting "filled with life, action and oratory." Discussion of the situation of the county court clerk drew the "most fireworks." Socialist J. N. Lassater was elected to the office in 1912, and upon his death Judge A. J. Curran named his widow, Laura A. Lassater, to fill the position. Mrs. Lassater was expected to fulfill the duties of her husband but planned on asking Socialist P. Louis Ziekgraf, a subordinate, to resign because they "could not see things from the same viewpoint." The county committee did not want to lose a Socialist position but finally agreed to allow Mrs. Lassater to "select a new deputy," and Ziekgraf would "hang out his shingle" to practice law. Caroline Lowe supported Mrs. Lassater in these "troubles."[61]

The *Worker's Chronicle* revealed one good reason why politicians of the two major parties were so concerned over the Socialist victory in 1912 and why they were so determined to oust these victors in 1914. Upon taking office, Guy Stanton, the county clerk whom opponents declared in the campaign to be illiterate despite being a schoolteacher, discovered a former district clerk, Clarence Price, owed the county $77.25 for collected fees he never deposited and that the recently deposed clerk owed the county $1,088.89 for the same reason. Samuel French, the former registrar of deeds, owed the county $1,281.20, and the county attorney had been instructed "more than six months ago to bring suit to recover the money" but had failed to do so. The writer concluded that the Socialists were the "one great harmonizer" for Republicans and Democrats, especially when "the ousting of a Socialist is the issue." The "illiterate" clerk had made a significant discovery.[62]

In the summer of 1914 the *Chronicle* disclosed the strategy of the two major parties to defeat the Socialists in Crawford County. They would both run a candidate for each office in the primary. After the primary the Democrat or Republican with the lowest vote would withdraw from the race, leaving only the Democrat with the highest vote to defeat the Socialist candidate or, in another instance, leave the Republican with the highest vote to face the Socialist. In either case all Democrats and Republicans would unite to support the combination candidate. The difficulty with this plan, of course, was whether the "machine fixers" could control all the combination candidates. In races in which they could not, the situation of 1912 would prevail, with the Democrats and Republicans splitting the opposition vote and the Socialists winning. The difference in this case was that there probably would not be a third opposition candidate in the races, a Bull Mooser, as in 1912.[63]

The Socialists did well in the primary elections, especially for county court judge. The Republicans were confident that incumbent judge A. J. Curran was quite safe, and they were delighted when the Socialist candidate, laborer Charles Cordray, decided to run. The accepted wisdom was that only a lawyer, or someone quite familiar with the law, could preside over a court. Cordray challenged this myth, arguing that the person most capable of administering justice was one who had witnessed injustice at the hands of judges trained in the law and one who could render justice "in the interests of human beings," rather than by legal precedent. Much to the dismay of the dominant politicians, Cordray polled as many votes in the primary as the combined tally of the two major candidates. To defeat Cordray in November, they would have to unite solidly behind one candidate and work diligently "to get out the vote."[64]

A merchant friend confronted Cordray with the issue of his ignorance of the law. Cordray responded that he had considered this question carefully and thought lawyers were too much hampered and prejudiced with technical law to make good judges. They relied too much on "precedent." A judge often has to decide "quickly" whether a certain piece of evidence should be admitted. Cordray noted that since the primary he had been "burning considerable midnight oil" examining this question. He believed that the fundamental rules of evidence should be based on common sense. The terms "incompetent, irrelevant, or immaterial" were used to determine the issue, and it was "not so difficult to decide whether the proper foundation had been laid for a question, or for the best evidence, or is it insulting to the witness." The merchant decided he would vote for Cordray.[65]

George Brewer, editor of the *Worker's Chronicle*, used his oratorical talents to present a Labor Day address in Wichita. He warned his fellow workers that the war in Europe, which had begun the previous month, might involve America in a war with Japan and subsequently in the war in Europe itself. He noted that Japan was "the leading competitor for the market in the Orient against American interests." This prospect alarmed him as Socialists opposed war in principle and especially this "imperialist" European war. He asked the workers to think in terms of class struggle, but he did not want to appeal to class hatred. He held no hatred toward John D. Rockefeller, he stated. Like the Irishman and the flea, he did not hate the flea but "detested the way he got his living."[66]

The "Great War" in Europe began in August 1914 and inflicted a serious wound on the Socialist movement throughout the world. When the Socialist county local of Crawford County met that month, the members resolved to go on record as "condemning warfare in general, particularly wars of aggression, usurpation, or invasion," and advocated "peace and good will among all classes of society." The famous "labor hater" Harrison Grey Otis of Los Angeles, on the other hand, expressed the opinion that fear of socialism "caused the rulers of Europe to plunge half a dozen odd nations into war," an interesting way of expressing his belief that "the throne of almost every ruler in Europe was in jeopardy" from this political movement.[67]

Debs spoke in Pittsburg a month before the election. Nearly forty Socialist candidates appeared on the platform with him. George Brewer, running for the Twentieth District representative, introduced Caroline Lowe, running for the next-door district, the Twentieth District of the state legislature, who briefly suggested the voters investigate the legislative votes in the last session, compared to the records of the two Socialist members. Charles Cordray "elicited an almost unanimous burst of applause when he was introduced." Debs passionately called for support of the *Chronicle* and for victory in the coming election against the newly formed combination of the two major parties. He described the Third District of Kansas as "a battleground of national interest," insisting that the voters should send someone from the working class to the national Congress.[68]

The *Chronicle* reported petty harassment of Socialists just before the election. The League of Women Voters was distributing anti-Socialist literature on a Friday night to people registering to vote in city hall, "under the nose" of the chief of police, which was forbidden by city ordinance. The following morning, when the Socialists began distributing their literature, the chief remembered the ordinance and ordered them to desist under threat of arrest. George Brewer and the Socialist city organizer decided to test the law and informed the chief that the distribution would continue, as he had permitted the opposition to do the previous evening. They called the chief's bluff, and he arrested no one.[69]

The editor of the *Girard Press* took this occasion to warn that "the hope of defeating the Socialists in Crawford County . . . rests with the women," who had received full franchise by state constitutional amendment in 1912. If they turned out to the polls and voted Republican, as they were expected to do, they would win. The editor predicted that the Republicans had selected a worthy slate and that it was the "duty" of the women to vote. The women were preparing to do this duty as a rush of people was reported at city hall to register to vote. On Saturday night the lines of people were growing, and the clerk had to bring in additional help. The new registrants that day brought the total up to 1,250, with four days remaining to sign up. The "colored ladies" of Pittsburg were organizing to form a voting league under the leadership of Mrs. T. J. Elias. There were over one hundred present, and over half were prospective members of the club. When Republican males supported the registration and voting of women in such numbers, including black women, they were truly desperate.[70]

Naturally, there were collisions of avid supporters at the political rallies of opponents. When Republicans gathered a crowd of two hundred at the Opera House in Pittsburg, they also attracted several Socialists who wished to question the speakers, the county attorney, and Judge A. J. Curran. When county attorney A. H. Keller assailed the Socialists, they returned his fire. J. A. Wayland's fortune became a political issue, and the whereabouts of the money *Appeal* editor Fred Warren had received for legal defenses was also questioned. After the meeting these discussion continued outside.[71]

Two days later another Republican rally was held in the small community of Hepler, where socialism was again the target. Dr. C. O. Pingrey assailed Socialist theories, and the county attorney resumed his attack by calling attention to Socialist disrespect for the American flag. J. A. Wayland's wealth again was questioned, with one speaker asserting that it was proof that a poor man could advance in America, in spite of being a member of the Socialist Party.[72]

When U.S. congressman Philip P. Campbell brought his campaign to his home district, he was pursued the following day by Ralph Roberts from Labette County, who had been imported to assist the Socialist campaigns. Just before Election Day, Socialists tried to break up a Republican meeting at the schoolhouse in the small Crawford County community of Idell. "It was a dismal failure," reported the *Headlight*. Republicans had scheduled several speakers at Idell, and when they arrived, they found the Socialists had also scheduled a gathering there and had "announced the meeting sometime before the Republicans had billed one." Roberts immediately claimed that the scheduled meeting "belonged to him." The school board member who had arranged his meeting was not present, but another board member claimed the Socialists had not received permission and said he would protect the Republican claim to speak. The Republican leaders finally agreed to recognize the earlier plan of the Socialists to meet and retired. Before they left, they announced another meeting at Idell for the following Saturday. Roberts and "his ruffians" appeared Saturday night, and after listening to several speakers, "some of the rough appearing men" left the room, and soon there was banging on the back door and windows. Roberts then ascended the platform and tried to speak. When told to leave, he insisted that they had agreed to a debate between him and the Republican speakers at the previous meeting. The Republicans persevered, and a school board member sustained them. Finally, Roberts and his supporters departed, "making a considerable noise in the schoolhouse yard."[73]

Democratic governor George H. Hodges presented a "red hot attack" on the Socialists while at the same time assailing his opponent, Republican Arthur Capper. He charged that socialism was not the friend of labor and that "the now defunct Kansas Society of Labor" had condemned him and Samuel Gompers for supporting the change to election, rather than appointment, to the state labor and mine inspector commission. Thus, he claimed, Capper was "lined up with Debs, Jake Sheppard, the *Appeal to Reason*, and the Kansas Society of Labor," while he was "identified with Gompers, UMW president John White, and the American Federation of Labor."[74]

Jake Sheppard's son, Jim, ran for county attorney in 1914 and won narrowly by 140 votes, one of two county losses by Republicans in that election. Sheppard "made a good clean fight for the office," and the city editor thought he would "make a good county attorney." When the Fort Scott Socialists met the following spring in the opera house, Jake Sheppard hinted that he had a big announcement to make, which attracted a large gathering. He dwelled on the need for union men to support Democrat C. F. Lowderback for mayor to ensure that the tenure of the chief of police, Mr. Monahan, would continue. Monahan, he reminded his listeners, had given them "money, food, and moral support" in their strike against the Missouri Pacific shops six years earlier. Other than this reason, Sheppard had little good to say about the mayor, criticizing him and the city commissioners for voting themselves salaries that were "entirely too much for a little town like ours." Damning the mayor with faint praise, he then portrayed him as "pure and white," in comparison with his opponent, P. C. Hesser, who had protected strikebreakers during the strife six years earlier. Following the meeting, spectators gathered on the street and concluded that Sheppard's attack constituted "payment" for the Democratic support of Jim Sheppard in his campaign the previous year.[75]

Socialist financial secretary John R. Stone took exception to Sheppard's support of the mayor. In a public announcement the next day, which the *Republican* was pleased to print on its front page, Stone strongly endorsed Hesser because Lowderback's administration had "failed to appoint a single Socialist to an appointive position." Socialists had been fooled earlier into approving the commission form of government, "thereby voting men of our own party out of office." Furthermore, the current administration gave itself a raise while further reducing the salaries of the city employees already at the bottom of the pay scale. He was for a change of administration. Hesser promised to be bipartisan in appointments and would reduce the commissioners' salaries, so he deserved support.[76]

The results of the elections of 1914 were quite mixed. As the *Worker's Chronicle* noted, "Socialist election returns come in by slow freight while Democratic and Republican election news travel over Associated Press wires." The enfranchisement of women also slowed the process of ballot counting. The Socialists did well nationally, with representatives elected to twelve state legislatures. Although Democrat Robert L. Williams was elected governor of Oklahoma, the Socialists increased their 1912 vote of 46,262 to about 70,000, making Oklahoma a two-party state. The *Pittsburg Daily Headlight* proudly reported that the Republicans had "swept" Crawford County. Judge A. J. Curran defeated C. H. Cordray, and Arthur Capper won the governor's race by a large margin, but George Brewer defeated the Democratic candidate, J. H. Cassin, even though Republican J. W. Montee had withdrawn from the race, as previously agreed to. Socialist John Turkington won reelection in the sheriff's race, as did John Dowd for probate judge, but Caroline Lowe lost her bid for a seat in the state legislature. Males had just given women the full franchise two years earlier but declined to elect a female to any important office that soon. The Republican-Democratic strategy of cooperation proved successful.[77]

The local Pittsburg Socialists took solace in proudly announcing that the well-known blind and deaf advocate and Socialist Helen Keller had been made an honorary member earlier that year. The woman contemporarily described as "the most wonderful woman in the world" wrote that she was "proud and glad" to accept their offer of honorary membership. She was pleased the party was "winning slowly but surely in the fight for the disinherited of mankind," and she expressed regret that her opportunity to serve the cause was "limited."[78]

Despite the success of the combination in 1914, the need to eradicate the future political danger of Socialists continued, and it was determined to eliminate the *Worker's Chronicle* because of its great influence on Crawford County miners. The editor broke the news that rumors had circulated of a bankers' boycott that would ensue after the election. A week later four of the five banks in Pittsburg called and ordered their advertisements discontinued until further notice. When asked if this was a "combination," they responded negatively and said that they would "advise" when they wanted to renew. They had carried the ads continuously since the paper began, and this abrupt cancellation was a terrible financial blow. If the *Chronicle* were to "stay on the job, then the Socialists would have to pressure the bankers with a boycott.[79]

In what was termed "the largest Socialist meeting ever held" in Fort Scott, three thousand people heard Eugene Debs speak for two hours on socialism. He and his brother, Theodore, were on their way to the "mountains" of Oklahoma for a vacation now that the strenuous political campaign had ended. George Brewer, one of the directors of the People's College and recently elected to the state legislature, introduced the great Socialist. "Hundreds were heard to remark," as they left the hall, "that it was the greatest lecture ever delivered" in that city. Debs remained over a day to confer with "the People's College promoters."[80]

A week later the *Chronicle* had to report that an "understanding" was reached by Pittsburg bankers, coal companies, and the *Pittsburg Daily Headlight* that the *Chronicle* "must go." The *Headlight* began with stories designed to discredit editor George Brewer, stating he was using the newspaper to enrich himself and using the Socialist Party and the workers "for his own selfish ends." The town bankers were quite aware of the *Chronicle*'s precarious financial condition because of its frequent need to "hustle around to meet small and insignificant bills" and how often the paper's bank accounts were overdrawn. It had been "skating on thin ice all the time," as the bankers well knew. Debs discovered this "silent conspiracy" and suggested raising enough money to pay the immediate delinquent bills and then figure out how to give it the full support it needed. "Call this your Christmas gift or holiday offering," he suggested.[81]

The conspiracy worked in other mysterious ways. When Judge Curran had appointed Socialist Alva George as court stenographer two years earlier, he told him "it was a matter of utter indifference" if he were a Republican, Democrat, or Socialist. "Your work has been more than satisfactory," the judge told him, and "I may find it difficult to get anyone who will be as capable and efficient as you have proved to be." When the judge asked him to resign after the election, he refused, and Curran fired him, "although politics had nothing to do" with his decision. According to Curran, this question had arisen during the fall campaign, and the *Chronicle* passed on to its readers the rumor that "certain prominent bankers entered into the protest and fought his re-appointment."[82]

The opposition struck back at the Crawford County workers in other ways. Republican senator Ebenezer Porter, who was given Fred Stanton's seat after his legal election in 1912, became apprehensive that the same workers might again reject him in the election of 1916 and decided to act before this happened. (At this time state senators were elected for four-year terms, and the legislature met every other year unless a special session was called.) Porter introduced a bill requiring all "alien" voters to register various pieces of information about their plans for citizenship with county clerks, and each time they moved they would have to reregister. This was a "direct slap" at Crawford County because it would apply only to counties with a population between forty-five and sixty-five thousand, a stipulation that fit that county. This measure passed the lower house by a vote of eighty-six to six. The congressman from Cherokee County sponsored the bill, and the second congressman from Crawford County supported it. George Brewer opposed it, and these congressmen engaged him "in animated conversation at the back of the hall" while the bill was being rammed through the lower house. They kept Brewer occupied so that he could not expose the actual contents of the bill to the members of the lower house. Section 2 was the key to the proposal, as it required candidates filing for office to pay 1 percent of a year's salary of the office to a special fund. This financial burden would have the effect of limiting candidates to political office to the wealthy or to those with rich supporters and would certainly mean the demise of minority parties.[83]

When George Brewer discovered the plot, he "rushed to Girard," and shortly thereafter the *Appeal to Reason* contacted H. G. Creel, its staff correspondent living in Oklahoma City, to catch a train to Topeka at once. The next day Creel, Brewer, and state secretary of the Socialist Party, G. W. Kleihege, were "racing with time" to get out the message of this "Republican intrigue that shall shake Kansas to her borders." Creel soon was able to report to the Girard office that "Republican, Democratic, and Progressive legislators, appalled at the audacity of the coup," had "emphatically" declared their opposition to the proposal.[84]

Brewer then visited Governor Capper and explained the contents of the measure. Capper agreed to use his influence against it, and Brewer persuaded Republican representative Donald Coffman of Morris County to move to reconsider the vote. The roll showed fifty for and thirty-seven against, short of the constitutional requirement of two-thirds, and the measure died because sixty-three votes were required for approval. Old members of the legislature expressed the opinion that "never before have such tremendous odds been overcome" by a lone despised Socialist. Senator Porter tried to resurrect his original bill in the Senate but failed.[85]

While he was the lone Socialist legislator that session, George Brewer discovered that one sergeant-at-arms, one doorkeeper, two stenographers, and one clerk were "closet Socialists." They approached him in the "ante-rooms, halls, and committee rooms during the session and successfully assisted, in secret, the working out of plans of campaigns on the floor of the house." Brewer was not alone in his fight after all.[86]

Five days after Brewer's huge victory, the *Headlight* printed a story that when the vital vote came on the bill to restore labor's election of labor and mine commissioners, Brewer was absent and labor leaders could not find him to vote. The paper insinuated this was "a traitorous trick" on Brewer's part, and the joint labor committee insisted that the *Headlight* retract its story and "undo this wrong you have no doubt innocently done this gentleman."[87]

Brewer offered a plausible explanation. The bill was introduced early in the session and had languished in committee until mid-February. At nine o'clock one evening Brewer asked the Speaker and floor leader if anything of importance would come before the body that night, and they said no. He then accompanied Representative Harley of Cherokee County, who took the bill to the proper committee. As soon as they left the floor, a committee report on the bill was debated and defeated, thus killing the measure. It was reintroduced, however, and debated again later in the session, and a majority voted for the proposal.[88]

Senator Porter, the "friend of labor on the campaign trail," was not finished. He introduced in the state senate a bill providing that any candidate for the position of district judge "shall have been engaged in the continuous practice of law for a period of five years." This was a direct attack on the failed candidacy of Cordray against Judge Curran in the previous election. It passed the lower house with only six dissenting votes. Brewer was the sole legislator to speak against it. The senate later accepted it thirty-four to one, and the governor signed it on March 24, 1915.[89]

In an effort to maximize its appeal to miners, and thus its influence, and perhaps increase revenues, the *Chronicle* began offering an "Italian department." Over six thousand Italians resided in Crawford and Cherokee Counties, "almost as many as all other alien speaking nationalities combined." For several months the newspaper devoted two or three pages in Italian to this constituency. Socialist A. E. Adin of Italy, born of Italian and French parents, became the editor. The *Chronicle* hoped to recruit "at least one thousand Italian readers in a very short time." This effort continued for half a year, until the paper had to suspend it for financial reasons because the expected expansion in subscribers failed to materialize.[90]

In October 1916 George Brewer had to abandon the financially strapped *Worker's Chronicle* because his time on the lecture
tour took too much away from his editing job. The new owner
and manager, A. W. Lovejoy, saw the immediate need to increase
circulation and to build on current job printing and advertising
patronage. He failed in this endeavor, and on August 3, 1917, the
paper was turned over to a laborers' committee.[91]

The Socialists in the Tri-State region continued to decline in
numbers and political clout after their zenith in 1912. They held
a big rally to end the 1916 campaign. Jake Sheppard of Fort Scott
and Philip Callery of Pittsburg spoke to a crowd of several thousand. Debs decided not to run that year because of the European
war, so the party did not hold a national convention but nominated
the lackluster Allan L. Benson by mail referendum instead. Sheppard and Callery told the assemblage what Debs would have said
had he been there—that the Democrats and Republicans claimed
to be friends of labor, but this was false pretensions. "The crowd
gave close attention to the speakers and applauded many times,"
the *Worker's Chronicle* reported. Alex Howat toured the mining
camps, telling miners to "vote the way you strike."[92]

The Socialists were "snowed under." They received over four
thousand votes in Crawford County but lost heavily outside the
mining areas, winning only township races and a scattering of
county positions. J. T. Coleman, the new editor of the *Worker's
Chronicle*, once again pleaded with miners to subscribe to the
paper, noting that the political campaign was over and he now
could spend his full time building up the newspaper. The Socialist local held a pep rally in the *Chronicle* office in early December
to discuss ways of promoting its cause.[93]

Under the headline "What's the Matter with the Socialist Party
Organization in This County?" W. C. Benton answered that there
was a "supposed conflict between democracy and authority for
delegated power." In the past the membership "had leaned too
far" toward delegating to the red card county meetings their final
decisions rather than relying on the principles of democracy. He
wanted to change the county constitution to provide for red card
quarterly meetings and call for "special meetings whenever the

circumstances may warrant." The ultimate question was whether the membership would meet the challenge of democracy.[94]

Early in 1917 the state convention tried to breathe fresh life into the moribund party. The state secretary reported the average membership was 1,318. "The failure of the party to advance," he noted, was that the membership paid too little attention to majority rule and looked too much to the State Secretary" and a few other officials to do all the work. The *Chronicle* read into this meeting a "spirit of optimism" that was not present. Discussions were held on the need for a state party newspaper, and the delegates instructed the state secretary to submit "the proposition of establishing such a paper to a referendum vote of the state membership." Nothing came of this move. The most interesting development came over changing the U.S. Constitution, which labeled as "treason" any red card member voting for anyone for political office other than an official party candidate. Finally, the convention accepted resolutions condemning the draft and any military preparedness program.[95]

The resolutions concerning the draft and military preparedness proved divisive for American Socialists. The *Chronicle* presented an article on the split among European Socialists over the issue of war: "It is already apparent that the same division is to come to America." When Congress declared war on April 6, 1917, the crisis came to a head. The "war Socialists" met in St. Louis soon after for the sixth national convention. When this branch of the Socialist Party endorsed President Woodrow Wilson's "Great Crusade," the move fatally ruptured the party, which would undergo revolutionary changes following the armistice.[96]

These political developments spelled the doom of an already fatally wounded *Worker's Chronicle*. Organized labor in Crawford and Cherokee Counties determined to take control of the newspaper and make it a purely labor organ. Leading local Socialists, including August Dorchy, A. W. Lovejoy, Lincoln Phifer, Jake Sheppard, and John Turkington, became organized stock subscribers. Two weeks later the newspaper was formally turned over to a workers' committee, which was determined to continue it under the same name. It would be a nonpartisan weekly presenting "the things which interest organized labor in Nation, State, and this coal mining district." The Kansas State Federation of Labor and Alexander Howat's District 14 designated it as their official organ, and Howat gave it his hearty endorsement. It finally went defunct on August 31, 1923.[97]

The salt miners of Reno County in south-central Kansas had a different experience. Salt was discovered in the Hutchinson area in 1877, when a seam of three hundred feet was found. Ben Blanchard was drilling for oil or gas when he penetrated the salt vein. A mining industry was immediately established and passed through various stages of development until 1891, when the Crystal Salt Company acquired control of the field. A decade later the Morton Salt Company was the principle producer. Finally, a modern extraction plant was erected in 1907, capable of producing eight hundred barrels of salt daily.[98]

There were great differences between the salt miners and the coal miners. Whereas the Tri-State Mining Region required thousands of workers and many had to be imported from Europe and the South to meet its needs, the census of 1885 reported some three or four dozen miners in the Reno County and Hutchinson area. They all listed their occupation as "salt laborer," except perhaps a dozen, who listed "salt raker" as their means of livelihood. Almost all were native white Americans, except for an occasional Swede or Englishman. They had no important union or leader, such as Alexander Howat. Reno County was one of those rather liberal areas that had voted strongly for the Socialist candidates before and after World War I, and Hutchinson provided sufficient leadership for the Socialists to warrant holding their annual state convention there in 1914.

Coal was mined in various parts of the United States, and labor issues, unions and strikes, and political issues were usually present. Miners would strike and often would deal with the companies bringing in scabs to continue the work. Violence often erupted during a strike, perhaps more so if black miners, known as "Exodusters" in Kansas, were imported from the South. Socialism tended to favor the working class, obviously, and miners, both American and immigrant, often saw it as their best choice for representation and assistance. The Socialist leaders played to that view, most of them honestly caring for miners' health and livelihoods. It was a long, rocky road as Socialist leaders and miners battled the American mainstream politicians.

1. Julius Wayland. Wayland's Girard Socialist newspaper, *Appeal to Reason*, was the largest Socialist paper in the country. Special Collections & University Archives, Leonard H. Axe Library, Pittsburg State University, Pittsburg, Kansas.

2. G. C. Clemens, the empathetic Socialist and lawyer. From Gideon Laine (G. C. Clemens), *The Dead Line* (Topeka: Advocate Publishing Co., 1894).

3. Henry Laurens Call, the Socialist aviator in Girard. Pen-and-ink drawing from the *Joplin Daily Globe*, December 13, 1908, reproduced in the *Library Bulletin* (Kansas State College of Pittsburg) 8, nos. 3–4 (Spring–Summer 1974).

4. Emanuel and Marcet Haldeman-Julius
took over the *Appeal to Reason* and created
a publishing dynasty, primarily through the
Little Blue Books. Special Collections &
University Archives, Leonard H. Axe Library,
Pittsburg State University, Pittsburg, Kansas.

5. Albert Parsons, Civil War veteran in the Confederate army and Chicago anarchist, involved in the Haymarket bombing. From A. R. Parsons, *Anarchism: Its Philosophy and Scientific Basis, as Defined by Some of Its Apostles* (Chicago: Mrs. A. R. Parsons, Publisher, 1887).

6. Josephine Conger, Socialist reporter and advocate. Special Collections & University Archives, Leonard H. Axe Library, Pittsburg State University, Pittsburg, Kansas.

7. Canadian-born Caroline Lowe (*front left*),
Socialist advocate, writer, and speaker, with
Socialist politician and union leader Eugene
V. Debs (*front right*). Special Collections &
University Archives, Leonard H. Axe Library,
Pittsburg State University, Pittsburg, Kansas.

8. Alexander Howat (*left*), Scottish-born miner and union leader. Special Collections & University Archives, Leonard H. Axe Library, Pittsburg State University, Pittsburg, Kansas.

9. Phillip Callery, Pittsburg, Kansas, lawyer and Socialist. Special Collections & University Archives, Leonard H. Axe Library, Pittsburg State University, Pittsburg, Kansas.

10. Eugene Debs, five-time presidential candidate on the Socialist ticket and contributor to the *Appeal to Reason*. Special Collections & University Archives, Leonard H. Axe Library, Pittsburg State University, Pittsburg, Kansas.

11. Eugene Debs speaking at a rally at an
unidentified location. Special Collections
& University Archives, Leonard H.
Axe Library, Pittsburg State University,
Pittsburg, Kansas.

12. Jacob Sheppard, Fort Scott attorney and Socialist. Special Collections & University Archives, Leonard H. Axe Library, Pittsburg State University, Pittsburg, Kansas.

13. Earl Browder, Kansas-born leader of the Communist Party USA. Special Collections & University Archives, Leonard H. Axe Library, Pittsburg State University, Pittsburg, Kansas.

5

THE SUCCESSFUL SOCIALISTS

Most Socialists pursued their goals through peaceful means. This meant winning elections, elevating their candidates to power, then watching the results slowly emerge while keeping their people in office. Most Socialist units in Kansas followed the trend of their national candidate for the presidency, growing in numbers slowly but surely until World War I.

Eugene V. Debs won 96,931 national votes for the presidency in 1900, and 1,605 of them came from Kansas. Four years later he polled 408,230 votes nationally and increased his support in Kansas to 15,494 votes, not an insignificant growth for a young third party. In 1908 he made less impressive gains, with a total of 424,488 votes nationally, 12,420 of them from Kansas, a loss of over 3,000 votes in the state. He blamed this decline in votes on the Democrats, who in 1904 were "chagrined" with their candidate, Judge Alton B. Parker, thus voting for socialism but returning to their party four years later. The Progressive year of 1912 saw him receive 900,672 votes countrywide, with over 25,000 from the Sunflower State. Debs declined to run in 1916 while the war raged in Europe, even though America had yet to jump in.[1]

G. C. Clemens began to build the Social Democratic Party in Kansas in 1898 after he renounced the Fusionist Populists and Democrats. By the spring of 1900 he was publishing a short-lived state Socialist newspaper, as state secretary to the party. Unfortunately, he was forced to cease publication after six issues because the funds were not forthcoming to support it. He was also busy running for governor and was losing patience trying to be secretary to a fractious party and its disputatious members.

In the first issue he reported growth of the party. Dickinson County had nine Socialists voting in 1898; by 1900 an "old soldier-comrade" secured 148 subscriptions to *Appeal to Reason* in twenty-four hours of effort in the county seat of Abilene. Lyon County cast three Socialist votes in 1898, but one farmer sold over 100 subscriptions to the *Appeal*. Neosho County, with three Socialists in 1898, had enough members in 1900 to name a county ticket. Osage County looked promising because its Populists were "willing to throw their heels through the dashboard, when things were not satisfactory," and were scaring the Fusionist politicians. Many of them were now turning to socialism.[2]

G. C. Clemens was the Socialist candidate for governor in 1900, while the Democrats named John Breidenthal to oppose incumbent Republican governor William E. Stanley that year. O. Gene Clanton notes that Breidenthal's sympathies ran with the Social Democrats but met the current issues squarely. After narrowly losing to Stanley with 47 percent of the vote, he philosophized that "while I am a Socialist, I am convinced that Socialism must be a growth . . . [or an] evolution or a development, that is to say, that we cannot inaugurate a complete Socialistic system at once, but that we must gradually become possessed of the different public utilities and natural monopolies."[3]

Many in the Tri-State Mining Region lamented the fact that Socialist E. R. Ridgeley of Crawford County wanted an office in Congress so badly that he was prepared to sell out to the Fusionists. Clemens reprinted a letter from "C. Lypscomb" to Ridgeley. "Although the press of the country often refers to 'Hon. E. R. Ridgeley, the Socialist from Kansas,'" Lipscomb could not call him "comrade" any longer because he had received training from Fusionists and had previously thrown support toward individuals and movements that conflicted with socialism. He reminded Ridgeley that Clemens "was in the same mire you are now in" and pleaded with him to abandon the Fusionists and the doomed Populists, as Clemens had done.[4]

Eugene Debs joined Clemens in a political campaign in the

Tri-State region in March, and the candidate reported "the mining camps ablaze with Socialist enthusiasm" in Cherokee and
Crawford Counties. One hundred Socialists were organizing in
Pittsburg, and the nearby small mining community of Midway
would have the largest branch in that corner of the state, with two
hundred members. Clemens was so enthusiastic after the excur-
sion that he predicted that Socialists in those two counties alone
"will get more than twice as many votes" as the ticket received
statewide in 1898.[5]

The Socialists in the Tri-State region felt confident enough to
hold a congressional convention in 1900 to name a candidate for
the Third District. The delegation from Wilson County drove
seventy miles in a horse and covered buggy to attend. Meeting in
Pittsburg in July, they drafted a platform and nominated Scottish-
born John G. McLaughlin, who had been a well-known Socialist
agitator in Hamilton, Scotland, before migrating to the Tri-State
region, where he edited a "radical labor-reform newspaper." The
previous year he had spoken in most of the Tri-State mining
camps, even speaking French to the French miners. McLaughlin had previously promoted the Populist cause but, as "a Karl
Marx and LaSalle [sic] Socialist," had abandoned them because of
their insistence on Fusion. The *Pittsburg Tribune*, a Fusion journal, described him as "one of the brainiest men in the district"
and predicted he would "draw a very large vote from the ranks of
the Republicans in Cherokee County" because the laborers there
who admired him tended to lean Republican in their voting.[6]

Clemens reprinted a story from the *Kansas City Times* that
2,000 of the 2,900 signatures to the nomination papers of the
Prohibition Party were cast by Republicans. This was done
to injure the Fusionists by helping the Prohibitionists. More
important, the same newspaper was cited as the origin of a story
that the Republican State Central Committee was behind the
drive to nominate Clemens as the Socialist candidate, again to
siphon off votes from the Fusionists and Breidenthal. While
they tried to keep their activities secret, deputy sheriff James
Bales and Marshall Clint Webb of Pittsburg were circulating
such a petition in Fort Scott. Crawford County, the story ran,

was "strongly Fusion," and Clemens's candidacy was "by far the cheapest way of diverting several hundred votes from Breidenthal." The strategy almost worked, and the final votes were Stanley 181,893; Breidenthal, 164,793; Clemens, 1,258; and Prohibitionist Frank Holsinger, 212, although the combined total for Clemens and Holsinger was not nearly enough to throw the election to Breidenthal.[7]

Two years later Clemens garnered 4,408 votes as the Socialist candidate for attorney general. That year railroad engineer A. S. McAlester of Herington, a division point on the Rock Island line, received 4,078 votes for governor. His hometown averaged twenty-seven votes for Socialist candidates but gave him forty-eight.[8]

The Socialists were gaining political strength in the smaller towns as well as the urban and mining areas. In the first issue of the *Western Socialist News*, Clemens reported that branches were being established in Abilene, Bayard, Fort Scott, and White City. In January of that year W. F. Foy of White City presented dictionary versions of *socialism* for the edification of the local editor and his readers:

> I ask your readers to turn to Webster's dictionary and there find the following definition of the term Socialism: "A theory of society that advocates a more precise, orderly and harmonious arrangements [*sic*] of the social relations of mankind than that which has hitherto prevailed." . . . Look up the Standard dictionary and you will find that says "Socialism is a theory that aims to secure the reconciliation of society, increase of wealth and a more equal distribution of the products of labor through the public collective management of all industries." Its aim is "to every man according to his deeds."

Foy offered these definitions, wanting to emphasize that "the great good Father . . . gave to all men equal rights to his [*sic*] free gifts that are being taken from His people by trusts and combines." He believed this appeal might correct the wrong impression in the minds of "many of your readers" that socialism "pertains to the equal division of property, not bursting bombs, burning buildings, rapine and plunder." Three years later the Socialists in Abilene were strong enough to nominate a full slate for municipal officers. D. J. Eisenhower, father of military general and president Dwight D. Eisenhower, was running for school board member of the First Ward (South Abilene). The *Appeal to Reason* ran the headline "Great Socialist Gains Everywhere: Socialism Now Recognized as a Permanent Fact in the Politics of the Nation," noting, "We have made greater gains in small towns than in the big cities."[9]

Kansas was emerging as a leader in the national Socialist Party, despite the fact that Socialists were still in the minority within the state, and other Kansans were taking up the banner of radicalism. Several of the Kansas "radicals" would play a part in the national scene through legal maneuvering, speeches, and writings. However, Kansas Socialists were failing to get elected into any major mayoral seat, the governorship, or the Congress or Senate. The Populists were very active in state politics in the late 1800s and early 1900s. When the Democratic Party faltered, the state then fell under the control of the Republicans.[10]

In the 1890s it is likely that no state in the Union was more radical than Kansas, a trend that lasted well into the 1900s, finally dying during World War I. Many Populists quietly shifted their views more to socialism than populism.

The slate of Socialist candidates for Decatur County in 1906 is indicative of the type of people recruited for office in rural areas. R. B. Thomas, running for the state legislature, was a merchant, as was J. E. Kulp, who was running for county clerk. Henry H. Adee, a farmer and teacher who had "been regularly admitted to the bar," stood for district judge. Robert Leake, running for the national House of Representatives, was a cattleman and farmer, as was H. W. Andrews, candidate for county treasurer who had already served two terms in that office. W. D. Beard, a liveryman, was campaigning for county sheriff. Elmer Van Fleet, a farmer and teacher, was nominated for superintendent of schools. The Socialists did not name anyone for the position of county attorney.[11]

As a result of its successes in these elections, Kansas Socialists concluded they needed to reorganize the party. *Appeal to Reason* publisher J. A. Wayland contended that the Socialist vote thus far was proletarian and an appeal should also be made to former

Populists who had not participated in an election for four years. A "slight test" was made of farmers in the Seventh District, which included the Tri-State region, and as a result, Wayland believed that the farmers of the state would "respond to the Socialist program with enthusiasm." The *Appeal* therefore "decided to enter the political arena with all the force and power of its army." Wayland delegated a staff member, Allen Ricker, to attend a meeting to tender the services of the *Appeal to Reason* and its "Appeal Army" to mobilize Kansas Socialists. He offered to pay $1.50 per day and expenses to solicitors, which would necessitate collecting dues from members. Speakers would be organized and authorized to sell Socialist literature, from which they would retain a commission. An all-out effort would be made in the elections of 1904.[12]

The *Appeal to Reason* believed that state and county conventions promoted party harmony. Delegates "from all over the state," George Brewer said in reporting on the 1906 conclave, believed they had reached the point where "every class conscious Socialist can rally and proclaim aloud the solidarity of our state movement." State secretary A. O. Grigsby reported the meeting to be "harmonious and enthusiastic," and they even received sympathetic words from the International Workers of the World, which "had been maliciously, brutally and criminally torn from their liberties and homes and thrown into prison," as the state secretary expressed it. Socialists focused on *Appeal to Reason* editor Fred Warren's race in 1906, in which he received almost three thousand votes in the campaign for Third District congressman.[13]

Walter Thomas Mills spoke to "the largest audience that ever gathered in Garden City to listen to a Socialist lecture." His speech was prefaced by the afternoon appearance of Paul D. Oakford, dubbed the "Boy Orator." Seven-year-old Paul created a sensation when he answered technical questions from the audience with "logical answers." Paul received letters from "New York to California and from the frozen region of Alaska to the tropical shores of the Gulf of Mexico," congratulating him or requesting lecture appointments. Paul was limited to speaking only during summer months, however, when school was not in session.[14]

In the elections of 1908 the national Socialist vote in Kansas dropped to 12,420, a decline of 3,000, but it rose in 1910 to 17,000 and jumped to 25,000 two years later. This proved to be the Socialists' second-highest point in the Sunflower State and the Tri-State region. Over 1,200 Socialists held office nationally that year (most of them in towns of 10,000 citizens or less), including 20 state legislators and just under 80 mayors in twenty-four states. These successes, which created a division inside the party due to Right-leaning national leadership, drove Big Bill Haywood from its executive committee that year over the use of violence, and he became the leader of the IWW, a splinter Socialist wing that advocated sabotage to achieve its ends. This group would subsequently develop an extensive membership in the Kansas wheat and oil fields.[15]

The smaller towns had less trouble with authorities. Socialists in the Decatur County town of Oberlin, in northwestern Kansas, held meetings for their candidates to promote themselves. Congressional candidates spoke on Saturday, Monday, and Tuesday in the small towns of Kanona, Jennings, and Dresden, respectively, and at schoolhouses in the area on Wednesday, Thursday, and Friday. These towns were too small to attract big names, but they advertised for people to turn out to hear Eugene Debs "on the 20th Century Phonograph" in addition to "selected concert music."[16]

Socialism was on the march in the state's largest cities of Topeka and Kansas City. The state legislature had expanded Kansas City by consolidating Armourdale, Kansas City, and Wyandotte into one unit in 1886, and four years later it surpassed Topeka and Leavenworth in population. At that time it had a heterogeneous male workforce of one-third white native-born; a third were immigrants or sons of immigrants from England, Germany, Ireland, Scotland, and Sweden; and the remainder were black Americans and scattered ethnic groups. White Americans dominated the professional workforce, as along with the capitalists and the skilled workers, but German and English immigrants also provided some of the skilled workforce. Irish made up about half of the unskilled laborers, while black Americans, including Exodusters, who had come from southern states, were at the bottom of the economic ladder. During the Populist period the Knights of Labor sought accommodation with the major political parties because the Populists stressed primarily rural issues and failed to connect with the laboring class. Many of these laborers and their leaders drifted over to socialism.[17]

As early as 1900, there were Socialist campaigns to elect candidates for local offices as well as to elect G. C. Clemens governor. In Kansas City, when Socialist Arthur Keep began haranguing a crowd at Seventh Street and C Avenue, a policeman notified him he was blocking the street and asked him to move. When he refused, the policeman pulled him off the stand. This did not seem right. This was America, where a man had the right to express his views, and a peaceful crowd had the right to hear him. The crowd then yelled and hissed, and fearing for his safety, the officer called for reinforcements. When thirty policemen arrived, Keep was again arousing the crowd, and he was arrested. Other Socialists who joined him were arrested, until finally six speakers were hauled off to jail. The audience grew rowdier, leading the officers to charge them with billy clubs, "hitting right and left" until they cleared the street.[18]

Two years later the Socialists announced a group of laborers and Kate O'Hare were running for county offices. Their platform included the usual push for government ownership of utilities and the means of production and distribution, organizing industry "on a scientific basis instead of the present anarchic disorder." It also called for higher wages, abolishing child labor, compulsory education, and the "relief of destitution," and it drew attention to the local "disreputable pesthouse" that cared for victims of smallpox.[19]

Late in 1903 Kansas City Socialists announced the opening of a "School of Socialism." It occupied "a dingy little room" that also served as party headquarters, and Walter Thomas Mills presided over it. "I want you to learn so that we may throttle this hideous Capitalism," "Prof" George R. Kilpatrick told the students. "I am sick and tired and disgusted with everything I see outside that window." Its one hundred students came from California, Colorado, Washington, Illinois, Iowa, Kansas, Louisiana, Michigan,

Minnesota, Missouri, Ohio, Oklahoma, Nebraska, North Dakota, and Texas. Kilpatrick had taught political economy at Ripon College in Wisconsin until he began studying socialism. It was not revealed whether or not he had left there on his own initiative.[20]

In 1904 the Socialists again held a convention and nominated people for county office, including Frank O'Hare for county attorney and several workingmen. M. R. Smith, an African American, was named for registrar of deeds. Their platform this time included free textbooks, a reduction in the workday, and a referendum on all legislative enactments.[21]

Greater political efforts resulted in a significant victory in Kansas City, Kansas, in 1905, when M. R. Smith won election as park commissioner. Comrade Smith became the first of his race to win an important office in a first-class city in Kansas. He was born in either 1861 or 1862 of fugitive slave parents. His mother finally made her way to Warsaw, Illinois, where young Smith "molded his own education as best he could," finally graduating from Warsaw Seminary, a racially integrated school, rare for its time. He moved to Springfield, Missouri, where he owned and edited the *Springfield Headlight* until 1896, when he became a Socialist. He migrated to Kansas City in 1899 and remained an active Socialist while practicing his new trade as a barber. This was his second candidacy for public office, and his election "came as a surprise to the old party politicians and as a valuable propaganda 'hit.'"[22]

The Socialists' success in 1904 emboldened them to anticipate the off-year elections of 1906, when turnout was expected to be lower. They were drawing such large crowds in Kansas City that the chief of police decided to ban further Socialist meetings because they tended to attract large crowds. Previously, they had been limited to selected spots where they could gather but not speak. The chief now announced that police in New York City and "other large cities" were arresting them at open-air meetings, so he would do likewise. If they wanted to gather hereafter, they would need to do so indoors.[23]

G. C. Clemens reported that the Socialists in Topeka were meeting "underground . . . imitating the early Christians of Rome." They held their gatherings in a barbershop and, as of April 1900, had held no public meetings. Despite this stealth, or perhaps because of it, they were recruiting new members. Clemens noted that Shawnee County cast only twenty-six Socialist votes in 1898 but believed the vote in 1900 "would have to be multiplied by two figures." Two months later he reported that the state committee was opening its headquarters in the Jewell Building in downtown Topeka, with the office of his newspaper on the same floor. "All comrades and inquirers [were] welcome," and Socialist literature was readily available.[24]

Popular Kansas author Elizabeth N. Barr addressed the Topeka Socialists with the message "If that's heaven, I will not go," an invective against the current social and economic order: "If heaven is the place for the elite to chant Hallalulahas [*sic*], I don't want to go there. I want to go to hell where everyone is welcome." She was pleased that the Socialist Party recognized women as political persons, asserting that there could be "no freedom for man without freedom for the woman." Socialism recognized that women have the same interests in government as men. She had talked to poor people, bankers, teachers, lawyers, preachers, "men and women in all walks of life," who were afraid to speak of what they believed "for fear their living will be taken away from them." "These people are slaves," she told the audience.[25]

The *Topeka Daily Capital* feared the Socialists "may poll heavy vote" in 1902. The party in Kansas "has been a good deal of a joke," it announced, but "it threatens this year to assume quite an important place in the political firmament." The party's growth resulted from those committed to it who had begun "quietly and earnestly to build it up." The editor believed that Socialist candidates for congressional seats "may have considerable effect on the outcome in close districts." Cowley, Crawford, Dickinson, Johnson, and Phillips Counties had already named county tickets.[26]

Issac Gilberg, a Russian Jewish immigrant and tailor, became a well-known lecturer and party organizer in Topeka. For years he "lectured and harangued, lifted and saved, pulled and pleaded." "Ike" and several like-minded Socialists concluded that every time the government fined a trust, the company retaliated by raising prices. Government control, therefore, was the wrong approach, as was government ownership, because a few men would gain control of "the money . . . as they do politics" in either case. This group of Socialists decided to form the Independent Socialist League and deal directly with wholesalers by creating a cooperative to buy for them.[27]

These Socialists soon found 230 other members, and the group decided to publish its own newspaper, the *Shawnee County News*. W. E. Bush, former secretary of state, joined the league and became editor of the *News*. He soon claimed eight hundred subscribers and predicted several hundred more would subscribe in the future. They also operated an institution for the three hundred victims of white slavers in Topeka but were soon forced to abandon it for lack of financial support "and the interference of the police department." When asked if he would give up on socialism if his plan failed, Gilberg replied: "Not on your life. I will simply give up trying to lead an ideal life in a world of human beings." After two years of this cooperative buying, though, he quit because he concluded that "the world don't want to be saved." It was time to stop, and "if he never pulls another stroke in the uplift boat," the editor insisted, "he ought to have a silver cup in the hall of fame built for the poor man's friend."[28]

One modern approach to the analysis of Socialist political success is to divide the state into quadrants, with today's Interstate 70 as the north-south division and Highway 81 as the east-west line. This leaves the northwest quadrant with the lowest population; the southwest one with the largest area and second-lowest population; the southeast quadrant with the Tri-State region and including Emporia, Salina, and most of Wichita; and the northeast quadrant with the smallest area but the largest population, with Topeka, Lawrence, Leavenworth, and Wyandotte County.

Debs won 1,605 votes for president in Kansas in 1900 and increased this tally to 15,494 in 1904, but in 1908, when running against Taft, the number dropped to 12,420. This followed a national trend in which Debs increased his total national vote by some 15,000 ballots but failed to meet the gains of several hundred thousand votes that his supporters expected. In 1912, when the Republican Party split over Taft's candidacy and Roosevelt's Bull

Moose race, Debs doubled his vote in Kansas over that of 1908 (table 1). When the Socialist vote for governor in these election years is tabulated by counties in the four quadrants, the results are not meaningful in some cases but are quite revealing in others, especially in the third and fourth quadrants, where the population was the largest and Socialist activity was high (table 2).[29]

Table 1. Kansas votes for Debs for president, 1900–1912

1900	1904	1908	1912
1,605	15,494	12,420	25,000

Table 2. Votes for governor by quadrant, 1900–1914

Quadrant	1900	1904	1908	1912	1916
I	146	1,433	1,408	573	2,604
II	102	1,908	1,479	559	4,784
III	529	5,355	7,220	2,927	13,193
IV	972	2,938	2,052	443	1,756

Milo Mitchell proved to be the best vote getter of the Socialist candidates for governor. Born in New York at the beginning of the Civil War, he migrated to Kansas and began farming near Kingman. Kingman County, in south-central Kansas, was one of the stronger Socialist counties in quadrant II, and he ran for lieutenant governor with G. W. Kleihege in 1912, gathering name recognition in the party outside his home county. His personality and popularity led the party to nominate him for the top spot in 1914.

It is a striking feature that Kansans gave more votes to Mitchell than any other Socialist candidate for governor when Debs was not running and almost double what they gave Harry Gilham, of Oswego, in 1908, when Debs received a small vote. The popular Henry Allen, editor of the *Wichita Beacon*, ran on the Progressive ticket in the off-year election of 1914 and won eighty-four thousand votes.

Not surprisingly, support for Socialists in quadrant I, in the northwest, was strong, although it contained only twenty-four counties and had the smallest population. It had been, however, a stronghold for populism. Quadrant II, in the southwest, had thirty-three counties and, with Dodge City, Garden City, and Hutchinson, had a larger population than quadrant I but had not been strongly Populist and did not produce the Socialist numbers that quadrant I did. Quadrant III contained Wichita, the Tri-State region, and Labette, Montgomery, and Neosho Counties, with the relatively large towns of Pittsburg, Parsons, Coffeyville, and Independence. This was the stronghold of socialism from 1904 to 1914, casting 13,193 of the 23,354 votes for Milo Mitchell. Quadrant IV, in the northeast, contained Topeka, Lawrence, Leavenworth, and Wyandotte County. Lawrence, a university town, and Manhattan, with the agriculture school, were never havens for Socialists, while Leavenworth, by contrast, cast only 284 and 304 ballots for gubernatorial candidates George Hibner and Milo Mitchell, respectively. Wyandotte County, or Kansas City, was the strength of Socialists in this section, giving Gilham 897 votes in 1904 yet only 644 for Mitchell.[30]

Did the presence of Socialist newspapers assist the growth of socialism, or did the large numbers of Socialists support their local journals financially? Hill City, in the northwest quadrant, had one of the more enduring newspapers for forty-four months, but this was in the early period, from 1897 to 1901. Dodge City's *Advance* was published from May 1900 through February 1901, again in the early period, but Ford County was never a strong Socialist area, unlike Kingman, Reno, and Pratt Counties, which lacked large towns. Iola's newspaper lasted fourteen months and strongly promoted socialism, but the *Lawrence Progressive Herald* was published for almost twice as long, twenty-six months, yet the county where it was located, Douglas County, was relatively free of Socialists. The *Worker's Chronicle* in Pittsburg appeared for seven years in the bastion of socialism.

The northwestern tier of thirteen counties reveals interesting statistics from 1914, when these counties cast 1,706 votes for Mitchell, while the remaining eleven counties of quadrant I gave only 1,840 to the popular Henry Allen. The ten counties in quadrant II that cast over 100 votes gave Mitchell 1,555 ballots, while the remaining twenty-three showed 5,847 votes cast for Allen, undoubtedly because his *Wichita Beacon* had influenced the counties' voters favorably. In quadrant III the eight counties of Bourbon (Fort Scott), Cherokee (mining), Cowley (Winfield and Arkansas City), Crawford (Pittsburg), Labette (Coffeyville), Montgomery (Independence), Sedgwick (Wichita), and Wilson (Neodesha) cast 8,643 ballots for Mitchell and 16,560 for Allen. The winner, Arthur Capper, received 33,252 votes in these counties, but the liberal vote here (which includes Allen) equaled almost two-thirds of his total. The region was truly progressive in this most progressive time period in Kansas history. The outstanding feature of the election of 1914 for the smallest but most populous quadrant, number IV, reveals it to be the most conservative and the bulwark of the Republican Party throughout Kansas history. As noted previously, quadrant IV gave Mitchell only 1,756 votes, while Arthur Capper drew 66,176 ballots. Only Shawnee County, with 238; Leavenworth, with 304; and Wyandotte, with 641, cast over 200 votes for Mitchell

In the summer of 1913 *Emporia Gazette* editor William Allen White wrote an editorial titled "The Chuckling Socialist," in which he noted that

> Kansas City, Kansas, voted to construct a municipal electric lighting plant. Yesterday, Judge Hook, of the Federal Circuit Court, approved a plan looking to the municipal ownership of the Kansas street car system. Last week Attorney General John Dawson declared that ice, being a public utility, should be controlled by the state. Last month a bill favorably considered by a committee of Congress provided for the construction of a government railroad in Alaska, and for the government ownership and lease operation of coal mines. . . .
>
> If you were a Socialist, wouldn't you hunt a cool, shady spot between two buildings where the air poured through and sit down in a kitchen chair and chuckle and chuckle and chuckle?
>
> The really interesting part of the situation is that about half of the American Socialist platform for 1904 is now on the statute books of one-third of the states, and much of it is in the platforms of at least two of the great parties.
>
> The Socialists are getting too conservative for this country. They will have to get a move on themselves or they will be without an

issue in 1916. The Bull Moosers have stolen the Socialist thunder, and the Progressive Republicans declare they are just as progressive as the Bull Moosers, and the Democrats say they are more progressive than the Progressives. Unless the Democrats and Republicans are lying about how progressive they are . . . the Socialist might as well go out of business, for all the great parties will be swiping the Socialist planks.[31]

A year after their successes in the 1912 election, Tri-State Socialists achieved a major milestone in establishing the People's College in Fort Scott. Walter Mills's International School of Social Economy in Girard merged with the new institution, financed in part by the *Appeal to Reason*. Mills had moved his school from Chicago to Girard in 1901 and promised students they would be given work and financial support while studying and promoting socialism. The new school was based on this premise. J. A. Wayland, in turn, was so pleased with the move that he put himself on salary and promised to devote all profits of his printing, after expenses, to the school. The People's College at Fort Scott would replace Mills's school.[32]

The staid *Fort Scott Republican* waxed ecstatic over the possibility of the town hosting another college, after having lost an earlier Normal School to Pittsburg. Headlining its first story "Will Put Fort Scott on the Map," the newspaper was certain the new school guaranteed the future importance of the old frontier fort city. Conceived by Jake I. Sheppard, chief counsel for the area Socialists, he was joined by C. B. Hoffman, Arthur Le Sueur of Minot, North Dakota, Caroline Lowe of Pittsburg, and George Brewer of Girard to secure a fifty-year charter from the state of Kansas to establish the college. In addition to offering correspondence classes similar to those of the International School of Social Economy, its charter authorized the college to operate "mines, farms, dairies, orchards, and gardens" and to manufacture and buy and sell merchandise, machinery, and tools. It would offer students "a practical education while giving them" an opportunity to support themselves on the college farm.[33]

In the next issue of the *Fort Scott Republican*, the city editor said he had had "quite a talk" with Sheppard about the proposed college. He believed the proposal had great merit, especially because of "the enthusiasm and keen interest with which Mr. Sheppard and his associates are taking hold of the project." The editor insisted that the college would prove highly important to Fort Scott "if only half the vision Mr. Sheppard and his associates are now seeing, is realized." The fast-talking Jake Sheppard informed him that the directors would "make it the greatest educational and vocational center in the world"—a preposterous claim that should have given pause to experienced businessmen and professionals. But, the editor noted, "look at the phenomenal growth and expansion of the *Appeal to Reason*."[34]

In the same issue Sheppard affirmed his belief that "Fort Scott will become, within a few years, the chief center of education in the world." The college had two stated objectives: to bring education within the reach of every man, woman, and child; and to teach from the viewpoint of the working class. The school would be worker owned and worker controlled. The college would erect the necessary buildings, but "our money will be spent rather to secure the best teachers and apparatus than to build for show." Sheppard expected the students to be "a splendid class of people . . . who come with a serious purpose and no time will be wasted by them in idleness." Workers everywhere would own the college, sworn statements of income and expenses would be published periodically by school authorities, and "every part of the civilized earth will contribute to the maintenance of the school and furnish students for it." After the first few months "thousands of strangers will be among us." He asked that all the town's residents be courteous and welcoming to strangers, as per the town's reputation.[35]

The college established a unique feature for raising money and for involving the community and workers everywhere in its operation. Planners immediately organized a "People's College Union," with annual dues of $1 for a five-year period. Each union member would have a voice in the management of the college. Half of this subscription rate would pay for the *College News*, a monthly publication that would provide announcements of the college's finances and its activities. The college would offer residential work as well as correspondence courses. Until the board of directors could acquire acreage on which to construct a building, the J. D. Hill property at Tenth and National had been secured to hold classes and house the administration. Sheppard predicted the college would "bring into Fort Scott the next year at least 5,000 people," and he confidently predicted it would double the population of the city in the next three to five years. The newspaper reported that Chicago had been considered as a site for the school, but Fort Scott was finally selected because of the influence of Jake Sheppard.[36]

Workmen were busy repairing the Hill property to make it suitable. Valued at one time at $50,000, it had deteriorated considerably. With new paint and papering restoration, it was brought back to a respectable appearance. Sheppard informed the locals, with some possible exaggeration, that there were now "something like 5,000 students already enrolled for the correspondence courses." He added that the current problem would be "to keep the students away from the city until the home school is really build [sic]." Meanwhile, many workers, both men and women, would be hired to work in the Hill house to deal with the expected large amount of correspondence.[37]

Two weeks later the trustees called a public meeting to discuss details of the proposed college. Despite inclement weather, meeting attendance was very good, with many people from outside of the Fort Scott area, as there was great interest in the school throughout the region. Sheppard introduced Miss Marian Wharton, a popular Chautauqua speaker. Wharton would serve as a student advisor in the college but would spend a majority of her time recruiting new students. Caroline Lowe, the sole female on the board of directors, spoke of the challenges facing the college, and the city newspaper was optimistic she would do her best in making the school a success. C. B. Hoffman, the college's first president, spoke of the purpose and benefits of the school. The board of directors met following this public gathering and elected officers: Eugene Debs, chancellor; Hoffman, president; Arthur Le Sueur, first vice president and treasurer; Caroline Lowe, second vice president; George Brewer, third vice president; and Jake Sheppard, secretary. Later it would add Charles Edward Russell, Fred Warren, Frank P. Walsh, Kate Richards O'Hare, and other noted Socialists as advisors. The greater the involvement, the wider the support. The board approved of a law course that had been developed, and the "correspondence course would start in a few days." By the beginning of September, courses in public instruction, parliamentary law, and English would be available.[38]

A week later the board of directors, who would do a masterful job of public relations, called another meeting to garner further support for the fledgling college. Jake Sheppard presided, introducing President Hoffman. The local editor conceded that Hoffman "might not be considered a great orator, but he shows breadth of business comprehension, honesty, and keen intellect." The editor also called attention to the fact that President Hoffman had been a successful businessman, first as a flour manufacturer, then as a banker. Hoffman told the crowd that he was now "on the other side of the counter." The editor also was impressed with Arthur Le Sueur, a "retired lawyer of independent means," referring to him as "hard-nosed, as the Scotch say." He "is everything before being a radical or an extremist," and "judging from a half hour's talk, he has a courage that is not afraid." Le Sueur was followed by George Brewer, Caroline Lowe, and Marian Wharton. The show served its purpose, judging by the *Republican* editor's response, of convincing the home folks that these "radical" Socialists were just plain people who had legal and business experience and were not crazy dreamers or incompetent pedagogues.[39]

Three days later Sheppard and his colleagues staged another pep rally. The *Republican* editor noted that the town's citizens were heartily "behind the People's College movement" and would "push it with all the vigor they can." The evening's meeting was called primarily as a reception for the college directors, but it included an appeal to the Fort Scott businessmen to continue and expand their endorsement. They expected an attendance of three to four thousand, with many people coming from the surrounding area. The city band played, and there were several speakers. The editor expected twenty-five or thirty businessmen to speak briefly and suggested that the businessmen, professionals, and working people should "keep up this keen interest until the college is one of the greatest institutions in the world."[40]

The following day the citizens of Fort Scott delivered an official welcome to the college, which was destined to become "the greatest educational institution in the world," as supporters expressed it. A thousand people heard the first speech, then a rain shower briefly drove many in the crowd to seek shelter. When the speaking resumed, Martin Miller, "one of Fort Scott's most progressive businessmen," was introduced. Miller was credited with the original call to assemble and welcomed the college to Fort Scott. The city, he said, "never will be able to repay Jake Sheppard for putting this city upon the map." Charles Griffith, a local popular orator, reminded his listeners that Fort Scott had once hosted a state normal school that graduated "10,000 men and women . . . who have helped build up this great state." Fort Scott had neglected the school, but given another opportunity to host a college, the citizenry should "boost it with all the vim that is possible." H. A. Strong, editor of the *Fort Scott Republican*, stated that "he was heartily in accord with the movement" and would help in any way he could to make the college successful. Community pride was so powerful for the new school that Mrs. Gilbert Blatchley, president of the local Daughters of the American Revolution (DAR), was induced to welcome the college that would soon be training young Socialists to overturn her capitalist society. As a national regent of the DAR, she assured her listeners they would do what they could to help the People's College. Finally, President Hoffman assured the hosts that "we appreciate this most cordial welcome to the fullest extent."[41]

Lawyer William "Judge" Biddle wrote a letter to the editor suggesting that "everyone contribute $25 to promote the college." Jake Sheppard quickly responded with the theory behind the People's College Union. It was too much to ask citizens for $25, so the college board of directors came up with the idea of selling $5, five-year subscriptions to the *People's College News*. It was important, Sheppard stressed, to reach a high enrollment in the union before August 10, 1914, because, under the current postal laws, the school was allowed to print two copies of the *News* for each union member, and the college would send the second copies "throughout the country" to advertise the school and recruit students. The board of directors, Sheppard explained, established this reasonable fee structure because it wanted "absolute good will and kind feeling for us among the people of Fort Scott." Sheppard concluded by noting he wanted his hometown to "furnish a larger list of members in the College Union" than Le Sueur's town of Minot, North Dakota, or Hoffman's town of Kansas City, Kansas.[42]

In mid-August the college mailed fifty-five hundred letters across the country and Canada to answer queries about the new school. The missive described college activities thus far, similar to the monthly news bulletin that would circulate later, and informed the reader about the College Union. The people of Fort Scott, the editor noted, were "not responding to the call as they should and therefore it is hoped they will forget the war in Europe long enough to go to the People's State Bank" in Fort Scott and "enroll in the Union." "This immense amount of mail," the editor was certain, demonstrated that "the college is getting along fine and within a few weeks will have a big increase in students."[43]

Fifty Fort Scott businessmen staged an organizational drive for union members, trying to visit as many people as possible in the town. The newspaper editor reported a current 1,300 members and said, now that the drive was completed, "It is hoped that those who were seen will drop into the People's State Bank and deposit their dollar for the year." The editor reported that very few people "of means" had failed to purchase a membership. The first weekend in October was set aside for Educational Day, on which workers "from all over the world" would gather and discuss the importance of education. The People's College planned a special meeting for this purpose, and Chancellor Eugene Debs sent a message "throbbing with the enthusiasm of a great ideal and the love of a great heart." Two programs were planned for that Sunday, at 2:30 p.m. and 7:30 p.m. There would be music and speeches by Jake Sheppard, Caroline Lowe, George Brewer, H. A. Rightmire (a former Populist leader), and Marian Wharton. The same edition announced that Chancellor Debs would move to Fort Scott the first of November "to take up People's College work in earnest."[44]

The college curriculum expanded slowly. Correspondence courses were first offered for six-month periods in business law, English, business English, and public speaking as well as a three-year correspondence course in law. The first two years in all programs were offered in correspondence courses, and the third year of work was taken in residence in Fort Scott for the degree.[45]

Arthur Le Sueur, vice president of the People's College, announced that Debs would speak at a fund-raiser on November 12, 1914. Admission would be ten cents and twenty-five cents for reserved seats. Because the funds would go toward financing the college, the town editor urged that "every man, woman, and child interested in the education of the working man should turn out for this meeting." Le Sueur announced the title of his address as "Socialism: Its Aims, Ethics, and Ideals." The sponsors were "anxious that every man, woman, and child of Fort Scott be present at this meeting and give the speaker a warm welcome to our city."[46]

The college directors continued to bring in special speakers for fund-raisers. In mid-December 1914 J. Stitt Wilson came from Berkeley, California. He brought with him "the reputation of being one of the greatest Socialist speakers in the United States." He was formerly a mayor of Berkeley, a Methodist minister, and currently a member of the People's College advisory board. Helen Keller could always be depended upon to draw a large crowd. The local newspaper billed her as "being blind, deaf and dumb at the age of 19 months and now one of the most educated women in America." Keller was making her first appearance in Fort Scott, and it was "in the interest of the People's College." She was preceded onstage by the story of her life by Mrs. Anne S. Macey (Anne M. Sullivan), the teacher and companion of twenty-six years who opened the gates of the outside world to Miss Keller. While attending Radcliffe College, the editor added, Keller "wrote the story of her life, which has since been translated into fifteen languages."[47]

Arthur Le Sueur, dean of the Law Department by 1916, that year headed the defense of seven "victims" engaged in the strike against the steel trust on the Mesabi Iron Range in Minnesota. The first case involved a striker who was charged with "interfering with an officer." Le Sueur argued that the fellow was being prosecuted for being a foreigner. The assistant county attorney advised the jury that "these foreigners must be taught to keep their place." Le Sueur responded that, unfortunately, "not every person has the foresight to do as Mr. Frank did, that is, select not only his parents but his birthplace." Anyone who asked for a conviction because the defendant was a foreigner "has a very narrow and provincial outlook unworthy of one who holds the position of prosecuting attorney." Le Sueur won the case and promised members of the college's law department that they would be doing "all over the country in a short time" what he had done in Minnesota.[48]

The fledgling college, with its inadequate financial support, was having a difficult time functioning at the level of expectations of its directors. As a result, Jake Sheppard undertook an extensive fund-raising trip in the East. The college directors had taken options on some three thousand acres of land in the Tower Hill area, and they would expire in August 1, 1915. They planned to build their "home school" there, and some of the "loyal citizens" renewed the options "without cost to the college." The board wanted to build dormitories for several thousand students as well as a sports field and a school for agriculture. However, this would require outside funding. Sheppard wrote back to the Fort Scott supporters that he had "worked harder in the last two weeks than ever before in his life, but that he is meeting with much success." He reported summer being a bad time due to the number of people out on vacation, including some heirs to soap fortunes, such as James Gamble of Procter & Gamble.[49]

In late July, Sheppard returned home and made a report to the Fort Scott supporters at an ice cream social. He had interviewed "a number of rich men" and believed the owner of the Larkin Soap Company of Buffalo, New York, would help the college, as would one of the Taylor brothers who had founded a Winston-Salem tobacco business and James Gamble. He arranged for "several of these financiers" to come to Fort Scott to help with building plans. However, it was difficult work to persuade capitalists to invest in a school to promote socialism. It hurt the school when President C. B. Hoffman died unexpectedly later that month, forcing Le Sueur to become president.[50]

Arthur Le Sueur, while still vice president, and with the assistance of Marian Wharton, had begun editing a monthly they called the *People's College News*, sent free to all members of the College Union. In the December 1915 issue Secretary Jake Sheppard informed readers that during the eighteen months the school had been operating, he had "only unstinted praise for my associate officers, our corps of teachers, and employees." He was especially proud of Le Sueur's Law Department, which had produced some lawyers that "the entire Nation will be delighted to honor."

The price of the law program was $100, and this included a fourteen-volume law library. The fee of $25 was payable when the student enrolled, then $5 monthly until it was all paid. Philip Callery proved to be one of its best-known graduates. He recalled that one day Jake Sheppard asked him why he did not become a lawyer. He responded that, first of all, he could not afford to attend law school and, in addition, he "had not received a college education sufficient to entitle me to enter a college or university for the study of law." "No problem," Sheppard responded, "we teach by correspondence so you study in your own home." That winter Callery began the course, and two years later he passed the state bar exam with a grade "ranking pretty close to the top." In his first three years of practice he made over $20,000 and then became legal counsel for UMW District 14 and drew a handsome retainer from the miners.[51]

The *People's College News* was filled with college activities, financial reports, and items of interest to Socialists. Frank P. Walsh reviewed Miss Wharton's book, *Plain English*, designed as a college text, and wrote a story about workers' institutes. Alexander Berkman visited Chicago as part of the International Defense League. He was scheduled to speak at the Hebrew Institute but found the doors locked. The students then struck in sympathy and, with the assistance of "a majority of their teachers, organized an institute of their own" called the Workers' Institute. The April 1916 issue noted the college received $2,333.22 from tuition and another $350 from the College Union and Miscellaneous. It disbursed an equal amount, primarily to salaries and supplies.

Two weeks before America entered World War I, a fire devastated the People's College. About 10:00 a.m. workers discovered the wood balcony on the third floor had caught fire. It was soon brought under control, but the water damage from the city fire department ruined the first two floors. Despite only losing a small amount of supplies, the damage was enough to require relocating to another building. They found a "commodious location" in the heart of downtown. The correspondence and files were saved, but students were reminded to accept the crisis and understand any delays that might occur until the transfer was completed.[52]

In July 1917, three months after the United States' entry into the war, the *People's College News* reported the net profits of forty-two large American corporations, comparing the years 1913–16. American Smelting and Refining profits had increased threefold during those years, while Bethlehem Steel's rose eight times. E. I. du Pont de Nemours and Company shot up a modest 700 percent, and U.S. Steel increased from $81 million in 1913 to $271 million in 1916. The smaller Lackawanna Steel and Republic Steel increased sixfold and fivefold, respectively. The profits of all these war-related industries increased from $204 million in 1913 to $730 million in 1916. These figures were taken from the *Congressional Record* of May 15, 1917.[53]

At the end of the war the college was preparing to establish a dairy program. Farmers, the newsletter noted, "are making big money on the sale of milk and milk products." The college was receiving inquiries from local landowners looking for farm partners or tenants. The trustees were establishing a "Farm Bureau" to bring landowners and prospective tenants together. "Back to the Land" was the rallying cry for this program. "If anyone tells you there is anywhere on earth a better Automobile and Farm Tractor School, than the one operated by the People's College," the newsletter advised, "deny it emphatically."[54]

American entry into the war brought added burdens to the college. The War Revenue Act of 1917 produced a host of "nuisance" taxes on coffee, sugar, and movie tickets but also postage stamps, which affected the college because of its extensive mailings. In addition, paper cost two or three times what it did in 1914. An editorial in the *People's College News* warned students that the nonprofit school would have to pass these costs on to them. The administration pleaded with the students to include a postage stamp with their letters that required an answer.[55]

By the spring of 1918 the college had expanded its offerings in correspondence considerably. It now had departments for stenographic, commercial, commercial normal, and civil service. The school still offered correspondence courses for plain and advanced English, penmanship, letter writing, domestic science, arithmetic, algebra, shorthand, typing, bookkeeping, office management, and law, and it was moving in the direction of establishing a business school. By the end of the war, it had enrolled students from every state in the Union and several foreign countries. Over ten thousand students had taken one or more of its courses, including appeal law. The college now operated a 160-acre farm and had plans to establish a modern dairy there.[56]

In January 1916 Jake Sheppard resigned his position in the college. When the war came to America, Jake later explained, "the school had a hard struggle for its existence." "Several times" since then school officials had asked him to return. With the end of hostilities, they again appealed to him to become president and offered him "full authority to reorganize" the college according to postwar needs. Sheppard yielded to their blandishments.[57]

On January 17, 1919, over two thousand people attended the grand opening of the Automobile Department of the People's College. Each lady in attendance received a red carnation. The department's garage on South National Avenue contained the "largest and best equipped lighting, starting, and ignition room in the world," with tools, machinery, student work benches, and a "comprehensive array of chassis of standard cars, stripped for instruction." Adjoining this garage was the College Eveready Battery Service Station. Professor H. D. Lloyd, the longtime head of the Rake School in Kansas City, accepted the position of principal for the Automobile Department at an annual salary of $12,000.[58]

Jake Sheppard and his staff and employees were present at the opening of the Auto Department to explain the various departments of the college. The college adopted the maxim "We are not interested in anything except in the welfare of our school and the progress of our city." Vanished in this new capitalist enterprise was the primary concern for educating the nation's workingmen and women in Socialistic premises. Jake Sheppard promised the citizens of Fort Scott that the People's College would become "the greatest school of its kind in the world." "There were none who visited the institution today," the local editor observed, "that doubted this assertion." Even the Commercial Department boasted a sign that read, "THE SCHOOL IS STRONG FOR FORT SCOTT." Unfortunately, the college collapsed due to inadequate funding.

Socialists had success in promoting municipal-owned utilities, or what was termed "gas and water socialism." As early as 1902, the *Appeal to Reason* called attention to the growing number of municipally owned utilities. Of the 1787 waterworks in America, half were city owned, and there were 460 municipal-owned electric plants. The average cost to users was $160 for privately owned companies, whereas this was reduced to $59 in municipal-owned systems, in which the profits were eliminated.[59]

Prior to the opening of the big producers in Kansas, natural gas was piped through interstate commerce and was expensive. Kansans were careless with the disposal of their garbage, which frequently contaminated their drinking water, leading to epidemics of typhoid fever. Municipal waterworks, therefore, often came with efforts to clean up the city's water supply. The secretary of the state board of health, Dr. Samuel J. Crumbine, led the way in this reform.[60]

Crumbine challenged much of society's folklore, including the maxim that running water purifies itself every seven miles. He and the state bacteriologist traveled the Kansas River in a small boat from Topeka to Lawrence, some twenty-eight miles, taking water samples periodically. When the samples were tested, they discovered that citizens of Lawrence were drinking Topeka sewage. They then investigated the privately owned Lawrence water plant, and their revelations helped reformers promote a municipal system. The issue dated back to 1914, when the city council tentatively agreed to purchase the private plant for $50,000 but the company refused the offer. That spring M. J. Wells ran for mayor as the public welfare candidate to buy the water plant at a reasonable price or "prepare to build a new waterworks." Developments were at an impasse six months later, so the city undertook a water survey. This report, plus Crumbine's recommendation, led Lawrence to build its own system in 1917. Meanwhile, Lawrence citizens and University of Kansas students were drinking polluted water.[61]

A private firm had built a water plant for Topeka in 1881. Some two decades later the city bought the system for $620,000. The city council found that whatever alternative it investigated—whether buying it or building a new one—it faced potential legal problems that could occupy the council for years. Pittsburg faced a similar dilemma: whether to buy their private system for $255,000 or to build a new one. Like Topeka, the town held a vote on a bond issue in 1907, but only 1,139 votes were cast, and 836 of them were negative. Four years later, however, the voters approved the bonds for both cities to purchase the old plants and modernize them.[62]

Iola, forty miles west of Fort Scott, was a progressive town and the home of the *Iola Cooperator*. As early as 1900, the city of Iola had invested just over $1.1 million in a new electric plant powered by coal and steam and in 1907 a natural gas system, but it was not until 1930 that its citizens decided to build a city water plant.[63]

The state's largest city at the time, the Kansas side of Kansas City, built a publicly owned steam-run electric power plant for $20 million in 1912 and a water plant in 1909 for $10 million. By 1940 the city could transfer almost $183,000 in profits from its electric plant to other city accounts and nearly $4,000 excess cash from its water plant. The issue of a municipally owned water system dragged on for several years. In 1904 the county newspaper announced that the existing private plant had been built for a city of ten thousand people, but the current population was six times larger than that. The editor thought it would be a wise investment for the city to build its own system. The city finally bought the private plant and in 1910 voted bonds to expand it to meet the needs of the growing population.[64]

A. S. McAllister, Socialist candidate for governor in 1902, was a railroad engineer from Herington. In 1908 his town bought a water system and updated it, building a diesel-fueled electric power plant that produced enough revenue to use $46,000 annually for other city purposes. Following authorization by the voters for a $43,000 bond issue, the city contracted with the Squire Electric Company to complete the system by September 15. In mid-August the city newspaper reported that only the cover for the new water tower remained to be completed. Railroad men proudly announced that the 121-foot tower could be seen from a great distance. The editor was happy to report that the construction was achieved without accident despite recent heavy storms and high winds.[65]

In the southwest M. M. Murdock, owner and editor of the *Wichita Eagle*, opposed municipal ownership of the water system. He noted that the city paid $10,000 annually for the private company's fire hydrants in order to lessen insurance premiums on property protection. This sum "would not pay half the interest on the bonds" required to purchase the system in addition to the costs of operating the plant. "Don't let the bond agents bind the hands and feet of this Wichita," Murdock pleaded with citizens. Despite his plea, or perhaps because of it, the voters approved the bonds by a three-to-one margin.[66]

Voters in Pittsburg approved bonds in 1911 by a five-to-one margin to purchase and modernize their private waterworks system. The revenue from the sale of water would pay the interest and still create a sinking fund to pay off the bonds at maturity. Those opposed to the bond issue resisted it because they thought "the city's best interest would be served" by building a completely new plant. Now that the election was decided, the editor surmised, "the citizens all will settle down to 'boosting' for Pittsburg."[67]

Voters in Coffeyville approved a bond issue of $20,000 for a municipal electric light plant in the fall elections of 1900. The following April the newspaper proudly announced that "the big machinery at the power house moved off without a hitch or jar and every light in the city was burning brightly in a few moments." Within a few years the system was producing $100,000 in revenue above costs that was being used to cover other city expenses.[68]

Chanute city officials, hearing of Coffeyville's success, visited the town two years later to investigate municipal ownership of utilities and proceeded to expand its municipal system. In 1900 the city had purchased a natural gas well, which eventually expanded into a $1.5 million system of gas, water, and electricity. The gas system was so profitable that in 1903 its fund loaned the city $30,000 to purchase a municipal electric system. Twenty years later these utilities had yielded almost $1 million in profits to carry on city functions. The city water plant was less profitable but "paid its own way."

In 1928 Chanute could divert $75,000 of its utilities profits to build an airport. Four years earlier these utilities furnished half the cost of $367,000 to build a municipal building. In addition, improvements were made in city parks, including a modern swimming pool, a baseball field, a large park auditorium, and a band shell. Following World War II, one could live in debt-free Chanute and not have to pay city taxes.[69]

In keeping with its name, the western Kansas town of Garden City carefully utilized water during its history to keep the town green and luxuriant. In addition to its municipal water supply, the town held a bond issue election in 1912 for a municipal light plant costing $40,000. The issue passed but brought on an investigation, possibly at the instigation of the Garden City Light Utility Company, a private organization, and the Kansas attorney general invalidated the election on a technicality and ordered a new one. The second election also carried. The city expanded its underground sanitary sewage system in 1917, which routed raw sewage into the Arkansas River. City officials expanded the water system in 1922, when the town opened a hand-dug reservoir that covered almost a city block holding 2.5 million gallons of water in reserve. Billed as "the world's largest free, concrete-lined municipal swimming pool," the children could enjoy it on hot summer days, and it could irrigate the city park during water shortages.[70]

Salina was rather late in accepting gas and water socialism. It was not until 1925 that voters decided 1,742 to 355 to buy the water plant supplying the town. They cast a light vote of one-third of those eligible, indicating apathy on the part of the citizenry. The local Nonpartisan League newspaper supported the purchase, pointing out that the user who paid $1 monthly for the service would be contributing sixty cents to retiring the purchase bonds. By paying the same amount of forty cents for the service, the city's profit would retire the bonds in twenty years and "have a nice surplus on hand." The editor expressed the desire for the town to expand into city ownership of other utilities in the future.[71]

Gas and water socialism in Kansas continued through the Great Depression, when New Deal agencies began assisting cities in building utilities through public works projects. The small town of White City, south of Manhattan, for example, applied to the Public Works Administration for help in constructing a water system. After receiving a 50-50 matching grant, women voters pushed citizens to approve a bond issue to finance the city's half of the costs, and the project was completed in 1938. Buoyed by this success, the city fathers applied to the Works Progress Administration and in 1940 received a 75-25 matching grant to construct a municipal sewage disposal system. They voted the bonds to cover the 25 percent, and the sewage system was completed on the eve of World War II. Other towns in Kansas also took advantage of this federal assistance.[72]

After the demise of the Populist Party, many agrarian liberals joined the emerging Socialist Party, but a new farm organization arose to carry on the work of the old alliances and many of the Socialist projects. Texas agrarian Newt Gresham persuaded some Texas neighbors to form the Farmers Educational and Cooperative Union of America. In 1904 three Populists, one Socialist, one Independent, and five Democrats became charter members of what became popularly known as the Farmers Union (FU). It spread rapidly, and by 1908 the national secretary claimed one million members. The FU pursued the goals of "cooperatives, collective control of marketing, and campaigns to withhold crops" for better farm prices. One writer described the Jobbing Association in Kansas City, Kansas, an offshoot of the FU, as "the largest cooperative institution in the world." While it was more cautious than the Populists in its policies, it supported the "radical reform" ideas of the Progressives between 1911 and 1915, "from nationalizing natural resources to outlawing child labor."[73]

Following receipt of a national charter in 1906, interested farmers met in Hutchinson and organized a unit in Kansas. The national president attended this meeting, as did James Butler of Topeka, who was a member of the national board. Attendees chose J. E. McQuillen of Heizer, a member of the state legislature, as state president. Kansas became one of the first FU states to establish a newspaper, the *Kansas Farmers Union*, in 1908. At first the South dominated the FU, but as it spread northward, there was a perceptible shift in membership and influence within northern states. By the end of World War I, FU-sponsored cooperatives were strongest in north-central states.[74]

The first few issues of the FU newspaper were published in Topeka until a suitable press was located in Salina. It was a monthly at first, then weekly before becoming a monthly again. It contained features on the co-op creameries, coyotes, trusts, tuberculosis in cattle, corn in India, purposes of the FU, the emergence of new locals, a story of instructors from Kansas State Agricultural College teaching farmers how to build a silo, letters to the editor, the activities of the FU's state lecturer, and setting hens. For a few issues the paper ran a special page for women. They carried advertisements for a lumberyard, an insurance company, and a harness shop. The editor insisted the newspaper would always be nonpartisan. In the May 1908 issue the editor announced that the FU had expanded to twenty-six states and had a national membership of 2.4 million.

The editor also became involved in soliciting members to petition the governor and the warden in the state prison in Lansing to continue producing binder twine. Following the lead of Minnesota and North Dakota, Kansas established a twine factory in the state prison in 1890. The warden claimed his factory was a losing proposition because farmers did not patronize it sufficiently, and some production remained unsold that year. The factory used convict labor, paying the men pennies daily, and the warden traveled to the Yucatán Peninsula in Mexico to arrange for a cheap supply of sisal (a fibrous agave plant used for rope) from the trust there, bypassing the regular source imported through New Orleans. Walter Thomas Mills used this factory as an example in his 1904 book on socialism and collectivist principles, *Struggle for Existence*. Although it was publicly owned and many called it socialistic in a free farm economy, he agreed that the use of convict labor and raw materials from the trust and managed by a capitalist political party "cannot be said to be either examples of Socialism or steps toward Socialism."[75]

When the FU held its annual meeting in Emporia in 1910, Sim A. Bramlette of Columbus, president-organizer of the Kansas State Federation of Labor, addressed the delegates. Bramlette made a special plea for cooperation between farmers and laborers, between the FU and the state AFL, as was happening in Arkansas, Oklahoma, and Texas, where laws were passed to "protect the common people from corporate domination and control." Bramlette believed such cooperation between the two groups could lead to more union men and laborers being elected to the state legislature and enacting laws to protect the "common people." His vision did not materialize, however, as the agrarian-dominated legislature continued to show its basic hostility toward trade unionists.[76]

Charles S. Walker, a Republican farmer from White City, became a forceful FU leader in Kansas. He left the farm in 1912 to work full-time for the FU, becoming state treasurer for a period and moving its headquarters to Salina. The state FU developed marketing cooperatives, including FarMarCo, and organized the Kansas Jobbing Company in 1912, which, by 1916 was doing $100 million in business annually. By 1919 FU elevator cooperatives controlled 50 percent of Kansas wheat. Some two hundred of these associations made plans to operate under their Jobbers Association in time for that year's wheat harvest. The Farmers Union also created cooperatives in gasoline, creameries, banks, and insurance companies. During the 1920s the FU split into two groups, one continuing the cooperative marketing and buying concept and the other attempting to bargain for crop prices much like collective bargaining for wages.[77]

Also at that time, Alexander Howat was successful in getting the judicial branch to declare the Kansas Court of Industrial Relations to be unconstitutional, marking a great Socialist victory. Supreme Court chief justice Howard William Taft, the former president, considered it to be a "novel constitutional theory" for the business of the butcher, the baker, the woodchopper, or the miner to be clothed in "public interest" and their wages and prices fixed by the state. Therefore, the state could not use that rationalization to interfere with property rights. This reading of the clause placed almost all businesses outside the reach of state regulation, until the court later reached a broader interpretation. The liberal justice Louis Brandeis told his chief he welcomed the decision, which discouraged the trend toward arbitrary compulsion exemplified by the Kansas law, as Alexander Howat had contended.[78]

The Tri-State coal miners, under Howat's leadership, successfully fought the Industrial Court of Kansas. The decade of the 1920s witnessed the widespread development of hydroelectric power and marked the decline of the coal industry. The Tri-State production was never a high-quality fuel, and eventually even strip mining could not compete with the new energy from dams and petroleum. But from 1908 through the election of 1916, in the towns and cities where there was a high percentage of them, miners proved to be the stronghold of the Socialist Party in Kansas.

6

THE WOBBLIES

The Socialist tenacity of opposition to militarism and World War I was a tribute to their dedication to principle but produced terrible results for individual party members and radical groups. The Industrial Workers of the World (IWW), commonly called "Wobblies," was an international union of revolutionary Socialists who were willing to use violence to achieve their ends. When they put their principles into action, their efforts were crowned by being punished severely by a Kansas culture caught up in the throes of political reaction. When America entered the war in April 1917, the official threat to Socialists from officials deepened. With opinion divided over American participation in the "capitalist" war because of losses in the Atlantic in the defense of neutral rights, President Woodrow Wilson determined to unite the nation through the Creel Committee. Chaired by Denver journalist George Creel, the Committee on Public Information became a powerful weapon in turning the European war into the "Great Crusade" for the American people, igniting a religious fervor in the public mind that boded ill for the Wobblies. The story of the Industrial Workers of the World belongs in a chapter by itself between the winning and the losing Socialists because, while never as successful as the winners, the union made a huge contribution to the welfare of those desperate migratory harvest and oil workers it tried to help.

Eugene Debs, along with Daniel De Leon, William "Big Bill" Haywood, and others, founded the IWW in Chicago, and the organization, with its radical approach to socialism, had a special appeal to the lumberjacks and miners of the Northwest, eastern textile workers, lumberjacks in Louisiana, and migrant agricultural and petroleum workers on the Great Plains. With the discoveries of natural gas and oil in Kansas, these workers flitted between following the wheat harvest and working the oil fields. Debs soon left the iww, and Haywood assumed leadership of the organization after the Socialist split in 1912 over the use of force, along with his violence-prone Western Federation of Miners.[1]

The Wobblies sought to unite all workers—black and white, male and female—under the motto that the working class and the employing class had nothing in common. Like all Socialists, they believed capitalists were parasites living off the labor of others and their system must be overthrown and a classless society established. The workers would own and control the means of production and distribution, and laborers would then enjoy the fruits of their labor. Debs left the iww over the use of sabotage to achieve its ends of revolutionizing the capitalist system. By this the organization meant pacific resistance to capitalism, but even this was too much for Debs and mainstream Socialists, who insisted the ballot box was the true means to the end. The iww insisted they were "at war against war" and opposed violence, but as the public attitude became increasingly reactionary, Kansas patriots concluded they were violent atheists and godless radicals. Their transient nature, of course, made them "more vulnerable to harassment and repression."[2]

Like the more conservative Socialists, Wobblies were vague about their goals. Made up of lumberjacks, miners, and migratory workers in the West, they represented the weakest elements in society. They pursued the simple goal of abolishing capitalism and instituting government ownership of the means of production and distribution, controlled by federated bodies of industrial workers. Haywood, however, insisted this aim could not be achieved through political means because "the wage earner or producing classes were in the minority" and "they are not educated in the game of politics; that their life is altogether industrial. . . . Between these two classes a struggle must go on until the workers of the world organize as a class, take possession of the

earth and the machinery of production, and abolish the wage system. . . . It is the historic mission of the laboring class to do away
with Capitalism." Wobblies, in other words, sought to achieve
Socialist goals through economic means, not the political process. When they settled on this course of action, they were at
odds with the Socialist Party.[3]

As a corollary, the iww would never participate in a legal process because this constituted political action. The Wobblies never
sought action in a capitalist court but when on trial would follow
what Mahatma Gandhi would later pursue, "passive resistance,"
a tactic frustrating to their opponents.[4]

Wobbly support was strongest among migratory men who lived
on the lower fringes of society, where violence was an accepted
part of life. No family, no franchise, no education, no dignity,
they felt impotent and alienated, bound together by a shared
misery. After a life of failure, beatings, and awful jails, they held
allegiance to nothing but their fellow sufferers.[5]

Legends grew, especially during World War I, that equated
the wandering hobo with the desperate criminal who used sabotage to cripple the war effort. Yet there was an interesting religious aspect to Wobbly philosophy, that of the gentle Christian
who viewed Christ as a passionate capitalist reformer who represented the epitome of social justice. Christ fought the Phari-
sees, threw out the money changers, and supported the masses
in their class struggle. The iww used the "unjust steward" parable of the man who was fired by his master and became destitute, found out how much his debtors owed, and reduced their
debts, then appropriated some of the difference, as Christ's way
of teaching that wealth should be divided among the poor. In
their literature and songs (Wobblies sang a lot) the union's members venerated Jesus as the first great Communist who taught His
followers to donate their possessions to society and live a communal life. Eugene Debs told a reporter who was interviewing
him in an Atlanta prison and saw a picture of Jesus near his bed:

> I told my friends of the cloth that I did not believe Christ was meek
> and lowly but a real, living vital agitator who went into the temple

with a lash and a krout [*sic*] and whipped the oppressors of the poor, routed them out of doors and spilled their blood and got silver on the floor. He told the robbed and misruled and exploited and driven people to disobey their plunderers, he denounced the profiteers, and it was for this that they nailed his quivering body to the cross and spiked it to the gates of Jerusalem, not because he told them to love one another. That was a harmless doctrine. But when he touched their profits and denounced them before their people he was then marked for crucifixion.[6]

To most Kansans this account was mockery of the vilest sort, and they viewed the wretches as denigrating sacred values of country, flag, and religion, especially during the war years. In Kansas authorities often arrested Wobblies for reading the Declaration of Independence from their soapboxes because the language sounded quite incendiary to the average Kansan who was ignorant of its contents. Most Kansans, including the governor in 1916, would agree with the editor of the *San Diego Tribune* when he argued in 1912 that "hanging is too good for them and they would be much better dead; for they are absolutely useless in the human economy; they are waste material of creation and should be drained off in the sewers of oblivion there to rot in cold obstruction like any other excrement." "Useless in the human economy," that is, except during harvest time, when their labor was vital.[7]

Nationally, the iww was not popular. But in Kansas its members were especially treated with strong suspicion and prejudice. In central Kansas sheriffs and policemen were holding open season on suspected and confirmed Wobblies. Once caught, lawmen held that the iww's constitution served as a call for force, and therefore they were considered guilty.[8] In early 1917 thirty-four Wobblies were arrested and had to wait in a dirty jail, subject to routine disciplinary beatings, for two years before most of them were convicted and sent to the federal penitentiary.[9]

War tensions led government officials to consider radical "aliens" (and many Wobblies were aliens) with a higher priority for deportation than German spies or agents. They held German spies in custody, of course, but the radical aliens were considered more dangerous, and "one-fourth or more" of those interned were in this group. To facilitate this process, the attorney general's office sought an even tougher law than the prewar statute that provided for exportation of any alien guilty of having committed a crime of moral turpitude within five years of entering the country. The new provision, ex post facto legislation, in May 1920 made the mere internment or conviction of aliens a deportable offense. This proviso applied to many who were merely members of the iww, even those certified as "peaceful and law abiding" but who were interned for "the moral effect on the community."[10]

Many superpatriots, of course, were dissatisfied with the slow speed of the criminal justice system and often took the law into their own hands. Although they did not resort to lynchings during wartime, they forced the purchase of government bonds, donations to the Red Cross, and lip service to support the war. They often kept people under surveillance who did not participate in these activities as fully as the patriots expected. They promoted the American Protective League, an agency sponsored by the Department of Justice that boasted 350,000 members in over six hundred towns and cities across the nation. Armed with a badge that impressed many with its similarity to those carried by Bureau of Investigation officials (later renamed the Federal Bureau of Investigation, or fbi), these people frightened even President Wilson. They examined people for loyalty, took censuses of alien land ownership, established an unofficial policy of "work or fight," and promoted various aspects of support for the war.[11]

The iww began with a conference in Chicago in 1905 of Marxian Socialists who drew up a constitution. Its preamble contained the observation that "there can be no peace so long as hunger and want are found among millions of working people and the few, who make up the employing class, have all the good things in life." A major split came in 1908 with the ejection of Daniel De Leon and his radical Socialist Laborites. Most iww members believed they should avoid politics and concentrate on direct economic action. This position added greatly to their image as a "nihilist cabal" in the public mind.[12]

Soon after the 1906 meeting, a group of packinghouse workers in Kansas City established an IWW unit, but the major activity in Kansas took place in Wichita in early 1907. Locals there asked the General Executive Board (GEB) of the Socialist Party for assistance in organizing workers, and in March they dispatched Lillian Forberg as a full-time organizer in that area. She immediately held evening meetings with workers and spent her days touring work sites. She persuaded metalworkers and bricklayers to organize and urged also furniture and cement workers to form locals. She continued to recruit sewer workers, but a significant split occurred in the city's locals over economic versus political activity, and Forberg took sides in the matter. The GEB soon ordered her to Minneapolis, and her successor, Clinton Simonton, a coal miner, moved the operations to Pittsburg, Kansas. He described this area as "rotten ripe" for the IWW and soon boasted a brick and tile local and another of smeltermen in the Tri-State Mining Region. Demoralized by the GEB's indifference, the Wichita locals quit paying dues, and their 1908 convention renounced all political activity. In Kansas those laborers who could take part politically did so, and this early movement died out.[13]

By 1912 public sentiment was beginning to turn away from the IWW because of its advocacy of economic action, or sabotage, and alleged radicalism. That year a group of "purported drunken Boy Scouts, recruited and aided by the Y.M.C.A.," broke up one of the IWW's meetings in Wichita with rotten tomatoes and watermelons.[14]

Conservatives and radicals viewed the 1912 convention as a showdown for control of the Socialist Party. Even Debs came out against sabotage, and "with mutual contempt and recriminations," the two groups split. The conservatives amended the constitution to condemn violence and voted to recall Haywood from the party's national executive board. Unfortunately, this anti-sabotage clause was "the ideological forerunner of the criminal syndicalism and the deportation statutes aimed at dissident members of the community."[15]

Big Bill Haywood's leadership of the IWW proved to be the major turning point for the Wobblies in Kansas when he determined to organize migratory farmworkers in the state. These unorganized laborers were terribly exploited, enduring deplorable living conditions, long hours, low wages, and physical danger from railroaders and in the "hobo jungles," as their camps were called. Riding the rails was dangerous. During a five-year period twenty-five thousand men were killed and an equal number seriously or permanently injured jumping aboard moving trains. Railroad crews often levied a dollar to "ride the rails," and the jungles were rife with con men and robbers out to get the workers' savings.[16]

The nature of the wheat crop and the total dependence on it for livelihood in some areas, especially in western Kansas, led to labor problems as most small towns could not supply extra workers for the short two-week period of harvest and had to rely on itinerants. Farmers and local officials advertised their estimated number of needed workers. Often they exaggerated the truth about numbers and expected pay scale because an excess of labor would hold down wages. Most Kansans were more concerned over rotting wheat, especially after the outbreak of World War I highlighted the need for food, than they were over unemployed migrant hobos. The migrants usually moved out of Kansas City to the wheat fields by boxcars, often freely provided by railroads; owners recognized the need for labor to harvest the crop to be hauled back east. This cheap transportation was dangerous, but the migrant could get a trip to his next job even if he lost his savings to gamblers or hijackers.

It was the bonanza farms, those with wheat fields of hundreds or thousands of acres west of approximately the 95th meridian, that required the greatest numbers of seasonal workers. These farms needed dozens of men, perhaps a hundred, during the harvest season and fewer during the plowing that followed. Before the coming of the combine in the mid-twentieth century, the wheat was cut with headers or binders, and the bundles needed to be shocked to ripen fully until threshed some two weeks later. Binding required at least three shockers for every two binders, and the fields of half-sections or larger needed several binders to cut the crop quickly before the seeds began to shell out on the ground.

The development of the Mid-Continent Oil Field around Tulsa, Oklahoma, in 1912 and the smaller portion of that field in Kansas near Augusta stirred this mass of abused workers who were ripe for unionizing. The petroleum development initiated a significant movement of migratory harvest hands into the oil fields each year after the harvest was completed. Haywood was determined to organize these workers into the Agricultural Workers Organization (AWO), later renamed the Agricultural Workers Industrial Union (AWIU), and the Oil Workers Industrial Union (OWIU) to promote better wages, hours, and working conditions. In 1917 Haywood appointed Phineas M. Eastman as secretary of the local in Augusta, Kansas, an appointment that would assume significance as America later prosecuted Wobbly leaders. The radical Eastman came to the IWW through the Louisiana Timber Workers.[17]

The United States' entry into the war in April 1917 presented many Socialists with a choice of patriotism versus principles. Wobblies easily chose their anti-war convictions. One Wobbly responded with a typical attitude:

> If your job had never kept you long enough in a place to qualify you to vote, if you slept in a lousy, sour bunkhouse, and ate food just as rotten as they could give you and get by with it; if Deputy Sheriffs shot your cooking cans full of holes and spilled your grub on the ground; if your wages were lowered on you when the bosses thought they had you down . . . . If every person who represented law and order and the nation beat you up, and railroaded you to jail, and the good Christian people cheered and told them to go to it, how the hell do you expect a man to be patriotic? This war is a business man's war and we don't see why we should go out and get shot in order to save the lovely state of affairs that we now enjoy.

Tensions mounted between Wobblies and authorities as the importance of wheat and oil production mounted and the Creel Committee whipped up patriotic emotions.[18]

Local business leaders depended on the farmers' harvest for their existence and took the lead in helping recruit sufficient labor supplies, in some cases feeding migrant workers who arrived in town too early for harvest. But the problem was too large for them, and the local authorities and the U.S. Bureau of Labor began a campaign of assistance. With a total migrant labor force of close to one hundred thousand in 1916, something needed to be done to bring order to the chaos, and the Wilson administration found the IWW to be "impalpable." But it was not until 1918 that the United States Employment Service was created to help resolve this problem of harvest labor needs. By that time the increasing use of automobiles would revolutionize this chaotic system. Before then, it was in shambles: farmers wanted a surplus of labor, and workers wanted a decent wage during the short harvest season.[19]

IWW organizers fanned out from Kansas City across the grain fields in 1914, enrolling new members in boxcars, jungles, and on the job. Before the end of harvest, they reported union activity around Dodge City, Fowler, Great Bend, Herington, Minneola, Pratt, St. Francis, and Tonapah. On several occasions farmers fired Wobblies for attempting to recruit other workers on their crew. Hoisington officials arrested two IWW members when they "spoke in public without a legal permit." But in some areas they were able to increase the wage rate from $2.50 to $3.00. The success of recruiting new members also meant prosperity for the national office as, for the first time since its foundation, it showed a strong credit line.[20]

Organizers experimented with methods of recruiting and found the "camp delegate" method used in California to be the most successful. Each chapter had a leader who spoke for his "gang," but he could not contact employers, and members could refuse to accept his leadership if they believed he was acting contrary to IWW policy. This experience, plus GEB member Frank Little's insistence that they needed "concerted and efficient action in the harvest fields next year," led to a revision of the organization's structure. Wobblies belonged to a local and purchased their cards and dues stamps from their unit secretary. These individuals could not handle the expected increase in recruiting, so the national office created a Bureau of Migratory Labor, with plans to meet in Kansas City in April 1915. There it created the AWO,

elected the experienced and efficient Walter Nef as national secretary, and chose Kansas City as the new site's headquarters. The
program included a ten-hour day, minimum wages with over-
time, good food, and clean beds—nothing particularly revolutionary there.[21]

Nef authorized between fifty and one hundred recruiters to fan
out across the wheat fields to recruit and handle the financial matters. The AWO advised them to solicit on the job and avoid "soap-
boxing" in towns. Some could not remain as quiet as instructed.
A group of recruiters from Oklahoma took control of a train and
directed its crew to take them to Wichita. They were successful,
however, in raising wages in the towns of Kinsley, Larned, Plains,
and Russell. Obviously, they enjoyed greatest success in the areas
where the recruiters had succeeded in 1914.[22]

This success generated fear and intense anger among middle-
class Kansans, and the mass media fed this hysteria with lurid
stories:

> They came to Kansas this year when the call was clarioned for thou-
> sands of harvest hands. The harvest hands came . . . also men of the
> wanderlust, wrecks of the slums, men at whom life has sneered and
> who seek to retaliate by sneering at life. Among the latter is [sic] the
> IWW agitators, ready to make the minds of the weak illiterates into
> warped molds, ready to fight, pillage, burn or murder. . . . They
> believe they are oppressed; surely fate has sneered on them and they
> seek vengeance against those whom upon fortune has smiled . . . a
> menace which threatens the wheat industry. . . . [They] take charge
> practically of the freight trains and demand that transients join their
> organization or be thrown off. They drive men out of the fields who
> don't have the card and several jails have been stormed . . . train-
> men officers shot . . . they make a cross like a Chinese laundry tag
> on fences and gate posts to mark houses where women have been
> generous with food.[23]

Henry P. Richardson, a former labor organizer from Chicago
with no IWW connection, took this opportunity to organize the
regular farmhands of Kansas. His "farm hand union," he declared,
would "educate the farmer to appreciate and respect the rights of

its members," although, he added, "a reasonable amount of force may be employed" if the employer proved recalcitrant. He pressed for a ten-hour day, which would relegate milking cows by lantern light and feeding the livestock before bedtime to the archaic era of "hoop skirts and poke bonnet." No more eighteen-hour days with a half-hour for lunch. "The Kansas farmer is rich and can afford it," he insisted, and can pay $45 monthly with room and board. "We intend to see that he does it—not by force but by education." Nothing further was learned of his success or failure.[24]

Once the AWO began organizing in 1914, conservative forces counterattacked. Cheyenne County officials, in the most northwestern county of the state, with relatively strong support for Socialists, sent a special story to the state's leading Republican organ. Officials declared that the county needed harvest hands but not "IWWs and paroled criminals": "We had rather handle our bumper crop at a loss than to be burdened with such riffraff." They disliked the idea of cities unloading "a lot of criminals upon the farming community under the guise of harvest hands, in order to save the cities the expense of keeping them." Six months later this county would cast 120 votes for Socialist Milo Mitchell, compared to 20 votes for G. W. Kleihege in 1912, but these farmers heartily disliked the Wobblies.[25]

Saline County, always rock-ribbed Republican, informed the Topeka newspaper that Salina was the "distributing point" for northwestern Kansas and that it was "combating the efforts of IWW organizers." The older migrants were doing their best in preventing their workers from joining "anti-work societies" and were meeting with greater success than the Wobblies. Some of the organizers, the story added, "hold union cards from the Federation of Labor in Colorado and took part in the labor troubles there last year."[26]

To protect their constituents' interests, many local editors sought to stimulate public fears over IWW activities and met with remarkable success. The editor of the *Salina Evening Journal* was representative of this breed of journalism. During the harvest season in 1917, he published many sensational stories of labor problems in the wheat fields. Salina authorities reported three businessmen having been arrested as spy suspects by secret servicemen. In addition, rumors sent a reporter "on a wild goose chase" to investigate "a munitions base, stocked with bombs, nitroglycerine, and gun wadding." It turned out to be an abandoned shack with no doors and "a heap of soup and baked beans cans." Another "tip" had a man murdered and his body hidden on a nearby farm because "he insulted the flag. . . . Everybody but the police and the man himself knew about the tragedy." That morning saw a damaged elevator, destruction of the crops, and "bomb setters were everywhere."[27]

Rumors grew more sinister. Two homemade bombs were found near the Standard Oil tanks in Hoisington. They were similar to some found the previous year during iww unrest. Other suspicious acts included the burning of two railroad bridges at Council Grove. America was in the war, and the Wobblies were being credited with all sorts of nefarious activities.[28]

The Salina editor warned later that summer of a "small army of them," headed right for Salina "before advancing westward." "Them" were iww scouts, and they "liked the city so well that they sent word back to the jungles to come on." The newcomers set up a jungle next to the Rock Island tracks, with the "knights of the ties" holding down the fort for the several hundred more expected. Police arrested three but were forced to release one of them, who convinced them he was not "subject to [draft] registration." The other two, "members of the iww contingency," were charged with vagrancy. Both were in the age range required for registering for the draft but did not possess registration documents. Ellsworth, Lincoln, and Russell Counties were making plans to keep the iww out. Based on their experience the previous year, "every farmer and village resident was cleaning up the family artillery . . . if the trouble gets beyond control." The same day the editor reported that the county sheriff had "routed" the twenty-five Wobblies in the jungle, "threw their equipment into the creek . . . and told them to hike."[29]

Three weeks later the Salina editor reported that Hoisington's Anti-Horse Thief Association was preparing to also protect the public from automobile thieves. The editor believed the association could be put to good use "when the IWWS get to causing trouble or during any similar disturbance." The previous day the editor told readers that Rock Island weight scales had been robbed of their brass beams at Bala, Broughton, Clay Center, Clifton, Concordia, Morganville, Vining, and Wakefield. The Clay County sheriff had arrested two men who were carrying "nineteen pounds of brass," the IWW constitution, and "the usual camping gear of the leisure class."[30]

The following month produced a bloodier tale. IWW members were assembling for dinner in their jungle at McPherson when a man named Emmett Hawk appeared. They sought to recruit him as a member. When he refused, they cursed him, and he drew a long knife and stabbed IWW leader Robert Sommers in the side, causing some internal injuries. Sommers was rushed to the hospital, and Hawk was jailed. Talk of violence grew and was promised, if Sommers were to die, and police "deputized citizens," making preparations "to stave off an attack" if the Wobblies resorted to violence.[31]

The next month the editor headlined the story that members of the IWW had bombed some railroad cars and otherwise were causing trouble in Miami, Oklahoma, part of the Tri-State Mining Region. Six Wobblies were arrested, and the Miami County attorney appealed to the U.S. marshal's office for help. Several suspects had been driven from the mining district for attempted dynamiting of freight cars. When similar occurrences took place, Wobblies received the blame. An old haystack west of Fabin burned from what could have been spontaneous combustion, but the Salina editor was convinced it was the work of the IWW. The stack lay in the center of a ripe wheat field, and "the suddenness of the fire and its rapid spread" convinced farmers of IWW complicity, the story ran, and "watchers are now set out and all suspicious looking persons will be questioned." When a violent explosion wrecked the threshing machine of a La Crosse farmer, many believed that it was the work of "an IWW agitator" who placed an explosive there to disrupt the work flow.[32]

The National Association of Manufacturers (NAM) demonstrated its willingness to go even further. When the Kansas Employers Association met in Pittsburg, K. P. Bird, general manager of the NAM, addressed the members on the fact that "labor is profiteering from the war" by their constantly striking, an interesting interpretation of the term *profiteering*. "Labor does not realize that this war is Labor's war," he asserted. Bird urged that pro-Germans and their sympathizers be interned and put to work "at hard labor" until deported. "Spies and traitors should be tried by court martial," he insisted, and "if guilty, should be shot at once." "No country on earth is so lax in its enforcement of regulations of this kind," he added.[33]

Faced with potential crises in the wheat belt, with grain a vital part of the war effort, the state of Kansas took action. In 1917 the state legislature enacted a vagrancy law that the farmers found effective in handling IWW members. In addition, Governor Arthur Capper advised communities to enact stringent vagrancy ordinances if they had not already done so. Capper held strong views on the IWW. Two years earlier he had urged the arrest of any members who stopped in his state and to levy a heavy fine because "if these men are made to work, Kansas will not be such a lure to them. Above all they do not want to work. They are disturbers and in a number of communities have intimidated people and destroyed property. As soon as a few hundred of these men can be employed on rock piles and in road building, I think the IWW will look elsewhere for comfort and these agitators will be kept moving."[34]

Samuel N. Hawkes, Capper's assistant attorney general, worked out a feasible plan for implementing general vagrancy laws. "In an effort to solve the IWW troubles which have caused much worry for farmers in the western section of the state," he said, the vagrancy laws should not mean jail sentences but fines. A justice of the peace, a municipal judge, or a county magistrate could fine the man for vagrancy, disturbing the peace, or threatening an officer and then force payment of the fine by working on the roads or "crack[ing] the rock" until the penalty was paid. All of this, the editor happily reported, "means sorrow and distress to the 'I Won't Work' crowd."[35]

The public scare attitude stemmed partly from a story headlined "I.W.W. Army Threatens War on Kansas Towns." When

Salina officials cleaned out their Wobbly jungle, one individual from the camp warned Major Fred Fitzpatrick of the Kansas National Guard to station troops around his armory because "he knew the plans that had been laid" by the iww. After two hundred Wobblies left the area, another fifty marched to Salina's city hall and demanded the release of their other two members. One of them possessed letters concerning "literature printed in different languages," and "thousands of pieces of literature have been scattered over the territory and it is all calculated to cause trouble." The iww leaders were reported to have telegraphed their headquarters in Chicago for five thousand more pamphlets and a request to "have 10,000 here in a few days."[36]

A posse of two hundred men ran known Wobblies out of Caldwell, and farmers within a three-mile radius of Turon armed themselves against the iww. Antipathy toward the union caused anonymous assailants to manhandle several Wobblies in Beloit, and a railroad policeman shot one in the arm at Wakeeny.[37] A mob deported 156 Wobblies from Junction City, and a Union Pacific policeman wounded another in the rail yards. On the other hand, fifty Wobblies pelted a Kanopolis train crew with chunks of coal. On four different occasions, fifty to two hundred Wobblies "bargained collectively" for the release of members in the Bunker Hill, Great Bend, and Salina jails. They used force to organize migrants, beating them and throwing them off moving freight trains if they proved obstinate.[38]

Because of persistent rumors, it was difficult for citizens to sift hearsay from true dangers. In early July 1916 some twelve thousand Wobblies allegedly were threatening to invade Wakeeny. The issue began when thirty "raiders" came to town to pilfer and one was arrested for possession of a weapon. That night about fifty iww members rescued him from jail and sent out a call for help, which came in great numbers. The mayor wired the governor for troops to protect his town, and Governor Capper responded that the militia was busy guarding the border from recent Mexican attacks led by Pancho Villa. Citizens and frightened farmers who had fled Wakeeny armed themselves for an invasion that never materialized.[39]

AWIU sabotage allegedly occurred at various points around the state, "displaying, by all accounts, an imaginative diversity of form." Fires around Hutchinson and Medicine Lodge destroyed wheat fields, while threshing machines near McPherson and Independence broke apart on hidden metal spikes. The town of Hiawatha, in Brown County, reported an attempt to poison the water supply of a harvest crew, and a Wobbly damaged a thresher at La Crosse with a bomb. Farmers were so obsessed with IWW violence that they blamed them in 1917 for the worst wheat crop in over a decade, ignoring the summer's adverse weather conditions.[40]

IWW recruiters were reportedly talking to workers building the new Camp Funston, adjacent to Fort Riley. Because of several instances of fire around buildings, the army had imposed a smoking ban. Two men, said to be members of the IWW, were asked to extinguish their cigarettes. The guard reminded them twice politely, but they replied that "they were using their own tobacco and papers [and] they would continue to smoke." Finally, the guard demanded they quit smoking and promised violence if they did not. The next moment the guard pounced on one of them, and the other fled. Workers reported that "IWW members in considerable numbers are loafing about the camp . . . seeking to stir up dissatisfaction and trouble." The workers, however, were reported to be satisfied, with carpenters making 65 cents hourly and laborers 37.5 cents with eight hours, "or as much longer as they desire."[41]

In one case IWW members received credit for a breach of military etiquette. A member of the National Guard unit in Kansas City, Kansas, wrote threatening letters to his commanding officer and explained he had taken "the idea from the I.W.W." Police judge A. J. Herrod announced he would thenceforth fine anyone $100 for the mere possession of a red card.[42]

Many states were moving beyond vagrancy laws to suppress the Wobblies. From 1917 through 1920 twenty-one states enacted criminal syndicalism laws to prosecute workers who employed sabotage or violence to achieve their goals. Many of these statutes included the teaching or aiding of unlawful acts. This type of legislation had its origins in the Espionage Act of 1917 and the Sedition Act of 1918, which were prompted in part by the Bolshevik Revolution in Russia. In turn, when the IWW noisily supported this revolution and began efforts to organize the Communist Party of the USA (CPUSA), public opinion swung even more to the suppression of the union.

The national Congress was equally suspicious of the Wobblies and eager to force conformity of patriotism on Americans. On June 15, 1917, Congress enacted the Espionage Act, which forbade aiding the enemy or inciting obstruction of duty in the armed forces. In addition, the postmaster general could exclude from the U.S. Mail any material he deemed treasonous or seditious. The following year, on May 16, Congress enacted the Sedition Act, forbidding any interference with the prosecution of the war. It outlawed willfully employing "disloyal, profane, scurrilous, or abusive language" about the American form of government, its flag, constitution, or the military forces. Penalties for both laws included a $10,000 fine and/or twenty years in prison. Federal officials liberally interpreted both statutes to maximize a concerted drive to destroy the IWW.

As the OWIU increased its recruitment efforts in the Kansas oil fields, petroleum company officials persuaded U.S. attorney Fred Robertson that the union must be crushed. Butler County's oil production was highly important to the war effort and, following the wheat harvest, was buzzing with IWW activity. The county attorney, Robert T. McCluggage, alarmed Kansans when he announced that three thousand IWW members in the oil fields "were threatening riots and pillage." Governor Capper began calling for federal troops, further alarming Fred Robertson, who needed no extra stimulus, as he had been exhilarated with the task of chasing draft dodgers, the teaching of the German language in public schools, and rumors of German sabotage and espionage activities in the Sunflower State.[43]

Becoming convinced, with assistance from petroleum officials, that the IWW planned "to tie up the entire industry," Robertson decided a good offense was a good defense: Wobbly officials needed to be incarcerated before they performed their nefarious deeds. Convinced of the accuracy of their own statistics, federal officials constructed a "large bull pen" in Augusta, and when it was completed, Robertson struck. In what was described as "one of the greatest roundups of IWW agitators ever undertaken in the Middle West," Robertson's agents arrested and charged twenty-seven Wobblies. Anticipating perhaps hundreds of arrests later, five secret service officials invaded the IWW tent headquarters and seized "much literature containing anti-war propaganda," charging those arrested with vagrancy. The "whipping of IWW members at Tulsa," the newspaper editor explained, had "augmented the IWW forces from Oklahoma" who came to Augusta. The raid led to "hundreds of agitators" being scattered, and they "were expected to land in other towns." Wichita was preparing for a number of them to arrive.[44]

After consulting with U.S. district judge John C. Pollock, Robertson finally indicted the men for violation of the Espionage Act by obstructing the recruitment of military personnel and the flow of the supply of war goods, namely wheat and oil. Once the men were incarcerated, Robertson was in no hurry to draft charges, and it ultimately took him two years to do the task properly, with the assistance of Judge Pollock, clearly a violation of the Sixth Amendment guarantee of a "speedy and public trial." Judge Pollock fixed exorbitant bail, ranging from $4,500 to $10,000, depending on what he considered to be their individual menace to society. After eighteen months of adverse publicity, Pollock relented and reduced some of the bail to $500, but the IWW still could not raise their bond.

The federal government had no facilities in Kansas in which to detain accused persons, so the victims were housed in Sedgwick and other nearby county jails. Some of these facilities were in such deplorable condition that adverse publicity, especially after exposure in a national journal, forced officials to move them to other facilities. A federal prison official described the Sedgwick jail as "unfit for animals." The roof leaked badly, the plumbing failed to work, and rats, roaches, and bedbugs were rampant. The most revolting aspect, though, was the thirty-five-ton giant cylinder to house prisoners. It consisted of two floors, each containing V-shaped cells six feet wide on the outside and twenty-two inches on the inside, six feet eight inches long and seven feet high. It was virtually escape-proof as the cage had to be rotated to align any cell with the single door on each floor. Living in this medieval institution was a nightmare, especially for those on the first floor. Some of the prisoners were finally moved to the Shawnee County jail, where the bathtub was described as "black as a boiler." A dungeon in the basement for "recalcitrant" prisoners alarmed inspectors. Health officials eventually forced a remodeling of these facilities, but it was too late for the Wobblies. After two years of living in this environment with victims of tuberculosis mingling with healthy inmates, the terrible wartime influenza struck them heavily. The inmates complained that the doctor was always tardy and drunk when summoned to treat them and always prescribed the same pink pill for whatever malady.[45]

While in the Shawnee County jail, they became acquainted with Pietro Perri, an Italian who had served an eighteen-month term in Leavenworth for preaching "sedition" to Michigan miners. While in prison, he and cell mates planned to assassinate the president. Two of the convicts revealed this plan to the warden, and Secret Service agents trailed Perri to Chicago, where "he had meetings with several alleged anarchists in a little statuary shop." The agents followed him for several weeks and arrested him in Cleveland. He was held in Topeka to await action by the grand jury, which indicted him and twenty-five other plotters. It was believed that Robertson had "at all times complete information about Perri" and the assassination plot.[46]

The Robertson delay in prosecution stemmed in part from the U.S. attorney's belief that the Wobbly menace had ended when the IWW leaders were jailed and from the IWW attorney delays in the hopes the federal government would relent on prosecution, especially after the war ended. Another reason was the federal strategy of prosecuting the national leaders in Chicago first and using those trials as a precedent. Once Judge Kenesaw Mountain Landis completed his sentencing in the Windy City, including Big Bill Haywood, who later jumped his bail and fled to Russia, those prosecutors moved to the Kansas City trials.[47]

Caroline Lowe assisted the chief attorney for the Wobblies,

George Vanderveer. The prosecutor presented confiscated books on sabotage from the Augusta raid as well as inflammatory IWW literature and two incriminating letters from IWW secretary Phineas Eastman denouncing conscription as "bloodsucking and cowardly." The final indictments charged them with violating the Espionage Law and the Lever Food and Fuel Control Act of August 10, 1918. IWW lawyers stunned the courtroom when the accused insisted they would offer no defense, a position in line with IWW philosophy that doing so constituted political action.

The Department of Justice, dissatisfied with Robertson's handling of the case from the beginning, finally appointed Samuel B. Amidon, a Wichita criminal lawyer active in Democratic politics, to assist him. During the Democratic National Convention of 1920, Amidon and attorney Jouett Shouse were described as two Kansans of national stature in their party. They were "part and parcel" of the Wilson administration, and "not a single move is made by [Virginia politician] Carter Glass and other Wilson leaders until the two Kansas leaders are consulted."[48]

Frank P. Wermke, shipped in from the Chicago trial as a paid witness, provided the prosecution's most important testimony as he asserted he had participated in Wobbly sabotage and violence. While working as a migrant farmhand, he claimed to have assisted in an IWW jailbreak and to have placed phosphorous in wheat stacks, scoop shovels in threshing machines, and bolts and spikes in wheat fields to break machinery.[49]

The case of *United States v. C. W. Anderson et al.* finally came to trial when the national attitude had changed from the ultra-patriotic spirit of the world war to the more invidious one of the "Big Red Scare," when Americans became paralyzed with fear of communism. National labor unrest fed hysteria over the spread of Bolshevism and revolution. The IWW added to these fears by strongly endorsing the revolutionary events in Russia and organizing the CPUSA. As early as the summer of 1918, Governor Capper sent a warning to mayors of Kansas towns to be on the lookout for Wobblies because he had heard that "a large body . . . were threatening to invade the state." If that happened, he expected to call out the home guards. "It has been clearly shown," he insisted, "that this organization is thoroughly disloyal in principle and in practice."[50]

In Reno County a vigilante committee of the local American Legion unit visited six suspected IWW members. The patriotic group explained: "We are doing what is not in line with law and order. Sometimes it is necessary to take shortcuts through red tape." The men swore they were not Wobblies and were released. The legion posted messages on main roads in the county declaring that "Hutchinson and Reno counties are, and we intend they shall remain[,] 100 percent American in every particular. We hereby serve notice that no IWW, 'parlor' Bolshevist or agitators may land in Reno." The Pratt County Home Guard began wearing uniforms and carrying guns with the expectation of being called out "at any time." They were drilling twice a week and planned to stand guard over the wheat after it was stacked and to keep an eye out for IWW members. Sheriff John H. Griffin apprehended and arrested ten men from Nebraska because he believed they were draft dodgers and one of them wore an IWW badge.[51]

Ten farmers, one banker, and one cattleman heard the evidence in the Wichita trial. Robertson quizzed all of them carefully to determine if they believed in established government and the laws of the country. Fred Robertson specifically asked each one if he was a member of the Nonpartisan League. Some of the evidence they viewed were "silent agitators" or gum-backed stickers that read, "Slow down the hours are long, the pay is small. So take your time and buck them all." The Butler County sheriff testified that these stickers were posted all over his county. Still, the jury deliberated a surprising twenty hours before delivering a guilty verdict.

After being incarcerated for eighteen months, one of the accused died of influenza, two of them were committed for insanity, and four who had been released earlier on personal recognizance failed to appear for the trial. Although Eugene Debs received a presidential pardon as a Christmas present in 1921, many of these Wobblies languished in prison for several more years as the federal government sought to punish the "political prisoners" long after the end of the war by forcing them to serve their full terms as an example of what happens to lawbreakers.[52]

The day after the Kansas IWW members were sentenced, a group of superpatriots met in Topeka and formed the National One Hundred Percent American Club. Dr. Frank L. Loveland became its leader, and other members included state attorney general Richard J. Hopkins and public utilities commissioner W. L. Huggins. The club announced its creed as "Autocracy Breeds Socialism—Socialism Breeds Bolshevism—Bolshevism Breeds IWWism—IWWism Breeds Anarchy—and Anarchy Breeds Hell." The preamble noted that the club's purpose was "to coordinate the work begun by [Seattle mayor Ole] Hanson, Coolidge . . . and the federal government." Its membership, they generously declared, was not limited to those who had served in the armed forces during the war, as none of them had either.[53]

A Wobbly soon tested the Kansas criminal syndicalist law. The Butler County attorney petitioned his district court to enjoin the IWW from operating in the Sunflower State, and the state supreme court sustained a permanent injunction against the union's activities. The high court stressed the importance of the production of oil and wheat, even though the war had ended, and noted that "if successful in their efforts, they could paralyze two essential industries, not only of the state, but of the nation." Their decision reached the state supreme court as *Fiske v. Kansas* in 1927. Harold B. Fiske of Washington state worked the wheat fields as an organizer for the AWIU. On June 30, 1923, he accepted two men into membership in the IWW. When arrested, he had IWW materials in his possession and freely admitted he was an organizer. The state supreme court conceded that the preamble to the IWW constitution did not advocate violence, but the jury could have properly found that Fiske might have interpreted it thusly when he explained it to new recruits. In an unusual interpretation the Kansas court held that Fiske's free speech had not been violated because "penalizing advocacy of violence in bringing about governmental changes does not violate constitutional guarantees." During his trial no evidence was introduced to demonstrate he had actually interpreted the IWW preamble to advocate violence.[54]

The U.S. Supreme Court unanimously reversed the state court. After carefully examining the IWW preamble, the justices found it did not advocate force or violence as a means of industrial or political change. The criminal syndicalist law had been applied to his activities without evidence that the Wobblies advocated "any crime, violence, or other unlawful acts," and his conviction was "an arbitrary and unreasonable exercise of the state's police power."[55]

Despite the loss of their state leaders in Fred Robertson's roundup, iww recruiting activity continued in the wheat fields in the summer following the armistice. William Benson was arrested in Yates Center on his way to the oil fields near El Dorado. He planned a committee meeting "at which the assassin was to be selected," the *Topeka Daily Capital* editor alleged, "to kill United States Attorney Fred Robertson [and this] has added weight to the iww problem." Although the Wobblies were active in the El Dorado area, with four tents as headquarters, they were left alone "as long as no violence was being committed." They had located there because efforts to reestablish the headquarters in Augusta "were futile." Several federal agents in the region reported conditions as "bad." Chief of police Mose Burch reported overhearing an iww official state that recruiting was going to proceed and that "they hoped to control the field this summer."[56]

The situation in the wheat fields continued to be serious that summer of 1919, primarily because of a shortage of available labor. Salina officials reported their area was 30 men short of need, and neighboring towns were calling for 1,050 men, an increase of "250 over yesterday." Harvest would soon begin west of Russell, increasing the demand of more workers. Patriots found only one iww member, and a veteran "took him roughly, and the idler left town with a black eye and other bruises." That meant one less hand for the Russell harvest. Hutchinson also reported a dearth of harvesters. "We can place 3,000 harvest hands at once alone if we can get them," reported one official. "Probably 150 farmers from Reno County spent the day with their cars parked around the depot awaiting harvest hands," said another. While only one or two iww members were found causing trouble, men who were caught loafing and refusing to work were told to leave town.[57]

On the other hand, high harvest wages were reported as beneficial in defeating the iww that summer. "With wheat dead

ripe," farmers "appear to have lost all idea of the value of a dollar" in their quest to find harvest hands. A farmer near Salina
offered seventy-five cents an hour for workers, and "a little further west . . . the going price was 80 and even 90 cents." One
Ellsworth farmer paid $11 a day, and in Hays it was $15. Between
Russell and Hays, one observer noted, "as far as you can see it is
one field of grain to be harvested." Even with their women helping, there was "only about one-tenth enough" labor to bring in
the crop. The report noted that the state fire marshal had a large
group empowered with enforcing the law, and this was the reason for "no disorder."[58]

On the same day "war to the knife" was declared in McPherson County, the county officers were given permission to arrest
suspects for any reason. Even the city police were questioning
and searching "all men who do not immediately go to the fields
upon arrival." The county attorney was prepared to "swear in any
number of special officers to get the desired effect" of sufficient
workers. One wonders if this policy might not affect the amount
of manpower available for the wheat fields.[59]

Robertson appeared before a special session of the state legislature to secure an emergency appropriation to fund federal-state
cooperation in meeting the IWW menace. Labor commissioner
John Crawford responded to Robertson's warning with the observation that the IWW "was not at work in Kansas." Following the
1919 harvest, however, officials in Hays arrested Harry Mallory,
who had "inside information from IWW headquarters" in his possession. Mallory allegedly was instructed to wait until two weeks
after the wheat harvest "before starting the campaign which is
expected to put fear in the hearts of the wheat growers" by destroying their crops and equipment. How this would hurt the harvest
two weeks afterward was not explained, but officials stated it was
thought that such destruction would occur after the fact, "with
greater safety to the men who apply the match." It appeared to
be a strange plot.[60]

Three months later an Oscar Swayze wrote the *Topeka State
Journal* that Caroline Lowe, in Kansas to defend the IWW, "was
very ignorant of this bunch of nondescripts, else their printed pro-

paganda is a mere camouflage." Their literature not only urged
the destruction of "property, government, and life," he insisted,
but "they also advise the bayoneting of babies, and the seizing
and use of pretty maidens to their hellish lust." This "lawyeress
woman ought to tell the truth," he insisted, "and not attempt to
gloss over the cussedness of the IWW."[61]

Selig Perlman and Philip Taft, in their *History of Labor*, began
a scholarly tradition in 1932, when they stated that the Wobbly
trials had cost the IWW its leaders, their organizational efforts
ended, and their rather abrupt decline commenced. This interpretation was maintained by later labor historians, but it does not
hold true in the West Coast states and certainly not in Kansas.
The early 1920s saw a resurgence in the IWW ranks, and it was
not until 1924 that a philosophical split among members led to
a decline from which the union never recovered. The organization was not "as dynamic as it was in 1916 or 1917," but it was
revitalized after the war and witnessed a significant increase in
numbers and influence.[62]

Education and IWW publications fired this resurrection of the
union cause, in addition to the continuing problem of maintaining Wobbly membership. Harvest hands worked briefly during
the summer months and either needed to save enough money
during that period to "winter over" in a cheap flophouse in Kansas City or, more commonly, to migrate to the oil fields, to the
garden crops of California, or to the forests of the Northwest to
seek work. For any of these choices, there was an obvious need
by the union to have the men maintain their membership. To
address this problem, the AWIU changed the use of stickers to con-
vey its messages in the war years to using leaflets of a more complex nature. With titles such as *You Need Industrial Unionism*, *The
Two Triple Alliances*, and *Agriculture, the Mother Industry*, the union
sought not only to arouse interest in improving immediate conditions but to "stimulate a collective class-consciousness" among
harvest workers by identifying their common cultural experience
as workers. This initiative, they reasoned, would focus workers'
attention on a future society that would meet their needs. Agriculture was the foundation of society, and the union must adapt

itself to this way of life. In 1922 the IWW published *Hang On to Your Life Belt*, which was designed to encourage the continuation of membership after the harvest was completed no matter where workers migrated. They established a universal transfer of membership for those who would winter over, migrate to other work, or become day laborers.[63]

The serious recession of 1920–22, especially in agriculture, added impetus to this new policy, when large numbers of urban workers in automobile and other manufacturing industries began migrating to seek employment on the Great Plains. It also opened opportunities for increased memberships. At the annual meeting in 1921, the AWIU endorsed the policy of seeking improvements for harvest workers; pledged support to fellow Wobblies still in prison; funded a permanent hall in Kansas City, Missouri; and agreed that mass membership conventions pulled workers off their jobs if they believed they had an obligation to attend. To alleviate this problem, they established a Republican form of electing delegates to represent them at annual or other meetings. Their strategy in Kansas that summer called for recruiters to avoid large towns and concentrate on the workers in the countryside. As a result, 1921 was a banner year for the IWW as the number of laborers who were harvest Wobblies pushed the wage up to $5 or more. But it was not all "sweetness and light" in the Kansas wheat fields; authorities maintained their opposition to the union that had begun during the war.[64]

Law officers continued to suppress the IWW during the 1920 harvest. Just before harvest began, 200 peace officers met in Hutchinson to plan countermeasures for the "trouble makers." If reinforcements were needed, the state fire marshal commissioned 250 special agents to maintain a round-the-clock vigil of the wheat fields. They were there also to sell fire insurance if the demand arose. At the same time a Butler County court invoked the state's criminal syndicalism law by reminding the Wobblies that its members were "restrained and enjoined from . . . carrying on their unlawful practices in the State of Kansas." The judge's timing for his pronouncement "made it impossible for the IWW to seek legal redress until after the harvest had ended."[65]

Officials reported a plethora of hands in 1920, with "overwhelming numbers and every freight train . . . bringing more hordes."
Anthony, Arkansas City, Caldwell, Medicine Lodge, and Winfield "were crowded with men," and county agents were discour-
aging further immigration. "Many of them had money to buy
a bed," it was noted, but "could find none at any price." It was
estimated that one hundred combined thresher-harvesters would
be operating in Kansas that year. Rock Island special agent Ben
Judkins arrested Steve Gain, an iww member, and the county
jailer found a membership card and some clippings from Wobbly newspapers in his cap. He had joined three days earlier and
was given number 719,283. Judge Rad M. Lee fined him $100
and gave him sixty days in jail on the charge of vagrancy. There
was sufficient labor, with 30 percent of workers veterans of World
War I and "a fair portion of students," to assist farmers and still
keep the going wage of seventy cents.[66]

Governor Henry Allen received letters from harvest hands that
restaurant owners were taking advantage of the surplus labor by
raising prices. They bought eggs at twenty-six cent a dozen and
served "two eggs, two thin slices of bread and a glass of water for
25 cents." There were no other places for the men to eat, and "the
prices are highway robbery." The labor commissioner, John H.
Crawford, received a letter from six men at Kingman who said
they had agreed to work for seventy cents but were being "jewed"
down. A convention of farmers in Hutchinson had agreed upon
seventy cents, the writer complained, and "if the farmers are going
to go back on their promise, is it not a fact that they are worse
than the iww they denounce?" Crawford thought this practice
"would give us a bad name among farm laborers next season."[67]

So many migrants could not find work that year that Hutchinson
was forced to reestablish its long dormant soup kitchen because
hundreds of unemployed workers were still there. The American Legion post gave the migrants free lodging, and the Salva-
tion Army was providing food. The advertisements for labor at
$7 a day attracted a large number of men, and the city finally
had to intervene and help feed them. Many of the men who had
been promised seventy cents refused to work for lower wages.[68]

Sheriff Alex Welz of Hays made a highly successful raid on a "complete IWW outfit" in the group's nearby jungle. He captured a ledger showing that "Gen Secy C. L. Johnson" had "taken in $4,420 since May first." The cache included "General Defense Stamps" of $7,430 and "IWW stamps" worth $11,750. Johnson escaped the raid, and W. E. Townsend, an organizer, was reported to have offered $2,500 "for possession of the black bag and its contents."[69]

The AWIU laid plans for the next year, raising the commission for new members from fifty cents to a dollar, hoping this would "spur the enthusiasm of the several hundred delegates" the union would place in the Midwest in 1921. Law enforcement officials counterattacked by arresting labor organizers "before they established a foothold." Police arrested "scores of IWWs in Kiowa, Hutchinson, Anthony, McPherson, and Kingman, but reports of concealed incendiary devices proved to be unfounded." The Wobbly drive was a huge success, with 13,000 new members that year, "4,000–6,000" of whom came from Kansas alone, "the greatest number of new initiates in the state since 1916." As a result, the union could renew vigorous bargaining for improved working conditions and higher wages. This, in turn, gave impetus to the OWIU in recruiting new oil workers in the Mid-Continent Oil Field area.[70]

Hot summer weather ripened the wheat crop at least two weeks early in the 1921 season, and the harvest was ready to begin, although there was a shortage of workers in the area. The Kansas State Farm Bureau had helped recruit labor in the 1920 season, so Charles R. Weeks, its secretary, sent out emergency calls to chambers of commerce and labor offices in eastern Kansas and western Missouri for additional labor. No state labor conference was held nor a wage pattern set, although several county and sectional meetings were conducted to agree on the wage scale of the previous year's $3. But the early harvest and the shortage of labor changed this calculation. As a result, local authorities began a "work or go to jail" policy in Hutchinson. Every man found "loafing" would receive police assistance in finding harvest employment. Harvest hands were reportedly "grabbed by farmers as fast as they arrive." Haskell County farmers were "meeting all trains" in nearby towns and "grabbing hands as they alight." Instead of $3, they were receiving $4, $5, "and even as high as $6 for good men." This meant, one report observed, that "the wage has practically doubled since the start [of harvest]."[71]

The state of Kansas declared war on "all iww organizers" in 1922. Governor Henry Allen and state fire marshal Lew T. Hussey called on sheriffs and county attorneys of fifteen wheat counties to meet in Hutchinson in late June "to deal with the menace." Twenty organizers had already been arrested, and authorities found "every indication that a concerted and well organized movement is afoot to terrorize the wheat fields." Authorities had been arresting men in Wichita and Hutchinson for two weeks under the state's criminal syndicalism law. The "terrorism" of high wages caused by a shortage of labor the previous year would not be repeated. "These organizers preach sabotage and incendiarism, urge the workers, no matter what pay is offered, to keep asking for more, and as soon as their demands are refused, then sabotage is supposed to start," decried the *Topeka Daily Capital* on June 27. In Colby and McFarland iww members suffered beatings, "a regression to the brutality of the immediate postwar years."[72]

In 1923 Harry Feinberg, secretary of the iww General Defense Committee, wrote "many letters" across the state asking citizens to protest to Governor Jonathan Davis that Wobblies were being prosecuted in Kansas without just cause. Attorney general C. B. Griffith responded that the Sunflower State would continue to be "an unhealthy place for reds" in the coming harvest. If evidence reached his office "that anyone is teaching these doctrines," the state law enforcement agencies would "have no hesitancy in continuing to . . . enforce the law [of syndicalism] against such activities."[73]

The success of the awiu provided support for a campaign of recruiting in the oil fields. By 1922 the owiu had forty-five men working alongside the oil migrant workers in the Mid-Continent Field. "In March that year their efforts had secured enough new dues payers to establish that union's financial autonomy for the first time in its existence." At the same time the owiu was emphasiz-

ing retaining members as much as recruiting new ones. It reduced
the payment of recruiters from a dollar back to fifty cents but set
a corresponding 50 percent cut in monthly dues, which "encouraged the migrants to remain in good standing" with the union.
While it declined somewhat in adding new recruits, it enjoyed
an increase of three thousand in the number of dues payments.[74]

The following year was again an active one for the AWIU. A
shortage of "1,300 men" worked to the advantage of the union.
"Reports here that higher wages are being paid in western counties" meant a shortage of hands in central Kansas. Salina had witnessed the arrest of only one Wobbly, Fred Van Etten of Denver,
who was soon released. One week after this report, fifty IWW
members "stormed" the Salina jail to demand the release of organizer A. M. Shea. They were repulsed and promised to return
with "500 members" the next day to force his release. The police
judge, however, soon released Shea.[75]

The state began a more aggressive campaign in 1923 to provide
a free employment service. Presiding judge John H. Crawford,
of the soon-to-be-defunct Court of Industrial Relations and federal director of the U.S. Employment Service, toured the Southwest and predicted a bumper wheat crop and high prices. Harvest
had begun, and "hundreds of harvest hands are being distributed
daily in this territory," he announced, by "the free employment
agency." Wichita authorities were pleased that police chief T. J.
Thompson's policy of "work or jail" was functioning well. Word
of it "spread among hundreds of floaters congregated around
railroad centers," and soon "not a single 'harvest hand' unwilling to work was found." "Over 100 floaters" left town "rather
than spend a few weeks on the municipal farm."[76]

By 1924 the automobile and the combine were beginning to
revolutionize the harvest fields. AWIU organizers began complaining about the difficulty of recruiting "auto tramps" into the
union. These workers utilized the mobility that a secondhand
Ford gave them to move from job to job, camping along the
highway at night. This mobility lessened their solidarity, and
their absence from the jungles meant less contact and less presence on the freight trains. The combine—the joining together

of the cutting and threshing processes—eliminated their wheat shocking jobs, although the large expenses of this machinery unfortunately reduced farm profits. Fifteen thousand combines were used in Kansas fields in 1927 and cut the farmers' harvesting costs in half.[77]

Curiously, the Fiske decision of 1927 contributed significantly to the disintegration of the IWW. The emergence of a dissident group, known as the Emergency Program, disagreed with the IWW's leadership. These purists insisted that legal defense activities were illegitimate and those who espoused them were "politicians." These people were expelled at the 1924 annual meeting, and they held their own convention the following year, resolving that "the recourse to legal technicalities, kowtowing to master class courts, and the building up of funds to keep a lot of worthless pie-cards in office has proved its uselessness." The IWW never recovered from this deep split and disintegrated, never again to become a factor in American labor history.[78]

The IWW had a significant impact on Kansas, especially in the wheat and oil fields and in their financial success. The AWO and AWIU branches provided half the income received by the parent union during their existence, and the OWIU became self-sufficient. Their apogee coincided with the World War I era of intolerance and the Big Red Scare afterward, and the public interpreted their weapons of protest and sabotage as signs that their members were disloyal and unpatriotic. The Wobblies greatly alleviated the situation of those abused migratory harvest hands, but as Peterson and Fite have observed, they were destroyed in Kansas by "a conservative people who displayed an intemperance that would do credit to the wildest of radicals."[79]

7

THE LOSING SOCIALISTS

Arthur C. Townley founded the Nonpartisan League (NPL) in North Dakota in 1915 and directed its activities for seven years before resigning. By that time the organization was no longer viable, but during its heyday it established the only state government to carry out the Socialist ideals of government-owned industries, yielded to the Farmer-Labor Party legacy in Minnesota, and had a brief, flamboyant struggle for existence in Kansas. It was killed in the Sunflower State largely because opponents were successful in stigmatizing it as pro-German and unpatriotic, similar to the fate they dealt the Wobblies.[1]

Townley was born on a farm in northwestern Minnesota, taught school for two years after graduating from high school, then joined his brother in farming in northwestern North Dakota. They first raised wheat but turned to the profitable crop of flax and bought expensive machinery. Then disaster struck one year with an early frost and unprecedented snowstorms. Townley went bankrupt, became bitter, worked as a plasterer's helper, and became something of a tramp, traveling from North Dakota to the Pacific Ocean. He joined the Socialist Party but seemed unable to get along with its members because they thought he was not "sound."[2]

During this period Townley learned firsthand of agricultural problems. The railroads were charging exorbitant fees, and elevators along their rights-of-way were cheating farmers on grading their grain and in charging drayage and other fees. Banks were levying interest on mortgaged farms and chattel of as much as 40 percent, which meant farmers could go broke easily with one bad crop year. The machinery and twine trusts, as the name implies, had monopolies on their products. Lawyers protected their clients, the railroads, the grain dealers, and the bankers, through legalities and lobbying and serving in the legislatures and regulatory agencies. The Republican Party had a stranglehold on all branches of North Dakota government. Townley once unburdened himself of his philosophy rather succinctly when he said, "If you put a lawyer, a banker, and an industrialist in a barrel and roll it downhill, there'll always be a son-of-a-bitch on top."[3]

Immediately after the NPL gained sufficient strength, North Dakota Socialists pursued a program of government-owned mills and elevators and a rural credits plan to loan money to farmers at low interest rates. Farmers were particularly frustrated at this point because they had twice approved referendums providing for state-owned terminal elevators and the legislature had taken no action on their proposals.[4]

Socialists soon discovered their approach was more popular in the rural areas (where voters dominated) than was their party appeal, so they created an "organization department" whereby nonmembers could belong without signing the red card. This arrangement was more to his liking, and Townley became an organizer for the new department, driving a Model T Ford around the countryside, holding meetings, and selling Socialist literature. Signers had to pledge to support political candidates who favored the state program. Soon the department had more members than the party, and it was discontinued because "the tail would soon be wagging the dog." Townley was disgusted over this development and over party political strategy but had another purpose for organizing farmers. He wanted to control the primary process through nonpartisan action.[5]

An interesting speaker, Townley's "persuasive influence was electrifying," whether he was talking to an individual or a group. Public speaking was not a strength, but he was able to engage an audience, and he spoke the "farmer's language." He excelled in dry humor, used ridicule effectively, and "woe unto him who tried the heckling game." Decrying corporate wealth, and with a dose of irony and sarcasm, he usually won the crowd over. He charged $16 to join the NPL, with $6 required up front; the fee was often paid with a postdated check for October, after the harvest. For this sum members also received the organization's newspaper, the *Ellsworth County Leader*.[6]

He sent organizers with training in psychology and instructions out in Fords to "find out the damn fool's hobby and then talk it. If he likes religion, talk Jesus Christ; if he is against the government, damn the Democrats; if he is afraid of whiskey, preach prohibition; if he wants to talk hogs, talk hogs—talk anything he'll listen to, but talk, talk, talk until you get his God-damn John Henry on a check for sixteen dollars." Everyone had a grievance against big business. Townley often let slip a cuss word against trusts, and this did not harm him in wheat country.[7]

Townley's concept was rather simple in principle: farmers were too busy and too scattered to act efficiently as individuals, so organize them, seize control of the direct primaries, elect league supporters of whatever persuasion, and teach the members to trust their leaders to make the right decisions for them. Farmers constituted a vast majority of voters but were exploited by professional politicians, who knew they could never stick together for long. Townley constantly asked, "Will you stick?" and after a lengthy haranguing, they would yell back, "We'll stick." Only "through tight organization could the farmers ever achieve their objectives," he once opined. Normally, farmers would be gathered into a local meeting wherever facilities could be obtained. There they selected delegates to attend a district meeting, during which shouts of "We'll stick" accompanied the stomping of boots. The league caucus would then select candidates to run or to support in the direct primaries, and the farmers would vote for them regardless of whether they were Republicans or Democrats. Their aim was to capture the primary and endorse the candidates who agreed to support the league's program. Often the delegates chosen were farmers inexperienced in politics when the league could not find a supportive major party candidate.[8]

The Republican State Convention in 1916 was held in Fargo in late March. Beforehand each delegate suggested candidates for state office, and their names were written on a blackboard. All were discussed thoroughly, with input from league speakers and organizers. The delegates then voted by secret ballot. Lynn J. Frazier, an unknown Republican farmer, was nominated for governor, and others who had expressed agreement with the league's program were named for state offices. The nominating process was followed by dozens of speeches, then a Saturday night parade of two thousand farmers, with bands and fireworks.[9]

A largely Republican state ticket could hardly lose in North Dakota, and Townley made certain of it by calling for precinct meetings "to canvass every nook and cranny" to get out the farm vote. Frazier won rather handily, and the league's supporters captured control of the lower house. The state senate, with longer terms, would have to wait two years to complete Socialist plans. In the elections of 1918 the NPL secured "a clean sweep of all three branches of the state government," along with approval of amendments to the state constitution giving the state power to enact the NPL's program.[10]

The legislature that met in January 1919 generally voted for the laws the league's caucus recommended. It created an Industrial Commission to manage state enterprises and established a state Bank of North Dakota to provide low-cost rural credits for farmers, to finance state departments and enterprises, and to serve as a clearinghouse for state banks. Another measure set up the North Dakota Mill and Elevator Association to install "a system of warehouses, elevators, flour mills, factories, plants, machinery, and equipments [sic]." This law left the number, size, and location of these units to the discretion of the Industrial Commission. The Home Building Association was a state-controlled building and loan business, and the state Hail Insurance put that system on an acreage tax basis. Unless specifically withdrawn from the system, this protection levied a flat tax of three cents per acre annually on farms, and a commissioner would determine how much additional tax would be needed to cover losses each year. Finally, taxes were removed on all agricultural improvements.[11]

These ideas were quickly exported to Minnesota, the neighboring state to the east. The program there was not successful, but the movement eventually emerged as the Farmer-Labor political party in the 1930s. The NPL was reported to have invaded South Dakota "in a forcible way." A friend of South Dakota governor Peter Norbeck told him they were coming in like "a swarm of grasshoppers." The Republican Norbeck cleverly outmaneuvered this movement in his state by taking the offensive. He persuaded his legislature to propose amending the state constitution to permit South Dakota to enter certain kinds of businesses. He then attacked Socialists as "radicals" and asserted that his program was "simply cooperative." After amending the state constitution, he persuaded his solons to establish a state-owned cement plant and a coal mine and, most important, a state rural credits plan. He appealed to Kansas governor Henry J. Allen, writing, "I believe the best way to meet the League proposition is to give the farmers every reasonable thing they ask for and to refuse to go with them on the impracticable." Allen rejected this sound advice and met the NPL head on, fighting their fire with the fire of patriotism. He ultimately won but with disastrous consequences for his state.[12]

Some voices and faces familiar to radical elements in the Sunflower State resurfaced when the NPL moved southward. Walter Thomas Mills, upon his retirement from league work and return to teaching in California, wrote a letter to both Townley and the NPL that the *Ellsworth County Leader*, the official NPL newspaper, printed on its front page. Mills had lectured all over the country for the NPL from December 27, 1917, to November 3, 1920. "During these thousand and forty-five days," he remarked, "I have spoken over twelve hundred times," a circuit that involved traveling seventy thousand miles, some twenty thousand of them in a Ford. He recalled his "framed-up arrest" and acquittal on charges of sedition and having been kidnapped twice, "on one occasion most brutally treated by mobs which had been expressly organized by the public authorities under the direction of [the] Chamber of Commerce." He would continue to work for the NPL but no doubt was eager to return to the peace and quiet of the classroom.[13]

Elmer T. Peterson charged that Townley and NPL secretary Arthur Le Sueur, who was an attorney for the Industrial Workers of the World and played an important role in the Mesabi Strike in 1916, negotiated an agreement with the Wobblies on July 21, 1917. Le Sueur was quoted as telling AWIU representatives that the farmers of North Dakota would be willing to pay $5 for a ten-hour day and if the union and the NPL could come to an agreement on this, the IWW and NPL would wrest control from state government. Le Sueur would later come to a parting of the ways with the NPL in North Dakota when he argued, rightly so, that the North Dakota Industrial Commission should be staffed with directors elected specifically to those offices. When Townley succeeded in holding out for a three-man board of state officials selected from different departments, Le Sueur promptly resigned in disgust because he believed the commission should not become involved in politics.[14]

The Department of Justice solicited the opinion of Kansas governor Arthur Capper on charges of NPL disloyalty. Capper reported that "the League was comporting itself in accordance with law and the war needs of the nation." Later, when the NPL was required to present written references to rent offices for its headquarters in Topeka, Governor Capper and Tom McNeal, editor of *Capper's Farmer*, "came to its assistance." This action "probably was partly responsible for Capper's carrying all of the 105 counties in the primary election" that year.[15]

Phil E. Zimmerman, a Lindsborg traveling salesman, told a different story. He had witnessed the league's operation in North Dakota and began speaking to Kansas civic groups about the NPL menace in the spring of 1918. He warned them "the Bolshiviki had landed" and described both the IWW and the NPL as "the tools of the Kaiser." During a presentation in Topeka, he quoted from a fictitious Wobbly oath that members must hold "in supreme contempt all institutions of Capitalism, including ecclesiastical and secular, and its laws, its flag, its courts, its codes, its churches and religions." Zimmerman carried on his campaign for three years, hitting the banquet circuit while serving the state fire marshal as a guard against IWW activities. Because of lack of financial support, the "field secretary of the Kansas Anti-Bolshivist campaign," as he was labeled, believed he had to move to another state to continue his operations. In three years his organization had received $7,500 in support. In contrast, he observed, the NPL "this year has separated the farmers in one Kansas county from more than $36,000; and from the entire state have taken out more than a half million dollars." He believed he could not expect success against those odds.[16]

This conservative success in pinning the IWW label on the Non-partisan League led a great majority of Kansas media to denounce the organization and its goals. Soon after the first local league was organized at Hedville in Saline County, on July 13, 1917, with A. J. Dille as the local chairman, William Allen White's *Emporia Gazette* denounced it as the "Hun-partisan League" because it was "pacifist and pro-German at bottom." He compared opposition to the league's principles as "the old Alliance fight twenty-seven years ago," back when he wrote his famous, or infamous, essay "What's the Matter with Kansas," only now he also applied the unpatriotic tag to the league.[17]

NPL organizer J. M. Brewer successfully organized locals in Ellsworth, Lincoln, and Rice Counties but did not have great success immediately as the farmers were busy with summer work. Robert Morlan states that Brewer's initial efforts in Saline County, with the FU headquarters in Salina and thirty thousand members, received "fairly strong Farmers Union and Cooperative backing." The *Kansas City Star*, however, noted that the FU had some similar ideas of state ownership but was devoting most of its energies "in a different way in organizing farmer-owned cooperatives" in elevators, mills, stores, coal, and lumberyards, and "similar institutions." Brewer, the journal added, "started his organization in the hotbed of the union." The FU would soon exhibit real hostility to the NPL.[18]

Maurice McAuliffe, FU president, became increasingly emphatic in denouncing the NPL. "There isn't any more chance of an amiable affiliation, either formal or informal," he proclaimed, "than there is of a unity of the moon and the sun, and the two associations are just about as far apart." The FU, he added, "has always fought the Nonpartisan League." The FU secretary, when asked about his organization, said the NPL "has views which are purely Socialistic—we are not in politics." While at first many FU members joined the NPL, they had "mostly all dropped out since," he added.[19]

R. L. Cooper, another league organizer, reported "a slick reporter came to the office the other day and represented himself as a young lawyer of this city interested in politics." As a result, he managed to acquire some of the literature and information. The NPL had to guard its literature carefully because "it is often misunderstood in the quarters of the profiteers," he explained. When the reporter's newspaper published his story on the NPL, "even the elevator boys in the New England building in Topeka did not realize the league had been officing there" since July 1917. Believing the opposition was out to cause him trouble, Cooper was defiant. "If they think they can drive me out," he said, "let them hop to it. I don't drive very easy, and I don't scare."[20]

The *Kansas City Star* carried an interesting story with a map of NPL membership in Dickinson, Marion, and western Morris Counties, an area with a heavy German population. Information on the league was difficult to obtain because the organization was "not using publicity." Memberships were sold for $16, but "nobody seems to know just where the $16 goes or how it is divided up," the story continued. Members informed the newspaper correspondent that some went to the organization's newspaper, the *Leader*, part went to the organizer who sold the membership, and part of it went "to the state and general organizations."[21]

"There are twelve hundred members of the League" in Dickinson County, "a well-known politician" told the reporter in Topeka. The correspondent believed that Dickinson County actually had 250 members. The league had about 200 members in Marion County and another 200 in Morris. Most of them were farmers who were very involved with county matters. Some of them supported America's involvement in the war, but it was believed that Germans made up a large majority in Dickinson County. In southern Dickinson, western Morris, and northern Marion Counties they were predominantly citizens of German descent, many with roots going back to the early days of Kansas history. Those in Dickinson, particularly in Herington, were said to be

as "bitterly opposed to the United States in this war as the subjects of the Kaiser in Prussia."[22]

J. M. Fengel, with "one of the best farms in the county," was
a member of the Abilene School Board for six years, a Mason,
a Shriner, and a member of the NPL. He was emphatically not a
Socialist but had joined the NPL "to force a square deal for the
farmer." He would not vote for a candidate who opposed the war
or for a Socialist. "I am a German," he said, "but I am strong
for the United States, which is my country." "Some of the old
Germans in this country are not right on the war," he admitted, because "they cannot break away from their old affections."
Another farmer, when recruited, asked for a list of members in the
area. He was shown a list of thirty, "and every one of them was
German, either by birth or by marriage." Most of the organizers
were either German or Norwegian from North Dakota. Fengel
remembered the organizer telling him "the League would not
go into politics in Kansas this year" because "we are not strong
enough to do anything" at present.[23]

The league never became strong in Kansas. Membership in
Minnesota reached 50,000 in 1919, 40,000 in North Dakota, but
only 11,300 in Iowa, Kansas, Oklahoma, and Texas combined.
The opposition leadership in Kansas was determined to keep it
this way. John Worley, prominent in Topeka affairs and member of the city council, announced in April 1918 that the United
Commercial Travelers of America (UCT), with 40,000 members
in Kansas, would be an active force against the NPL. This organization was certain the league was "disloyal in its acts and propaganda, not only in Kansas but in other states." Worley was named
chair of a special committee to investigate the league. Every member of the UCT "will explain to the thousands of country merchants and other customers" the insidious work of the NPL and
discourage farmers from joining. The NPL was "playing farmers
for suckers," Worley asserted. The league, it was charged, had
twenty organizers working in Kansas and claimed about 30,000
members across the state.[24]

By this time the media had alerted Governor Capper to the
danger the NPL posed to his state. He gave a "patriotic" speech in

Canton, warning its leaders "to remain a patriotic organization" or authorities would deal with it "severely," as it had done with the iww. "In a crisis like this," he warned, "there should be no question about anyone's loyalty." He asked his listeners for German propaganda and suspected seditious acts by NPL members. "We cleaned out the iwws in Kansas last summer," he reminded the audience, "and we are ready for any other crowd that is not absolutely and thoroly [sic] loyal to the government. . . . You have got to line up with Uncle Sam or leave Kansas." He had almost one hundred state guard units who would prevent disloyalty from spreading throughout the state.[25]

One week later the NPL *Leader* fired back a reminder to Capper that he had "placed his approval stamp" on the organization. "Interest was aroused," the state's leading Republican newspaper noted, "in the strange ability of the organizers to separate the farmer from sixteen dollars for a membership card which seemed to promote the millennium, when the same farmers wouldn't waste the gasoline in his family car to attend a Republican, Democrat, or Socialist rally." The NPL was suspect, however, because of its close relationships with the iww and other suspicious groups. L. M. Sheldon, Oklahoma manager of the league, saw "nothing wrong or alarming" in Governor Capper's threat to have the Council of National Defense investigate the NPL. The *State Journal* the next day denied that Capper had ever "directly or indirectly endorsed the league but stated he had directed the Council of Defense in each county to "make a thoro [sic] inquiry into its operations and report to him any utterances or actions . . . that savor of disloyalty in the slightest degree."[26]

The thirty-six business and professional men occupying offices in the New England Building in Topeka were horrified to discover they had a "seditious" neighbor and petitioned the owner to ask the NPL to vacate its office there. The petitioners included "a number of the most prominent attorneys in the city, insurance agents, and others." The owner noted that he could not order the league to vacate as its annual lease had five months yet to run before it expired. "Records of the Red Cross headquarters here," the story noted, failed to show that "Cooper, the state manager and secretary made a contribution to the second war fund drive," an ominous sign of disloyalty.[27]

The first open threat to the NPL came in mid-1919 in Ellis County. League officials in St. Paul sent August Luttenken to recruit in Kansas, and the headquarters in Topeka assigned him to this wheat-producing Democratic county laden with German and Russian farmers. The war had been over for six months, yet Luttenken complained that Ellis County sheriff Alex Weltz had called him to his office and made threats to break up the league in his county because its members were disloyal. Accompanied by labor leader James O. Stevic, Luttenken took NPL literature to the office of attorney general Richard Hopkins and requested that he and Judge S. M. Hawkes extend them protection. "We haven't violated any law," Luttenken asserted, "and have only organized for the future work of the League." How many members do you have in the county? he was asked. Stevic replied, "We have 464 members in that county." He was then asked how many members there were in the state. He carefully responded: "It has been claimed that we have 60,000 members in Kansas. We have not tried to deny that claim and so far as the public is concerned, it can continue to place the figure at 60,000." Judge Hawkes told Luttenken that as long as he did not violate any law, "he should not be interfered with," and he wrote a letter to that effect to Ellis County attorney E. C. Flour.[28]

James O. Stevic was elected president of the Topeka Industrial Council five times and was widely known and respected within organized labor circles. The president of the Kansas State Federation of Labor called a "nonpartisan political meeting" in Emporia in April 1919, and Stevic attended. At this conference he was chosen as temporary chairman of the First Congressional District League unit, and at a meeting at Horton two weeks later, he was elected permanent chairman. He became enthused over the NPL cause and soon became a highly popular speaker for the movement. After traveling the state extensively, he reported that "labor is really getting into action for the coming campaign [of 1920]."[29]

The league grew rapidly in Kansas immediately after the war. Some three thousand farmers attended a rally in Victoria on October 19, 1919, a gathering too large to hold in the hall. Seating was hurriedly thrown up, with the speakers addressing the audience from the hall steps. A sixteen piece farmers' band warmed up the vast crowd for Minnesota labor leader Francis H. Shoemaker and Montana NPL member R. B. Martin, who spoke for three hours. Phil Zimmerman, the "knocking lawyer," as the *Leader* called him, was present, saying "caustic things," but declined to address the throng when given the opportunity.[30]

In a preview of what would happen later, a group moved south to seize O. E. Wood of Lincoln, Nebraska, a farmer and organizer for that state's FU who was describing to an audience in Stafford County how the Nonpartisan League actually operated in North Dakota. Several dozen men rushed in and accosted the chairman, whereupon they "forced a sack over his head, threw him in a car, and with a revolver on each side of his head, drove about four miles in the country to a straw stack, where he was manhandled, the clothes practically torn off his back, and he was forced to go through other degradation." He finally convinced the mob he was not the man they were seeking, and they took him home. They then returned to the meeting and "renewed their attack" with iron bars, two-by-fours, and small projectiles. Meanwhile, the mayor, the sheriff and his deputy, and the city marshal were nowhere to be found. Stevic accompanied Wood to Topeka, where they reported the attack to attorney general Richard Hopkins. He assured them "he had faith in the County Attorney of Stafford County."[31]

It was difficult for the league to win in the court of public opinion or with state officials in Governor Allen's administration. A lawsuit was brought in Stafford County for the kidnapping of a league organizer. The *Topeka Daily Capital* reported that the litigation "really developed into a trial, instead, of the Nonpartisan League itself." The court sustained a motion of the defense to quash the case when the prosecution failed "to show any connection of the defendants with the alleged kidnappers" of the organizer. When the defense attorney asserted that the NPL was "traitorous to the United States and is seditious and unlawful," the crowd "broke out in loud cheers." The reporter did not record the judge reprimanding the lawyer or the crowd. When the prosecutor attempted to prove league loyalty by quoting assistant U.S. secretary of agriculture Carl Vrooman, who had said, "There are more loyal citizens in the Nonpartisan League than in the Republican Party," his assertion "brought an uproar from the big crowd in the courtroom."[32]

In October 1919, 150 farmers first incorporated the *Ellsworth County Leader*. The greatest number of them came from Ellsworth, McPherson, Ottawa, and Saline , Counties, with one-sixth of them from surrounding counties. This area had a higher percentage of foreign-born residents than the state average in 1920, with Czechs, Germans, Russians, and Swedes predominating. Describing itself as a "nonpartisan" supporter of the NPL, it emblazoned on its front page "We Are Of the Farmer; By the Farmer; and For the Farmer; not to the detriment of others, but for the *betterment* of all." The *Leader* resembled the official national paper and offered numerous editorials, news coverage, and cartoons, presenting the aims of the league and the evils it was fighting. It spent a great deal of space denying that the NPL was "Socialistic, Bolshevistic, and sympathetic to the IWW." The newspaper pointed to the state-owned printing plant, which had saved the state "$90,000 each year on the state's printing alone," as an example of exemplary socialism.[33]

After the league headquarters moved from Salina to Topeka, editor M. L. Amos and the *Leader* promoters decided to move the paper from Ellsworth to the larger town of Salina, after some Saline County farmers pledged further financial support. One hundred and fifty-two shares, "represented in person," voted unanimously for the move, and they asked each subscriber to solicit one new reader to help defray the costs of the transfer. The newspaper was renamed the *Kansas Leader*.[34]

M. L. Amos, Walter Thomas Mills, Stevic, and Jay McFadden of Stafford were scheduled to speak at an NPL picnic in Ellinwood, in the central Kansas county of Barton. The league was gaining strength in Barton County, with 606 members; Dickinson ranked second, with 359; Marion had 340; and Saline had 317. The opposition became increasingly concerned over this growth. T.

B. Kelley, chairman of the Vigilance Committee of Great Bend, wrote to George Klein, the NPL organizer at Ellinwood, that the veterans of Great Bend would not tolerate the meeting of the league. "We do not desire any violence," he wrote, "and so take this means of informing you of what we intend to do." Veterans were to be on hand to help prevent the NPL from staging a public event. Three hundred veterans heard Mills speak, and "after a lively battle," the "mob" took Mills, Stevic, and Amos prisoners and drove them to Great Bend. While there, they were "subjected to innumerable indignities," held in the stockyards, then taken to the train station. On the way the three were carrying the American flag when the mob rotten-egged them.[35]

The *Hutchinson News* carried a story that certain documents were found on Stevic and Mills that purportedly demonstrated that the NPL was "scheming to get control of the state." Copies of *Solidarity* were found, as was a letter written by NPL organizer J. L. Coates of Greenburg to Stevic explaining the plan. The NPL had a married woman in Kiowa County, a forty-year-old schoolteacher who belonged to the NPL and was a "good talker." Perhaps she could be persuaded to run for the state legislature, not as an NPL candidate but "simply as an ambitious person." The same tactic could be used throughout the state where NPL members were to be found. This plan did not constitute a radical plot "to gain control of the state," as the headline proclaimed.[36]

The following day the *Great Bend Tribune* editorialized that "if the Nonpartisan League grows and prospers in Barton County it will be only after the last member of the American Legion, and they are several hundred strong, are safely dead and buried." Farmers organized a boycott of Ellinwood storekeepers who supported the mob action, promising "they will starve before they will buy a cent's worth from these merchants." Editor Amos expressed his contempt for "the mob, dressed in the soldier uniform egged that [U.S.] flag until egg dripped from its folds . . . in the interests of patriotism and 100 percent Americanism."[37]

Mills, Stevic, and Amos visited the state capital, with Amos proudly displaying the "spoiled hens' fruit" on their banner. The governor was in the East campaigning for the Republican nom-

ination for the presidency. Attorney General Hopkins could not
arrange to see them "until late this afternoon," and the governor's
secretary, Emmett George, would not commit the governor to
action. Grinning broadly, Mills compared the state government
to "a Mexican province which is without organized government
every other day." "Why, I have been a Republican for two and
a half years," Amos chided, "surely we ought to have some con-
sideration." "Do you want military protection?" he was asked.
"Why not?" Amos replied. "Didn't the Governor send his troops
to the coal fields [to break the coal strike in 1919]? Hasn't a man
who discusses the issues of the day the same right to protection
as the man who digs coal?" Stevic asserted that a man in Great
Bend had promised a written declaration that the governor had
authorized the rough treatment with an expression of "give 'em
hell." The mob of veterans also stole a document from the organizers showing the membership figures of the league in Kansas
of 3,209 for 1919 and 6,230 in 1920.[38]

County sheriff Jeff Yancey, George Klein, and "six other farmers from Barton County with German sounding names" traveled
to Topeka to plead for an investigation of the incident. The governor, now back from his travels, instructed the attorney general
to take their testimony, promising not to allow visitors during
the process and not to make their names public, fearing reper-
cussions if they were identified. The farmers refused to file complaints against any American Legionnaire but just wanted "to
restore order in Barton County." Klein admitted he was no longer
a member of the NPL but complained that "a bunch of hoodlums
in uniform was terrorizing the county." Nothing further came
from the investigation, which did not surprise those who were
aware of Governor Allen's hostile attitude toward the league.[39]

Shortly after the egging episode, H. A. Dykstra, a Canadian
citizen, was talking to his employer, a Hudson farmer. A mob
gathered and began questioning him after they discovered he was
a foreigner. He told them he was for "the right to assemblage,
free speech and a free press" and that those who had egged the
farmers at Ellinwood and covered the American flag with rotten
eggs "were guilty of mob violence and violated the law." At this

point "the mob seized him, beat and abused and kicked him," and drove him out of town. A few days later four men appeared at his employer's farm, seized Dykstra, and took him to St. John, saying on the way that if he returned, they would "put a bean through him." They "rushed him to Dodge City where he spent ten hours in jail" before another group drove him to Garden City. From there another crowd took him to Syracuse, where "still another bunch of men" took him to Holly, Colorado. He brought suit against the city of Hudson and planned to sue the towns of Dodge City, St. John, and "later probably Garden City, Cimarron, Lakin, and Syracuse for damages."[40]

Walter Thomas Mills, however, gave an address at Ellis a short time later without incident. Perhaps his stature and national reputation protected him from violence. Two weeks after the Barton County mobbing, "a bunch of mobites" informed an NPL member, William Snare, that he had two hours to pack and leave Dodge City. A fight ensued, with farmers trying to protect Snare from a group of two hundred. A farmer broke the jaw of one protester and the arm of another, but the two hundred finally prevailed. They took Snare "without hat or coat" to Hutchinson. The next day the farmers faced Mrs. Snare and gave her money to get to Hutchinson to join her husband. Mrs. Snare, instead, went to Dodge City, where the mob seized her and promised to send her out of town like "they had done with Snare's son who was working in the city." Nearly three hundred railroad men "came to her rescue, however, and guarded her house," with the promise that there were "600 railroad boys of Dodge City who could be depended on."[41]

Late in December 1920, Arthur Townley came to Kansas to support the drive for members. The *Kansas Leader* stated that reporters were "red balled to Salina the past week because . . . [it] has become the most important city in the state" with his arrival. Kansas newspapers immediately heralded his coming as "an abdication of his leadership in North Dakota." Kansas farmers who had talked to him, the editor asserted, "found a quiet, unassuming gentleman in contrast to the tales that the newspapers have been pouring forth to their readers in the past two years." It was not known how long he would remain in the Sunflower State, but "it is certain that a large number of farmers will in the future pay little attention to the newspaper falsehoods that have been spread in the past" about him.[42]

Governor Henry J. Allen owned and edited the *Wichita Beacon*, a staunchly Republican newspaper. "In a widely quoted signed article on the front page" of his paper, Allen joined forces with the American Legion. He attacked Townley as one who had "worked to weaken the country at home" during World War I. "Townley and his tribe fought war drives, opposed the sale of Liberty Bonds, refused contributions to the Red Cross," he asserted. "Lacking the courage to go to war for Germany," Allen charged, "Townley and the NPL became friends with Germany" and worked for a Hun victory. He insisted the league tried to "spread to agriculture the same spirit that IWWism has spread to labor."[43]

When Allen ran for reelection in 1920 against Democrat Jonathan Davis, the NPL supported Davis. Amos wrote an editorial for the *Leader* close to election time that he headlined "FOR GOVERNOR; ALLEN WITH MOB RULE OR DAVIS WITH LAW AND ORDER." Farmer meetings were "broken up under the instigation of BUSINESSMEN, ALLEN IS A BUSINESSMAN," Amos proclaimed. Farmers advocated "free speech and peaceable assembly and DAVIS IS A FARMER." When the votes were counted, normally Democratic Ellsworth went solidly Republican, and Allen was reelected by a margin of three to two statewide. Allen was in the Governor's Mansion in 1921, when an episode in Great Bend between the American Legion and the Nonpartisan League would focus unwanted national attention on the Sunflower State.[44]

The *Literary Digest* noted that Townley sent his organizers into Nebraska and Kansas because his "troubles were thickest at home." While Townley was delivering one of his speeches, delegates from the Farm Bureau, the Farmers Union, the Grange (a state farmers' support organization and part of the National Grange of the Patrons of Husbandry), the Equity Union, the State Horticultural Society, the State Board of Agriculture, the State Livestock Association, and the Farmers' Cooperative Grain Dealers Association held a meeting to plot strategy to defeat the league. The *Literary Digest* reported that the *Kansas City Star*, widely circulated in eastern Kansas, suggested that farmers "can adopt any good thing devised by the Nonpartisan League without swallowing either the organization or Mr. Townley himself." The farmers' organizations were trying to devise "any good thing" to promote their cause.[45]

The American Legion emerged as the most effective weapon conservatives had against the NPL and its organizers. The legion as an organization was prohibited from taking political action directly, but many hundreds of its members decided they could do so as organized individuals. Thomas Lee, the legion's early historian and state commander, noted that the NPL "made an invasion in force" into the north-central area of Kansas, and this created trouble there from January through March, when the situation became "extremely critical." The Salina American Legion post "had some friction" with the league in that town. O. A. Kitterman, the Salina post commander, and Dr. S. L. Nelson informed the department executive secretary that, following its investigation, they had determined that Townley had been convicted of disloyalty (on circumstantial evidence of urging conspiracy to discourage enlistments) and that member organizers were found "to be in accord with his radical and un-American views," had "invaded the state," established their headquarters in Salina, and had "brought about a condition of stress that endangers the peace of the community and challenges the patriotism of the loyal men and women of Salina." The *Salina Post* had notified them that they were unwelcome guests of Salina; therefore, the paper said, the state unit "urges each member of the American Legion to perform his full duty as a citizen according to his own conscience and understanding."[46]

At this point Frederic W. Galbraith, national commander of the American Legion, wrote to Oscar Kitterman that the organization's constitution forbade political action of its posts and that the Nonpartisan League was regarded as a political organization. The opposition, Kitterman responded, would shift to the Constitutional Defense League, an organization of former servicemen that would be maintained "by popular subscription."[47]

In the melee that followed, Thomas Lee insisted that "too much credit cannot be given" to Dr. George Wilson and the local post officials "in holding down those members . . . who believed in direct action and who preserved the state from violence." Nelson, post commander Kitterman, and Matt Guilfoyle, a department executive committeeman from Herington, organized a unit of the American Defense League, elected Kitterman its president, and conducted "a campaign of publicity" that was successful in preventing the Nonpartisan League from taking over the Kansas government.[48]

Both sides gathered their forces. The American Defense League sent telegrams to legion posts throughout the state asking them to send a former serviceman and one other citizen to attend a planning session in Salina. Governor Henry Allen also was invited. Townley responded to this development by saying he had not intended to make speeches during his trip to Kansas but that "the publicity demanded it." He agreed to present the principles of the Nonpartisan League, what it had accomplished in North Dakota, and what it could achieve "if permitted to follow out its original plans."[49]

Governor Allen seized this moment to attack Townley in his efforts to "defeat the country at home" during World War I, and his "socialistic policy justified any body of men who loved the state in their hostility to 'Townleyism.'" He asserted that Townley had sold North Dakotans "on a lot of dreams that seemed real but the weakness and cost of his scheme have finally been exposed and Townley is hunting new fields" to conquer in Kansas. He assured listeners that the former servicemen "are opposing Townleyism with orderly propaganda," and so long as they "express their opposition with the brave self-restraint which they now exhibit," Kansans would be "grateful." This was not the speech of a concerned leader throwing cold water on a superpatriotic fire.[50]

Meanwhile, supporters could not find Townley. Some said he had gone to Kansas City, while others insisted he was in a Ford out in the countryside promoting the NPL. Then he appeared, saying he had been on a business trip to Minneapolis, Kansas, and called a meeting in Salina. The convention hall was packed that night, with two thousand in the hall and another one thousand waiting outside. Most were farmers and "labor union men." Plans were announced that recruiting efforts in Dickinson, McPherson, Ottawa, and Saline Counties would continue and the work would be extended to Geary County. Opponents said they expected Townley to work southward through counties to the Oklahoma line.[51]

The American Legion countered with a mass meeting two days later, also in Salina, of farmers and members of the American Legion posts of Abilene, Concordia, Great Bend, Gypsum, Herington, Junction City, Lindsborg, McPherson, Minneapolis, and Solomon. J. O'Brien, president of the National Constitutional Defense League of Racine, Wisconsin, addressed the gathering. The object of the meeting was "to convince the farmers" that they were being misled by the NPL. County sheriff Ernest Swanson, antagonistic to Townley's organization, demanded "there be no violence of any kind."[52]

The Townley supporters brought in their heavy artillery. North Dakota's attorney general, Jerome T. Brown, and Townley aide William Langer visited the Sunflower State. Townley supporters "declared that the entire brains of the Townley movement will be in Salina in a week," then the NPL would be ready for whatever its opponents were willing to throw at them and at any level, local to national. The NPL headquarters, both state and national, would move to Topeka.[53]

Soon afterward FU president Maurice McAuliffe denounced the *Emporia Gazette* for being responsible for the NPL "invasion" because of a previous editorial about Kansas farmers "being ground between the millstone of higher prices for farm labor, machinery, and high rates of interest above, and low prices of farm produce below." Editor William Allen White wrote that this was nonsense, and the *Gazette* and the FU agreed on the problem. The difference lay in the *Gazette* demanding something be done to resolve the dilemma—but what, White asked, is McAuliffe "doing about it?" "Get busy or cam [*sic*] down," he declared. White supported the effort of the Grange, the FU, the Farm Bureau Federation, and "farmers otherwise unorganized" to unite, but McAuliffe's FU "refused to federate." When the NPL leader arrived in Kansas, the FU leader put the blame on the *Gazette*. McAuliffe, White charged, had been "just as wrathy about the farm bureau as he is about the Nonpartisan League."[54]

The planning session of the legionnaires met in Newton and adopted resolutions denouncing Townley, as expected. They resolved that he "stands convicted in one of the state courts in Minnesota for acts of disloyalty during the war" and that his recent activity in Salina "endangers the peace of the community." They commended the "officers and members of the Salina post for the orderly manner in which they are conducting the campaign against Townley and other radical agitators." The tensions between the two forces continued to escalate through February 1921 and then exploded in early March, when NPL organizers went into McPherson County searching for angry farmers. The Lions Club of Arkansas City had unanimously endorsed the actions of the Salina American Legion, but the Ministerial Union tentatively agreed that the ministers would not preach on the subject of the Nonpartisan League.[55]

The crisis came to a head on March 12, 1921, when former U.S. senator J. Ralph Burton and "Prof George Wilson" were scheduled to speak in support of the league in Ellinwood. On their way they stopped for lunch in Great Bend, and opposition forces "escorted" them out of Barton County. In addition, James O. Stevic and NPL state secretary A. H. Parsons received a coat of tar and feathers the same day. The historian of the early legion in Kansas described the altercation as having unfolded when NPL members "invaded" Great Bend to demand that the sheriff permit Burton to continue to Ellinwood. An NPL member struck a former serviceman and "called him a vile name." A melee ensued in which "nearly everyone in the courthouse square" became involved. The "worsting" (losing) Nonpartisan Leaguers left for Ellinwood and on the way met five former servicemen from Lyons and "took their wrath out on them, beating them badly." The Lyons men, in turn, went home, recruited reinforcements, and drove to Ellinwood. They found the group that had attacked them and returned the beating, then managed a tar and feathering.

The mob kidnapped and drove Stevic and Parsons to Great Bend, where another gang took them to an isolated area. Two men each held their arms while they were "fearfully beaten" by others. "A circle of automobiles ringed about us," Stevic said, "and tar pots applied." After being tarred and beaten, the victims "staggered away, hearing another mob was after us." They found temporary shelter "in a straw stack," then walked to Great Bend, following a railroad track for twenty miles.[56] The Associated Press (AP) account told of Stevic and Parsons being compelled to roll on the ground after two hundred men applied tar to them, then they were given their clothing and ordered out of Barton County. The mob was "said to be" members of the American Legion from Great Bend, Ellinwood, and Lyons who had been "summoned through bugle calls." Stevic's hair, face, and shoulders were "matted with tar, two black eyes, injured backbone, twisted thigh, and bruises," according to a report in Larson's "Kansas and the Nonpartisan League." In addition, Parsons suffered "three broken ribs [and] probable internal injuries."[57]

C. O. Parsons, state chairman of the World War Veterans of Minnesota, complained to the national commander of the American Legion about the mob action, charging that Dr. S. L. Nelson had led the mob who tarred and feathered Parsons and Stevic.[58] Governor Allen ordered the attorney general to investigate after Stevic described the men's ordeal. "We underwent horrible treatment," the labor leader declared.

The *New York Times* picked up on an AP release, and this account was less detailed. According to the paper, the mob broke up an NPL meeting and seized Stevic and Parsons. The two had returned to Ellinwood after driving to Great Bend to find out why Burton had not appeared as scheduled. Upon hearing of this, the former servicemen traveled to Ellinwood and seized Stevic and Parsons, reminding Stevic that he had been warned twice not to return to Barton County. No effort was made to stop the mob proceedings by Sheriff Sam Hill, who was one of those "who earlier in the day had warned the two to keep out of Barton County." Hill also was the deputy U.S. marshal who had led the raid on the IWW at Augusta in 1917. "A cauldron of tar was brought up," but feathers had been forgotten, so the two were forced to roll in the grass. After the prisoners had gained a thorough knowledge of Barton County's attitude toward the NPL, their clothes were returned, and "the mob left with a parting word of warning."[59]

The following day the *Times* reported Burton's statement of denunciation in which he called the incident "the blackest of all crimes on the calendar—the suppression of free speech by force." Burton intimated that it was "almost entirely an American Legion affair" and appealed to the Allen administration in Topeka "to bring the leaders of the mob to justice." The governor requested that his attorney general investigate the episode. Burton was furious and, after a week of no results, declared that "Governor Allen is a mob Governor, Richard Hopkins is a mob Attorney General, and Judge D. A. Banta of Barton County is a mob judge." "Would you go to hell to prosecute an imp," he demanded, rhetorically, "with Satan presiding on the bench?"[60]

Governor Allen was kept busy with his "investigation" of the sad episode. He received a telegram from George H. Mallon, state manager of the NPL, stating that he, Burton, and George Wilson were scheduled to speak at Marion but that when they arrived, they were informed that the mayor, J. C. McIntosh, had forbidden the meeting. Mallon's loyalty could not be questioned, as he was a veteran of the Spanish-American War, three years of service in the U.S. Army in the Philippines, and a captain in the American Expeditionary Force who had received the Congressional Medal of Honor in France, given to him by General John J. Pershing. Among other actions he and his squad of nine men had attacked a German machine gun nest. After the ammunition ran out, Mallon attacked the enemy with his fists, and the Germans surrendered, with over one hundred prisoners being taken in this sortie. His military service was a primary reason that he had been chosen to head the league in Kansas, to blunt charges of league treason. Allen then told Attorney General Hopkins to telegraph the mayor, county sheriff J. C. Hannamon, and county attorney John E. Wheeler to appear in the capital "to make explanations." "It is my intention," intoned the governor, "to exhaust every power of my office to prevent future disorders and to protect the name of the state and the rights of its people under our laws guaranteeing free speech." He admitted he was "utterly out of sympathy with Townleyism" but that their "specious doctrine" should be countered with "logic and the orderly presentation of the objections to the movement."[61]

The Marion County officials answered the summons and met with the governor and attorney general in a closed session that the NPL was forbidden to attend. The mayor explained that he was prepared "at all times" to allow the league members to speak, but "he considered it within his discretion to decide for what use city property can be put." In addition, he feared the city could be held responsible if a riot broke out, so he refused them use of the city park and street corners. At a separate meeting Marion County officials and league representatives reached an agreement, and Governor Allen concluded that "both sides were misunderstood."[62]

John N. Floyd of Arkansas City, a member of the American Legion State Executive Committee, quickly exonerated the legion "from all blame for the Great Bend incident." Floyd, also a member of the legion's Americanization Committee, "made a thoro [sic] investigation" and was satisfied that the members of the local post had nothing to do with the demonstration. Yet he readily admitted that "several members of the Legion were in the party."[63]

J. M. Kennedy, a farmer with no ties to the NPL, wrote the Journal editor about Floyd's explanation. Floyd admitted there were Legionnaires in the mob, but "they were outnumbered two to one." This meant, Kennedy asserted, that there were sixty-six members of the American Legion present, and Floyd was "trying to cover up their disloyal acts and their violations of our state laws." Farmers had the same right "morally and legally to organize as you Legionnaires have," he insisted, "and they are going to continue to organize regardless of the legion's mob tactics." He noted that Judge Dan Banta said Stevic was responsible for his assault by "returning to the city after being told to leave and not return." This "happening," Kennedy retorted, "was deliberately planned and executed with the apparent knowledge of every county officers [sic] in Barton County." After studying NPL literature he had obtained from Bismarck, he was ready "to endorse the whole program" and expressed the wish that Stevic, Townley, and Burton would come and explain it to the Shawnee County farmers.[64]

The *Topeka State Journal* was convinced that Burton was using this happening to run for governor in 1922. The former senator, the editor noted, retained his "stinging sarcasm and much of his old fire as an orator." The NPL was seeking control of the Republican Party, and Burton was obviously promoting the league cause to farmers. Burton and Stevic were posing as "martyrs" in the tarring incident, the newspaper insisted, and their combination of farmers and laborers gave candidate George Snow over 25 percent of the votes cast in the last Republican primary. This came despite the fact that Snow "was under parole from the state hospital for the insane, was without a dollar for campaign expenses, had never seen the inside working of a political organization, knew nothing of politics or its manipulation, and might easily confuse the Magna Charta [*sic*] and the Jewish synagogue in a discussion of public issues." "Give this Snow strength to the adroit, versatile Burton," the editor added. If they could split the primary vote between perhaps a dozen candidates, add the rural discontent from slumping prices, and "disgruntled Democrats could cross over in the primary," this could cause trouble for the Republican regulars. The editor also called attention to the unpopularity of the NPL and suggested if the league could dominate the Republican primary, the Democrats could benefit from "thousands of Republicans" moving to the "Democratic column when they voted in November."[65]

A week later the newspaper continued this fantasy by noting that Burton solved the mystery of the organized opposition to the NPL, suggesting Republican leaders were not worried about the league and its loyalty. "That's all bunc [*sic*]," he wrote, but they were "scared the League would get its senses to working and will control their party and that the farmers will run things in the state." When asked if he would be a candidate for governor in the primaries, Burton responded that he was "not deciding political policies of the League in Kansas" and that he was "not even a member" and did not agree "with all its principles." There would have to be some understanding, he added, before

"I would consider running for anything." "I am almost tempted to buy a farm," Mrs. Burton injected, "that I might be eligible for membership in the league." In the election of 1922, of course, Allen retained control of the Republicans and won reelection.[66]

On the invitation of organized labor, Mallon and Burton spoke to a large gathering in Topeka on the issue of league activities. David L. Chandler of the Topeka Industrial Council, comprising fifty labor organizations, introduced Mallon, who briefly outlined the league's work and "exposed those who were fighting the farmers' organization in Kansas." He "spoke feelingly" of the American Legion and "placed the blame for its misguidance on the shoulders of the politicians." Burton, as usual, gave his "Mob Law v. Free Speech," which he was trying to ride into the governor's mansion. In his indictment of state officials, though "the big audience burst forth in its applauding support," indicating they were sympathetic to the league problems and agreeing that the administration was not handling the situation with impartiality. The governor and attorney general were invited to the gathering but failed to appear. The attorney general had stated publicly that unless the NPL "produce some evidence" of the mobbing, he would "let them do all the posing as martyrs they desire."[67]

As the NPL continued to gather rural support, Governor Allen spoke to a large gathering of Kiwanis Club members and urged them to help farmers "block" the league. He predicted that in the following year Kansas would "have its greatest fight against radicalism." If steps were not taken to "curb its activities, Kansas may find itself in as bad a condition as North Dakota." North Dakota was doing fine at this time, with New York financiers buying state bonds at a premium, and a majority might have been surprised to learn that conditions in their state were "bad." E. L. Chase, lieutenant governor of the Kansas-Missouri Kiwanian district, responded to Allen that his club did not "stand for radicalism," nor did it "take issues in political or religious controversies."[68]

Bruce L. Larson made a study of press reaction to the "affair at Great Bend" and found that a majority of area small-town newspapers supported the American Legion but that the press in Kansas, "by and large," condemned the mob action. The *Emporia*

Gazette insisted that Burton and Townley should be punished if they "violated the laws of sedition," but if not, they should be protected in their right to free speech. The *Lawrence Journal World* warned that the incident "may be expected to rally a lot of support for the league from persons who were undecided and who believe there should be full and free discussion." The *Salina Daily Union*, however, "minimized the incident," observing that "these things have no effect one way or the other."[69]

The *Pink Rag*, a Topeka newspaper, praised both the *Topeka Daily Capital* and the *Topeka State Journal* because they "editorially condemned the brutal outrage, and just at the time that isn't the popular trend." The *Manhattan Mercury* quipped that Barton County "may be a good place for wheat but it is a poor place for Nonpartisan Leaguers to attempt to take up homesteads." The *Dodge City Daily Globe* attempted humor with the observation that the mob had to stop with tarring as "there were no feathers available," for "it seems the hens had been called upon to equip an egging in another county." The *Abilene Daily Reflector*'s editor, Charles Harger, opined that when "a few more Nonpartisan League paid organizers are stripped and tarred they will get the idea that Barton County does not want them to orate in that section of Kansas." This was Burton's hometown and a stronghold of the NPL.[70]

Governor Allen's *Wichita Beacon* questioned the validity of reports of tarring parties, suggesting that it was possible the report had been sent out by a NPL sympathizer "for outside consumption." The editor added that "the files of Nonpartisan League papers contain dozens of tarring parties that never occurred." It is amazing that he would even suggest to readers that the secretive NPL would open its files to its enemies. The *Beacon* asserted that the accusations against American Legion members were "unjust and entirely without foundation in fact." Besides, members of other organizations had participated in the mobbing. Neither the American Legion nor the American Defense League favored the "use of force and violence," Allen's newspaper insisted.[71]

The governor of Kansas condemned the NPL and stoutly defended the American Legion, saying "he was proud of these brave American Legion boys who are standing shoulder to shoulder . . . and saying to the people of this state there's no room in this commonwealth for teachings of that kind." Townleyism, he insisted, worked "upon prejudices for the purpose of creating a class warfare which will benefit no one, except as it may enrich the pockets of Townley and his crowd to the extent of membership fees." The *Ellsworth County Leader* later gleefully reprinted the story of former Speaker W. P. Lambertson, who described Allen as a "political double dealer" and "public official skin flint." Allen was the candidate of the packinghouse industry, which had donated $1,500 to his campaign in 1920, and he had responded by pressuring the state legislature to pass the stockyards bill. This account was submitted as evidence that the governor was "not sincere in his pretensions of being a friend to the farmers," as the law worked against their interests. When he asked Lambertson what kind of a House of Representatives they had to work with in 1921, the Speaker said that it was "mostly made up of farmers." Allen responded that this was "about the worst kind . . . we could have." This farmer-dominated legislature gave him his prized legislative possession, however, the Industrial Court of Kansas, which completely alienated organized labor from the Republican Party.[72]

At this point H. E. Bruce, publisher of the *Marquette Tribune*, printed a retraction. In reporting the Great Bend incident, he had described James O. Stevic as "the backbone of a harvester laborers' strike in Barton County two or three years ago when the farmers were brow beaten into paying enormous wages right in the middle of harvest, when sabotage was used to force terms, when grain was burned, machinery destroyed, horses poisoned and the women folk terrorized." Stevic had been warned then to stay out of the county and "had himself to blame for being mobbed." After careful inquiry, Bruce had discovered that Stevic "had nothing to do with that strike." Stevic, in fact, was part of the organized labor structure then and had nothing to do with the Wobblies or migrant farm labor.[73]

Allen ordered attorney general Hopkins to make an investigation of the events in Great Bend. Hopkins notified county attorney

Will J. Weber, asking him to subpoena some witnesses in Barton County and take their testimony under oath. A later report indicated he had summoned twenty people but that "none of the testimony secured would be sufficient to warrant any arrests." The NPL men involved refused to testify out of fear of retaliation, and the investigation never went to court.[74]

The *Topeka Daily Capital* supported Allen in his handling of the event. It editorialized that he was "to be commended for promptly requiring an investigation" and pointed out that "the law is supreme" but that "there is no right for citizens to assume to themselves the government or suppression of opinion." Allen's *Beacon* again affirmed its stand against mob violence but emphasized that the newspaper had "pioneered the anti-League fight in Kansas and it always and consistently opposed and deplored the use of violence and mobs."[75]

The labor newspaper the *Worker's Chronicle* was critical of the governor, comparing his handling of the "incident" with his role in confronting the strike action in the coalfields in 1919. "Our Governor is against justice to the workers," it declared, "and gives his approval to mob violence." If the situation of the NPL and the legion had been reversed, the *Chronicle* insisted, then the governor and his attorney general "would have thrown forty fits, and sent the leaguers to prison." The *Kansas Leader*, now edited by the Great Bend tar-feathering victim James Stevic, was critical. Stevic let Townley speak for the newspaper's attitude. Townley asserted that "if local or state authorities . . . fail to act, there are still the courts and the federal authorities," and he stressed that the league would pursue the matter "until justice is done, if it takes years."[76]

Some farmers urged the governor to allow justice to prevail. Henry Nelson of the Saline County Farmers League insisted that his "investigation be thorough and the guilty parties brought to trial." He admitted that the farmers, as a whole, seemed to distrust the governor and the police. A mass meeting of Saline farmers, including representatives of the Wheat Growers Association, the FU, the Farm Bureau, and the NPL, wired the governor a resolution condemning the "recent mobbing" of the NPL organizers, asking him to conduct "a real investigation and bring to justice those criminals who violated every principle of constitutional rights and Americanism, for which our boys died in France."[77]

The American Defense League invited William Langer, discredited politician from North Dakota, to tour Kansas and speak against the NPL, which he had strongly supported as a Townley lieutenant before breaking with his leader. The former North Dakota attorney general had just been defeated by Lynn Frazier for governor of North Dakota, and he did not fare well in the Sunflower State either. FU president Maurice McAuliffe announced that Governor Allen, Elizabeth "Lizzie" Wooster (the first woman in Kansas to be elected to a state office), and Speaker of the House William W. Harvey would speak at the FU function. Allen spoke for twenty minutes, then introduced Bill Langer. When the North Dakotan "took the platform, two-thirds of the audience walked out and only a handful remained till his address was finished."[78]

Organized labor did not submit a legislative program that year. They were interested in the workers' compensation proposal but "did not want to precipitate a fight by submitting a separate measure." Other than that issue, organized labor was "principally interested in the program of the farmer members for the benefit of the farmers." The representative of the state federation of labor, W. E. Freeman, stated, "We will try to help the agricultural interests." The NPL endorsed Democrat Jonathan Davis for governor. Laborers and farmers "stuck" together in this election, and Davis became only the third Democrat thus far in Kansas history to win this office.[79]

Five months after the Great Bend episode, Arthur Banta, lawyer and son of Judge Dan Banta, was found shot to death beside his automobile on a lonely country road. "Are these the fruit of the mob spirit?" asked the *Kansas Leader*. The IWW was the first to be blamed for the murder, then "many other wild rumors" floated through the county. A short time later a prominent physician, Dr. W. A. Nixon, and Roy Hayes, a Standard Oil employee, were arrested for the crime, and Nixon was ultimately convicted. Legion commander Nixon had recently attended an NPL meeting at the Elks club and was reported to have said, "If you will send Townley to Great Bend, I guarantee that you will not be bothered with him any more."[80]

The American Legion in Great Bend invited Townley and NPL apostate Langer to debate the merits of the league in North Dakota. Recent presentations of Langer in Kansas, however, had not impressed the American Defense League, and the *Great Bend Tribune* announced that its American Legion post had retracted the invitation. As a result, Langer was "not only a 'dead' one among all political factions" in North Dakota but also among those who earlier in the year were gleeful over his challenge to meet Townley in debate "anywhere at any time." It was reported that Langer's services cost someone in Kansas "$500 per week, and it was a large amount to squander on worthless words."[81]

In September 1921 some one thousand NPL delegates met at the annual convention in Salina. They lowered membership fees from $18 for two years to $5 annually, with ladies' fees at $1 but no annual dues. The membership of the state committee was increased from five to nine, with one elected from each congressional district and one at large, with the at-large member becoming president. They named a committee to purchase the *Leader* plant but were unable to finance it sufficiently.

Fred J. Fraley struggled to keep his newspaper afloat financially. In January 1924 he printed a story on the front page that the *Leader* needed to raise $2,000 quickly and sent out recruiters for the NPL to help. Then, prior to the election of 1924, he hit upon the idea of staging a contest to win a $2,000 Essex automobile. The person sending in the highest number of new subscriptions to the *Leader* would win. This move tided the journal over for a period, but Fraley found in early 1926 that he needed another contest. This time the prize was a $1,100 Star Six Landau car and a $1,412 cash prize. Again the prizes were too costly for the gain in subscriptions, and the *Leader* printed its last issue on May 27 of that year.[82]

The NPL declined significantly when Townley began serving his prison term in Minnesota on charges of sedition during the war, and in May 1922 he tendered his resignation. The national

Leader cut back on publishing to save money, and in fourteen months it ceased publication. The league ceased to be a factor in Kansas after the victory of Davis in 1922. Following this election Fred W. Knapp, defeated in the Republican primary for governor that year, blamed Henry Allen for the party's defeat. Allen had characterized the members and officers of the taxpayers' organizations as "red card radicals, Socialists and Democrats" and said it was time to "discard such leadership and tactics." Ben Paulen managed to unite the torn party in the election of 1924. The NPL had ceased to be a political factor in Kansas. On the national level Robert La Follette assumed the leadership of the league, the Farmer-Labor Party was formed in Minnesota, and "in weakly organized states of Iowa, Kansas, Texas, and Oklahoma there was a gradual drifting back to former alliances."[83]

Railroad brotherhoods, along with representatives of splinter groups such as the NPL, took the lead in organizing the conference for Progressive Political Action in Cleveland in 1922. The group nominated Robert La Follette the elder for president in 1924 on a platform basically opposing monopoly of all types. The Republican Calvin Coolidge largely ignored his Democratic opponent, John W. Davis, and concentrated on lambasting La Follette, labeling his program "Red Radicalism." The Wisconsin liberal ran third, with close to five million votes, but carried only his home state in the Electoral College. His campaign was supported by Alf Landon, and Kansas gave him almost 15 percent of its vote.

Fred Fraley, running for the U.S. Senate on this ticket, used his newspaper, the *Kansas Leader*, to promote the La Follette campaign. He advertised good speakers—W. E. Freeman, president of the State Federation of Labor; Philip Callery; and William Mahoney, who told listeners about the Minnesota Farmer-Labor Party. Fraley featured a story that Helen Keller had written Senator La Follette of her support in his fight. She had hesitated to write because she knew that opposition editors would "cry out" at "the pathetic exploitation of deaf and dumb Helen Keller" by "the motley elements" but believed that his fight against the current economic system deserved her support.[84]

La Follette ran strongest in Crawford County, with 31 percent of its vote, but also ran well in "several counties with relatively strong union membership," such as Sedgwick and Wyandotte. Farmers looked upon his candidacy as a labor, not a farmer, endeavor. Fraley won almost a thousand votes, compared to Arthur Capper, who won the race for the Senate with over sixty thousand votes. It would be almost another decade before Kansas witnessed another surge of radicalism, this time during the Great Depression.[85]

For a state rife with radicalism, Socialists, and other agitators, the Nonpartisan League was met with distrust, if not fear, by many in the state. Its success in other states is evident, but Kansas citizens did not hesitate to resort to minor violence, private and public beatings, and gang violence to let the NPL know that it was not welcome in Kansas. NPL members did not give in easily, and many suffered for it. Kansas, it seemed, would tolerate some radicals in their midst, but when they seemed more hard-lined, the public rose up and met them with more resistance.

8

THE DEPRESSION RADICALS

Despite Eugene V. Debs's impressive vote count of almost one million while running for the presidency from an Atlanta prison in 1920, socialism seemed dead or at least largely moribund, until the Great Depression offered new hope for the restructuring of American society. During the Roaring Twenties the Big Red Scare took its toll, although the Wobblies remained active through 1924, despite enforcement of the Kansas criminal syndicalist law until it was declared unconstitutional. The former *Appeal to Reason* press in Girard was churning out Little Blue Books at a small but ultimately handsome profit for Emanuel Haldeman-Julius. The old Kansas leadership was still in prison, aging, and bereft of new ideas. Kate and Frank O'Hare led a group of some fifty radicals to Mena, Arkansas, to reorganize Commonwealth College. This was a resurrection of the People's College concept whereby a student needed only $100 for annual tuition to enroll. Room and board could be earned by working in the shops and on the college farm.[1]

A new leadership was emerging, though, under Earl Browder, James P. Cannon, Presbyterian minister Norman Thomas, and Ernest F. McNutt, who were ready for radical action in the 1930s. Socialist Party membership rose from 9,500 in 1929 to 17,000 in 1934, before it began to decline. In 1932 Thomas received 800,000 votes for the presidency but only 187,000 in 1936, with 18,276 and 2,766 ballots in Kansas, respectively. The New Deal programs that were resuscitating capitalism were co-opting the appeal of militant socialism and creating an ensuing constant struggle for control of the leadership of the party.[2]

In the Soviet Union, Kremlin leadership ordered a "Popular Front" in 1935, instructing all Communists to cooperate with any group fighting fascism. Pursuing this policy, in 1936 Kansas-born Earl Browder sought to take advantage of the split within the American Socialists. Their convention that year divided between the liberals and conservatives, or Old Guard, who believed the Leftists under Norman Thomas had "Communistic tendencies." Yet the followers of Thomas unanimously rejected Browder's offer to join campaigns with Thomas running on the top of the ticket and Browder campaigning for the vice presidency. The Communists then emphasized Browder's Kansas background when he ran on the Communist Party USA label. "Our candidate is the blood and bone of America," bragged a Communist leaflet in 1936, and the Communist Party USA even composed a song about him titled "That Man from Kansas."[3]

James Cannon's father, John Cannon, was a brickmaker in Rosedale, Kansas, until he became a small entrepreneur in insurance and real estate. He was a member of the Knights of Labor, then joined the Socialists, but he had little to do with raising his children. His wife, Ann, a devout Roman Catholic, had a great effect on the children, with James becoming an altar boy and developing a social conscience. James worked summers in the nearby Swift and Armour slaughterhouses until forced to work full-time after completing grammar school. In his teens he worked for the Missouri, Kansas, & Texas Railroad (the "Katy Railroad"), then as a printer's helper. Ann Cannon died when James was fourteen, and his grandmother moved in to help with the family. When his father took another wife, James moved out on his own. He read voraciously, especially Upton Sinclair's *The Jungle* but also Bellamy's *Looking Backward* and his father's Socialist publications, the *International Socialist Review* and the *Appeal to Reason*.[4]

James saved his money, enrolled in high school, and had almost completed his diploma when finances again forced him to work full-time. During these formative years he became a good debater and later a skilled orator. He joined the Socialists in 1908 but remained "unfocused" until 1911, when he joined the International Workers of the World, where he found his niche in this radical wing of the Socialist Party. In their Sunday afternoon classes he was introduced to the writings of Daniel De Leon as well as Marx and Engels. Surviving on short-term employment, he took to the soapbox, exhorting crowds, recruiting Wobblies, and selling IWW literature, slowly making a reputation until, by the end of the decade, he was foremost in the ranks of the American Trotskyites, an influential wing during the Great Depression.[5]

Following World War I, he joined Earl Browder in recruiting in Kansas, Missouri, and Nebraska. They published *Workers World*, and for a few weeks Browder edited the journal; when he returned to prison for sedition committed during the hostilities, Cannon took up the editorial duties. The young editors used Ella Reeve "Mother" Bloor, Ralph Cheyney, anti-war radical Scott Nearing, John Reed, and other writers for their weekly journal, with news from the European front, activities of Wobblies, and U.S. intervention in Soviet Russia. They closely followed the speaking tour of Horace Traubel, recently returned from a trip through Germany and Russia, where he interviewed Lenin and Trotsky.[6]

Earl Browder was the son of a Wichita Socialist who homesteaded in the 1880s near Medicine Lodge. Living in a dugout, the family saw their farm ruined by drought, lost it through mortgage foreclosure, and moved to Wichita, where Earl's father, William, taught elementary school. Moving from populism to socialism, William and Martha raised their children on Tom Paine's *Age of Reason* and relentlessly urged them to read in order to expand their horizons. Born in 1891, Browder and his siblings related to the "have-nots" in life. When his father became disabled, the ten-year-old Browder went to work as a department store errand boy. His formative years occurred during Eugene Debs's heyday, and he joined the Socialist Party, peddling its literature. When he reached twenty-one, he left home for Kansas City, where he met James Cannon.[7]

Declining an offer to join the political machine of Thomas J. Pendergast, Browder edited the monthly *Toiler* for syndicalist William Z. Foster's Trade Union Educational League. He also headed the American Federation of Labor local Bookkeepers, Stenographers, and Accountants Union and later managed a farmers' co-op. When World War I arrived, Browder joined a group of intellectuals opposed to the war. He and his colleagues urged young men to resist conscription, and on May 30, 1917, authorities arrested him, his brother William, and a future brother-in-law, Thomas R. Sullivan, in Olathe. They each received a one-year sentence and served their time in a Platte County, Missouri, jail because federal facilities were overcrowded. Never before had Browder been free from worrying about "where the next meal was coming from," and it was not an unpleasant experience as their jailer, happy to receive federal money, allowed all the privileges the law permitted. Browder used his time to write an accounting pamphlet.[8]

Freed between October 1918 and the following July, pending his conspiracy appeal, Browder joined James Cannon in publishing *Workers World*. They lost their appeal, and that July, Browder, his brother, and Sullivan began serving sixteen-month sentences at the United States Penitentiary, Leavenworth. Unlike his former incarceration, this was not a pleasant experience. Although he could play chess with Big Bill Haywood, before Haywood was released and fled to Russia, Browder faced "the strictest military regimentation" and backbreaking drudgery, and the encounter left him bitter and hardened. It also taught him the "self discipline necessary to champion a highly unpopular cause," helping to make him a mature radical.[9]

While in prison, his party split into three types of Communists. The Communist-Labor Party followed the radical iww model, the Communist Party, and the Soviets ordered the two to unite into the third, the Communist Party USA. Browder was paroled on November 15, 1920, ready to promote Leninism full-time. At this point a Soviet delegation came to America to recruit for the Red International of Labor Unions. "Liking Browder's Midwestern and AFL background," they invited him to Moscow. On the voyage over, Browder was reunited with Haywood, who was escaping to Russia after having skipped bail while waiting for results of an appeal on an earlier conviction.[10]

During this visit Browder impressed Bolshevik revolutionary Solomon Lozovsky, and he used this contact in 1926 to join a Soviet international labor organization in China. While there, he edited the *Pan Pacific Monthly* through 1928, created Communist labor unions, and was "politicizing workers." Back in America the CPUSA spent these years leading labor groups that were being ignored by the AFL. When Browder returned home, he was promoted, with Lozovsky's support, to the American Troika that ruled the CPUSA. He wrote most of the *Daily Worker*'s political articles and editorials until 1932, when the Kremlin made him chairman of the CPUSA.[11]

Browder returned to an America in the throes of the most devastating economic depression in history. Following the stock market crash in October 1929, the economic system almost collapsed. Unemployment rose to 25 percent in 1933, farm income declined by 58 percent from that of 1927, with wheat selling at thirty-three cents, corn fifteen cents, cattle four cents, hogs three cents, and eggs ten cents a dozen. Nature added insult to injury with terrible droughts and dust storms in 1934 and 1936. Basically an agrarian state, Kansas suffered like the industrial states to the east, and farmers, failing to maintain a sustenance level, desperately needed financial assistance, just like their urban cousins. The crisis was ready-made for radicals to spread their ideas.[12]

Relief was soon forthcoming, when President Herbert Hoover's Reconstruction Finance Corporation (RFC) began its loan policy for state relief work in early 1932. With constant reminders that the money constituted loans to states, although they were later forgiven, governors were urged to apply to the RFC after all other sources of revenue, including private charitable organizations, had been exhausted. In Kansas at that time poor relief was handled through the county commissioners, who either furnished "poor funds" or maintained a degrading "poor farm" or both. The enormity of this type of relief problem, though, soon bankrupted the system, and federal assistance became vital to prevent starvation for many.

President Hoover's program required accurate information on unemployment and expenditures, so Governor Harry Woodring established the Kansas Emergency Relief Commission (KERC), a bipartisan group of twelve to gather necessary statistics. The commission chose John Godfrey Stutz as its executive director. Stutz proved to be an exceptional person and politician. Born in a dugout house on the plains of Kansas, he traveled to Kansas State Agricultural College after finishing elementary school. He completed a high school course and received a college degree in four years. His studies at the University of Kansas were interrupted by service in World War I. Following the armistice, he enrolled at the University of Chicago for a time and then became executive director of the Kansas League of Municipalities.[13]

The league loaned him to KERC, where he insisted that relief work should suffer no political interference. This position was in line with New Deal relief policy, and he quickly found favor with the Federal Emergency Relief Administration (FERA) officials, a program established in the early years of the New Deal. The FERA field administrator wrote his chief, Harry Hopkins, that "we now have in Kansas one of the best State Relief Administration setups." Hopkins, who took pride in running his relief programs without political influence, agreed and wrote the postmaster general's office that he believed Stutz to be "thoroughly competent and in the main the decisions that are made represent his best judgment." Among other innovations that Kansans found difficult to accept, Stutz began forcing county commissioners to hire professional social workers and to keep accurate records.[14]

The election of 1932 brought significant changes in the approach to relief. By that time over one million people in the Midwest were on relief of some type, and others were receiving commodities from the Federal Surplus Relief Corporation (FSRC). Schooled in the philosophy of "rugged individualism," many farmers found Hoover's assistance through loans to states to be distasteful "and felt confused, guilty, and ashamed" over receiving it. The New Deal philosophy, by contrast, emerged with the passage of the FERA in May 1933. This approach provided direct grants to states to permit their relief agencies to increase their spending efforts. Kansas chose to use its relief grants for building roads.[15]

By March 1935 the KERC was handling 113,519 relief cases,

and in 1936 the agency estimated that it had distributed over $1.3 million in federal surplus relief commodities. The devastating dust bowls of the period brought another change as drought produced starving cattle as well as hungry people. Livestock were dying by the tens of thousands, and Harry Hopkins's temporary Civil Works Administration (CWA) began purchasing cattle in 1934 with factories in Kansas City, Parsons, Topeka, and Wichita processing 107,000 head. The canned meat was distributed as surplus commodities in poor relief programs. As of June 12, 1935, the federal government had butchered 520,676 animals in Kansas at a price of over $7.6 million.[16]

Dust bowl problems became so acute that a conference of agricultural college representatives from Colorado, Kansas, New Mexico, Oklahoma, and Texas met in Garden City on April 16 and 17, 1935. The conferees recommended an emergency program to control soil erosion. Their report noted that many people had abandoned their farms and more were planning to move, and when they did, they would "become relief charges, wherever they go." The following month Harry Hopkins pledged an increase of $6 million monthly in aid until the drought broke. That September, New Dealers promised to use Public Works Administration (PWA) funds to employ farmers on work relief. The KERC established transient camps in Kansas City, Topeka, and Wichita to handle this type of poverty, and by 1935 the Works Progress Administration (WPA, renamed Works Projects Administration in 1939) was employing 13,700 Kansas men and women, many of them of rural origins.[17]

Wichita witnessed a serious riot in 1934 directed at the Sedgwick County relief administration. The disturbance was sufficiently violent for Mayor Schuyler Crawford to request that Governor Landon dispatch National Guard troops there. Protesters demanded the removal of poor commissioner B. E. "Gene" George, and some invaded the relief headquarters. When county commissioners quizzed them, they complained that social workers had been insulting and insensitive. John Stutz immediately shut down CWA relief projects temporarily, with Harry Hopkins complaining that people striking on a work relief program leads "the public to think they don't need work or they wouldn't strike." An investigation revealed that the protesters were justified, and the county had "a cellar to garret house cleaning." This episode revealed what disgruntled workers could do when united, a concept not lost on future angry workers on a broader scale two years later.[18]

Another transition in New Deal philosophy took place in 1935 with an increased emphasis on work relief rather than assistance through "make work." On April 25 Congress approved the Emergency Relief Appropriations Act, under which President Franklin D. Roosevelt established the WPA, and he named Harry Hopkins as its administrator. The KERC immediately gave the WPA its work relief clients. Without these new federal relief funds, one authority wrote, "life itself would have become impossible" in drought-stricken southwestern Kansas. The law also empowered the president to create the Resettlement Administration (RA) to build community settlements for low-income suburbanites, called "Greenbelt towns." It also sought to aid marginal farmers by granting loans to purchase farms and machinery.[19]

The WPA established guidelines stipulating that work projects had to have local sponsors and be useful, be conducted on public property, and be completed by the end of each fiscal year. It implemented Hopkins's philosophy about the human need to earn one's pay, articulated in his statement "I don't think anyone can go on year after year, month after month accepting relief without affecting his character in some way unfavorably." His WPA was designed to save the dignity of unemployed workers. As Hopkins explained it, meaningful work "preserves a man's morale. It saves his skill. It gives him a chance to do something useful," a philosophy his boss had promoted since he was governor of New York in 1929, when the Great Crash unfolded. Although not stated, the program would also eliminate insensitive caseworkers "snooping" in "reliefers" homes for evidence to prove that they did not need assistance. The WPA spent approximately 85 percent of its funds on labor, striving to secure workers "a security wage" of thirty cents minimum or the prevailing local hourly rates, whichever was highest, with an average monthly schedule of 120 to 140 hours of work. Despite his determination to avoid politics in his relief programs, Hopkins was forced to violate his philosophy because of political developments in Kansas.[20]

The election of 1932 brought change to Kansas government with the rise of Alfred M. Landon to the governorship. Nicknamed the "Fox" by his University of Kansas fraternity brothers for his adroit ability to lift chickens off their roost without raising an alarm, Landon continued playing the role of the fox in obtaining relief funds for Kansas. He found a staggering 235,000 unemployed people in his state out of a population of 2 million. When Kansas received its first FERA allotment, Landon asked Hopkins for additional funds. He pleaded that in his "largely agricultural" state, not only did his farmers suffer from low crop prices, but drought created severe conditions in eighteen to twenty-nine counties, resulting in losses in garden crops in three-fourths of the state. Most important, Landon emphasized that the Kansas constitution forbade the state from assisting counties in their poor relief programs. The governor, therefore, requested additional assistance up to 40 percent of his total relief needs rather than the required three-to-one matching ratio, or the 25 percent that FERA grants stipulated.[21]

Hopkins approved his request with a penciled note at the bottom of Landon's letter that read, "Yes 40 percent ok Hopkins." A month later KERC secretary John Stutz asked Hopkins for "a stay of execution on the rule of 40-60" in case the special legislative session failed to comply with Landon's request for permission for counties to increase their level of relief spending. Otherwise, some counties would have "a shortage of funds." Although it was difficult for members of the agrarian-dominated legislature to understand why hungry people did not feed themselves from their gardens and livestock or why their relatives declined to help them, the solons grudgingly fulfilled their obligation and voted to allow counties to use their relief funds on road construction. Hopkins's generosity undoubtedly was prompted by the work of Stutz, as the field representative of FERA who asserted that "we now have in Kansas one of the best State Relief Administration set-ups." All this FERA staff admiration of Stutz was not completely correct, of course, because Stutz was well-known for his favoritism toward Republican relief applicants, yet his administration of this federal program won the staff's approval.[22]

When the special session of the state legislature approved authority for county and state highway construction, Attorney General Ronald Boynton declared the action unconstitutional. He cited Article 7, Section 4, of the state constitution that "the respective counties of the state shall provide, as may be prescribed by law, for those inhabitants who, by reason of age, infirmity, or other misfortune, may have claims upon the sympathy and aid of society." He argued that while this clause authorized counties to provide for relief, it forbade state financial assistance in those endeavors, an interpretation Governor Landon happily accepted. Landon told Boynton to challenge the law authorizing the Highway Department to borrow money to finance work relief to supplement the county spending on highway construction in a quo warranto proceeding, asking for a declaration of finding as to the law's validity. Much to their consternation, they won *State ex rel. Boynton v. State Highway Commission* when the state supreme court declared that the constitution "nowhere prohibits the State from making provision for the poor and needy." "To the extent, therefore, that the bill in question attempts to or does furnish relief to the poor and needy," the justices added, "it violates no constitutional provision." The Landon administration failed to relay this decision to federal relief authorities.[23]

One year later L. L. Ecker sent a memorandum to Aubrey Williams, a trusted Hopkins lieutenant, on Kansas relief spending. The state had "fared comparatively well," considering it had never allotted money for unemployment relief. In February 1935 the lower house of the state legislature appropriated $775,000 for the succeeding twenty-eight months to pay the salaries of state administrators for supervision of relief. Stutz then had to prompt the reluctant state senate that if senators failed to approve the measure, federal relief officials would withhold federal relief assistance "tomorrow." He reminded the lawmakers that the national government had contributed $30 million to Kansas relief, while the counties had raised only $6 million as a matching amount.

The senators approved the appropriation but only after informing Stutz they were "tired of being told what to do."[24]

Local Kansas governments had spent over $13 million in the
previous thirty-three months, compared to the state's contribution of "only 3/10 of one percent of all relief expenditures from
public funds," which went toward the administration of the programs. This arrangement upset FERA officials because it placed "a
serious hardship" on local financing and also because federal law
required that both state and local ability to contribute should be
exhausted before federal spending becomes available. Thus, by
maintaining the fiction that the state constitution forbade state
spending for relief, the federal government had provided 73.7
percent of the state's relief requirements, excepting administrative costs, during the previous thirty-three months, rather than
the legal 25 percent.[25]

Exacerbating the situation, Landon wired Hopkins at this point
that his public schools were in dire financial circumstances and
the current drought precluded county and local governments
from meeting the crisis. The governor pleaded for more money
despite the state having $1.5 million in unencumbered cash at
the end of fiscal year 1936, compared with $900,000 the previ-
ous year. He had fooled Hopkins once; perhaps he could do it
again. When a reporter suggested Landon's presidential candidacy was being boosted by his balancing the state budget, Hopkins exploded. Ignoring the fact that Landon had persuaded the
state legislature to enact a cash-basis law, which required all state
agencies to present budgets showing their expected sources of
revenue and expenditures and then hold public hearings, Hopkins snapped that "the state has not put up a dime for unemployment relief. Its Governor has made no effort to do so, as far as I
know," adding that Landon "was trying to get enough from me
to keep his schools going." Unfortunately for Hopkins, many
agreed with a *New York Times* editorial that falsely accused the
bureaucrat of not only having his facts wrong but of making an
unnecessarily partisan assault on the innocent Kansan.[26]

Emanuel Haldeman-Julius, the Little Blue Book publisher in
Girard, informed his readers that the state constitution required

a balanced budget. Landon had managed to balance his every year with help from the federal government. "If the money spent by Uncle Sam had really been spent by Landon," Haldeman-Julius explained, "the state treasury would have gone several hundred million dollars in the red." The Socialist editor was pleased with the great improvement in roads and bridges in Crawford County as a result of federal funding. In addition, the New Deal provided the county with a $65,000 fairgrounds, a new fire station for Girard, and a $15,000 swimming pool, and work would soon begin on a $35,000 gymnasium. The local Civilian Conservation Corps was building "a vast artificial lake, . . . which will give this county a wonderful summer resort." While Landon was posing as the financial savior of Kansas, he resisted all efforts "to call a special session of the legislature to amend the Constitution" to permit "the state to shoulder its share of the necessary expense." Landon's balanced budget, he noted, is "all splattered with blood."[27]

When Congress included a proviso to an appropriations act in 1936 that all federal appointees with $5,000 or more annual salary required senatorial confirmation, the Roosevelt administration concluded the lawmakers were trying to politicize the WPA. Hopkins declared that "there was nothing for it but to be all-political." When Democrat Walter Huxman was elected governor in the Roosevelt landslide of 1936, Evan Griffith of Manhattan served as WPA director until the new governor appointed him highway commissioner and Democrat Clarence G. Nevins to direct work relief in Kansas. Nevins had accumulated experience in relief work while serving on the KERC under Stutz. The *Topeka State Journal* called attention at that time to the importance of federal relief to the state. In 1934 Kansas received almost $22 million in relief funds compared to over $118 million for the state's agricultural crops.[28]

Meanwhile, dissatisfaction and dissension arose over the unemployment crisis, both because the problem was so widespread and because for the first time the federal government injected itself into what had been solely a state and local issue of relief. Groups began to form spontaneously to assist and lobby for those unfortunates who could not help themselves by acting singly. They evolved from sharing philanthropic and charitable goals to banding together, similar to unions, in order to achieve greater strength and empathy for those who could not find work.

The Unemployed Trading Post was chartered in Wichita on May 10, 1933. Those who were able contributed new and used merchandise, which was made available to the needy at reasonable prices. The poor, in turn, accepted whatever jobs were open to earn trading post dollars to purchase needed commodities. As the crisis worsened, this type of agency evolved into organizations to assist in the promotion of public works and to protect members from any discrimination, injustice, or favoritism of agency personnel who distributed relief or relief work unfairly.[29]

In the fall of 1933 Olaf Larsen founded the Worker's Education and Protective League of Kansas and began recruiting direct and work relief men. On the day the Civil Works Administration was terminated, 1,500 of his followers answered his call and held a protest meeting, demanding the firing of Shawnee County poor commissioner Lyle O. Armel and John Stutz. The demonstrators, including men, women, and children, marched peacefully through the capital city, escorted by two police motorcycles. Mayor Omar B. Ketchum congratulated them on their orderly demonstration, and Governor Alf Landon addressed them with assurances that the coming special session of the state legislature would discuss their problems. This mobilization demonstrated "how a large group of unemployed, most of whom had time to spare, could be effectively mobilized."[30]

Ernest F. McNutt, Kansas secretary of the Communist Labor Party of America, listed fifty-three such organizations as having been founded from 1933 to 1935, but this number includes only those that sought charters from the state. Many decided not to register, and all existed for various lengths of time. Answering McNutt's call, representatives of twenty-five of these groups met in Emporia on June 7–8, 1935, and organized the Kansas Allied Workers (KAW). One year later this organization agreed to affiliate with the Workers Alliance of America (WAA). The radical WAA was organized in 1935 and met again the following year to hear chairman David Lasser call attention to "the more and more frequent resort to the armed forces of the state, the use of tear gas bombs [that] indicates the determination of the masters of our industrial system to crush the labor movement." The WAA was most active in New York and New Jersey, but Lasser noted that he had spoken to "more than 50,000 unemployed and relief workers in eastern and midwestern states" and found "a deep-seated resentment against the new wage scale [of the WPA]." He proposed a campaign to aim for a $1 pay scale with a thirty-hour workweek.[31]

The WAA tried to bring uniformity to programs and actions of unemployed groups that were pressuring the national government. The *New York Times* was unsympathetic to its goals. The editor wrote that this new pressure group "represented a threat of governmental action controlled by organized minorities [that] will be broader and more disquieting than before." The editor was convinced that "this rising political mischief should be firmly dealt with in its very beginnings": "The right to strike by men who have made themselves wards and direct beneficiaries of the Government should be declared to be no right at all, but rather a public imposition."[32]

Lasser lamented the fate of the current fourteen million unemployed, and the WAA endorsed the Lundeen Bill, introduced in Congress in 1934, which would provide unemployment insurance to both unemployed laborers and farmers. The American Federation of Labor opposed this measure because it included farmers, and the organization wanted to cover laborers first. It also sought to obtain recognition from the government to represent unemployed men and women. The KAW established its headquarters in Topeka and elected McNutt as its secretary-treasurer and general factotum. He had been chosen a delegate to the National Emergency Convention of the Socialists in Chicago in 1919. He stated publicly then that he favored support of the Bolshevik uprising in Russia. He later joined the CPUSA and made his living as a printer. Both the KAW and the WAA endorsed government ownership of monopolies and a vast federal housing program. These stances made it easy for groups to label them communistic. Undoubtedly some members, such as McNutt, belonged to the CPUSA, but claims such as a writer made in the *Topeka State Journal*—that "national alliance members have been whooping it up for Leon Trotsky, booing the American Federation of Labor (because they opposed including farmers in the Lundeen Bill) claiming that capitalism is dead"—made it easier to apply the label loosely to the entire organization of seven hundred thousand people, including the seventy thousand members in Kansas.[33]

The Kansas Allied Workers lobbied for a state law setting fifty cents as the minimum wage and free school textbooks. It also endorsed the Lundeen Bill, demanded codrivers for safety reason on all trucks and buses operating on Kansas highways, and stressed the need for improved relief, both in amounts and procedures. When Governor Landon called a special session of the legislature to consider constitutional amendments to permit the state to assist in relief efforts, a power the state supreme court said already existed, KAW leaders met with him. They sought his permission to present their "demands" to lawmakers, including action to relieve the distress of old people during the interim before they became eligible for Social Security benefits, a crisis that would unfold later. Landon told them this action was beyond the scope of the executive branch, but he used his office to arrange a meeting for them with the house speaker and lieutenant governor to discuss their concerns. The effort proved fruitless, and KAW members staged a "sit in" of the legislature until it adjourned without helping them. All these activities received extensive coverage in the national and state press.[34]

Many people, including President Franklin D. Roosevelt and numerous KAW supporters, foresaw the advantages of realigning political coalitions during this economic crisis. In June 1936, months before the presidential election and one month after affiliating with WAA, a special committee of KAW officials met and heard political speakers espouse the concept of a Farmer-Labor party in Kansas. T. J. Tidler, representing "certain elements in the Socialist party," urged this coalition because "the present political organizations" appeared inadequate in the current crisis. Max Salzman of the CPUSA recommended that the "most pro-

gressive movement . . . among the farmers and laborers and the
middle class" work toward the same goal. Finally, Joseph Morris spoke for the "organized unemployed," or the KAW, suggesting that these people "should be the first to accept" such an idea
although this goal had failed in the past "because of the working
class people's failure to take a stand." Again they failed to take a
stand, and the concept never took root, except for Minnesota's
successful Farmer-Labor Party.[35]

These organizations, especially KAW (renamed Kansas Workers
Alliance in 1937), were always ready to lend protesters a helping
hand, such as was needed in the Tri-State region. The Depression hit the coal industry particularly hard, and soon Cherokee
and Crawford Counties were overwhelmed with relief problems.
After termination of the CWA in March 1934, dissension arose
over employment of needy workers and the use of a steam shovel
on the airport project in Pittsburg that displaced them. Led by
Alexander Howat, aggrieved workers formed the Farmer-Labor
Union (the local newspaper labeled it "Legion"), marched on the
airport in protest, and had a peaceable meeting with the county
commissioners in which they discussed their grievances. When
the issue first arose and the men walked off the job, Stutz canceled
their work project, a preview of what he would do in the future.
They informed the commissioners they could accept use of the
steam shovel and requested them to inform Stutz of the conces-
sion so he could revive the project. The committee also complained of men who had received work relief but did not need it
and that other needy workers were ignored. One commissioner,
in defense, asked them rhetorically, "How can anyone pick 1,200
of the most worthy men among 3,000?"[36]

A week after the first protest, Stutz telegraphed county poor
commissioner Marie Youngberg that he was ordering resumption
of the work project. This was great news to all sides as women and
children were suffering from want of food, and there were wor-
ries that unrest and violence might occur as a result. With news
of a settlement, the relief office in Pittsburg opened on Monday
morning, and everything proceeded smoothly, although Stutz had
stipulated that guards must be on hand to prevent violence. This

settlement, however, did not resolve the basic problem of further mine shutdowns, which resulted in the unemployment of 2,200 miners. The county commissioners, Youngberg, and President Henry Allai of District 14 of the United Mine Workers (UMW) telegraphed Harry Hopkins, pleading for more relief money for the area. They expected it to take several days for his response, but he quickly increased relief funds for the May quota when he heard about the layoffs.[37]

Five men were put on trial for their actions in the preliminary riot at the county commissioners' office in Pittsburg. Rudolph Smith and Frank Leavitt were charged with having led the "mob" amid calls of "Get a rope" and "Take care of him," before throwing a chair at Commissioner W. A. Beasley, seriously injuring him. On the witness stand Beasley exposed his back, showing "a large area still black and blue with large welts still standing out." One clerical worker identified Albert "Blackie" Lewis as the person who had shouted, "Let's hang him." The relief situation in Pittsburg was alleviated when John Stutz recommended separating relief activities from the local Red Cross. Acting on this suggestion, county commissioners replaced Youngberg as poor commissioner, and she retained her position in the Red Cross office in Pittsburg.[38]

Emporia faced a similar crisis the following summer, and by then regional Communists were becoming directly involved in the unemployment issue. At the same time a meeting was called in that city to form a state organization, the Kansas Allied Workers, and Emporia workers went on strike. While the local leader of KAW was not directly involved, he urged the men to seek more evidence of working conditions before striking. The 150 protesters demanded that WPA wages be raised from thirty cents to what they claimed was the prevailing Lyon County rate of forty cents, to offset reduction in hours allowed. In addition, the strikers "demanded" grocery orders, milk for children and the sick, and free medical assistance. William Burnley of Kansas City, Kansas, opened the meeting, saying he was a member of the National Executive Board of the American Workers Union (AWU), and he urged his listeners to support the Lundeen Bill.[39]

The AWU was a unit of the Socialist Party in St. Louis, where

Frank and Kate O'Hare were members. A large union with both employed and unemployed members, it enjoyed its greatest success in Wyandotte County, where it claimed 2,700 members. It began branching out and at the Emporia meeting agreed to affiliate with the KAW in 1936. John Hester was named state organizer, and his wife, Helen, was a delegate to the Emporia gathering. The mother of a three-year-old boy, Mrs. Hester was a former Beloit social worker who had been fired for her organizing activities. Officials found CPUSA literature in her possession at the Emporia meeting, but no one charged her with being a Communist at that time.[40]

Poor commissioner Shirley Prior notified the strikers that John Stutz was demanding more evidence that the prevailing wage rate was forty cents and that she was only following orders. The next morning, while Mrs. Hester addressed a crowd of seventy-five workers, a telegram from Stutz was read that said a local committee had set their hourly rate and it must be implemented, which received a positive reaction. When asked why they were clapping over this "serious" setback, they responded: "Let him cut off relief, that is just what we want. It will bring a showdown."[41]

At a mass meeting two days later, local strikers made it known to KAW leaders that they wanted to handle their own situation. They appointed a special strike committee to direct activities and care for "anyone suffering from lack of food," and they discussed setting up a soup kitchen. Despite their desire to control local developments, Mrs. Hester continued to address their meetings. She denounced the Stutz statement that he could not guarantee the forty-cent wage scale. "Don't you see what they are doing?" Mrs. Hester shouted. "They are afraid to come through with this wage now for it would hurt their forthcoming plan to put the workers on a slave labor basis of 20 cents an hour and a forty hour week next month." She urged the strikers to extend their walkout and to send people to other counties to expand the strike. The KAW asked for a meeting with strike leaders, and Mrs. Hester announced their decision to accept the invitation. Jack Shaw, "another American Workers Unionist," addressed the crowd, "assailing government policies in general."[42]

When interviewed, Mrs. Hester explained that her "chief interest was traveling place to place, speaking to the unemployed." The Hesters had no home and did not know where they would go next. Mrs. Hester denied rumors by KAW leaders who were asserting that Jack Shaw, R. Gillespie, and William Burnley of Kansas City were Communists. "I never met the young men before the unemployment convention," she asserted, "but our economic ideas are the same." This denial is interesting as she explained that she and her husband were members of the AWU, headquartered in St. Louis and that, while attending the unemployment conference, "it was purely an accident that I took part in the strike situation here." Yet she and her husband were officers in the AWU and surely knew whom they had chosen to accompany them on the trip.[43]

There were strikers who wanted to return to work, so the county commissioners telegraphed Stutz, asking him to relent and reopen the project. He refused, and strikers held another meeting at which the men voted eight to one to continue to hold out. Commissioner Prior announced a week later that work had been reinitiated for those who wanted employment at thirty cents and deputy sheriffs would guard the project. Strikers finally voted to return to work "under protest," and the holdouts gradually yielded.[44]

In early August 1935 the FERA cut work relief funds by 67.5 percent, or from $225,000 to $80,000, for the next five weeks in Wyandotte County, the area of greatest AWU strength. The WPA would not be ready to hire those who were employable until early September. On August 6 roughly one hundred relief workers marched on the county courthouse, seized control, and declared they would not vacate it until their demands were met. (This was some five months before the nation witnessed the first "sit-down" strike, a work stoppage by autoworkers in Flint, Michigan.)

The striking workers sent out members in automobiles to nearby work relief projects to invite others to join their protest, and soon a thousand people were demonstrating, a group that eventually swelled to two thousand. Workers confronted Frank M. Holcomb, chairman of the county commissioners, with shouts of "drag him out" and forced him to agree to consult with the other commissioners to increase county funding to make up for the projected FERA reductions. They wanted the full amount in cash for the relief cards they had signed on July 12, or more than $30 rather than the reduction to about $10 monthly, and a 25 percent increase in the county relief budget until September. They also insisted on free milk for children, the aged, and the ill and that ice water be made available on work relief projects, all "doable" demands. But the marchers insisted that all county employees with salaries of $100 or more must donate one month's pay and all others a half-month's pay to the county relief fund, which hit home with officials' pocketbooks and was summarily rejected. Marchers demanded there be no eviction for failure to pay rent and that their water and gas supplies be kept running during the five-week interim. They endorsed the radical Lundeen Bill, and they included the interesting requirement that the county provide them with food and beds during their occupancy of the county courthouse.[45]

The strikers sang, tried to sleep, and managed to remain calm and peaceful the first day and night. They wired President Roosevelt that 6,500 families in Wyandotte County were facing starvation and eviction from their homes. The group, led by the Reverend Francis J. "Frank" Paine, chairman of the county's Old Age Pension Society, or the Townsend Club, appointed twenty "policemen" to maintain order, keep the courthouse clean, and eject Communists from the movement. The second morning in Kansas City, Kansas, they staged a march to Seventh and Minnesota and back to the courthouse. On the third day state senator Joseph S. McDonald negotiated an agreement with the KERC and current state WPA director Evan Griffith to persuade Washington DC officials to continue FERA funding until the WPA projects were under way the following month. John Stutz began distributing an additional $225,000 to Kansas counties "on the basis of need." All these demands, as well as the milk and groceries for those who were literally starving, were fulfilled. The county commissioners agreed to offer office space for use of a committee of protesters in the old county jail. On August 11 Reverend Paine addressed the crowd, telling them of the successful conclusions, and adjourned the gathering.[46]

They were not entirely successful in keeping out Communists. Authorities arrested Jack Shaw with Communist literature in his possession. When Paine tried to disperse the peaceful crowd, Helen Hester informed him they were not finished with their business, insisting the crowd march on city hall and free Shaw. "Stay until we starve," she shouted, "stick with it until we get relief, no matter how long it is." Paine warned the group that these were "outsiders trying to cause excitement," and he left the meeting. Others were tiring of the demonstrations, having been there two long days, and they also left. When some demonstrators arrived at city hall and refused to leave, officials arrested Hester, William Burnley, and three other radicals. Authorities searched Burnley's house, where the Hesters were staying with their son, and found "a quantity of alleged Communist literature." On August 12 the radicals were fined $50 for vagrancy. Those who were outsiders were ordered to go home and not return, and this ended the Kansas City demonstration.[47]

The KAW met its first major test in a different situation while supporting the "drought farmers" of Shawnee and surrounding counties in March 1937. This proved to be a new development with farmers using union weapons to demand "rights." In the most rural counties of Kansas, farmers and farm laborers were the principal clients on work relief. The "Shawnee County Farmers Rebellion" arose when the drought farmers were cut off from their WPA jobs and before the RA was fully operational. Part of these layoffs stemmed from machinery replacing the work they and their horses had performed. Their livestock was starving, their families were hungry, and now they had lost their work relief. When conditions worsened, they met with Governor Landon to discuss their problems. They asked for reinstatement of their WPA jobs and a minimum thirty-hour workweek at fifty cents hourly. Landon, they claimed, *"deliberately washed his hands"* of the unemployed workers and busted farmers of Kansas. "The KERC and WPA heads [Stutz and Griffith] treated us the same way," they complained.[48]

The issue came to a head when President Roosevelt ordered a retrenchment in WPA funding. A deficiency appropriation bill of $789 million was passed to carry the WPA through June 30, 1937. To attack this deficit problem for the next fiscal year, a layoff of six hundred thousand employees was proposed. Governors of six major states called for a meeting at the White House to discuss the crisis. David Lasser insisted the issue arose because FDR had failed "to redeem his promise to provide WPA jobs for all employables on relief rolls." Lasser, in turn, met with the president and demanded a 20 percent increase for the WPA instead, in "security wages." Eventually, the WAA staged a massive march on the U.S. Capitol Building in August 1937 and saved three hundred thousand jobs. Meanwhile, this created an emergency in the Kansas relief rolls.[49]

Discussing their plight with county commissioners proved unsatisfactory as these officials already faced too many demands for their limited relief funds, so the farmers called a protest meeting in the KAW hall in Topeka, where some 250 farmers from Shawnee and surrounding counties gathered. They sent scores of telegrams to Roosevelt, Hopkins, and WPA officials lamenting that "our children and livestock are starving," to no avail. It was not until after Governor Walter Huxman's inauguration in 1937 that they finally saw action, when he arranged a meeting of the distraught farmers and Cal Ward of Omaha, the regional director of RA. "With so much pressure," KAW secretary McNutt wrote, "the resettlement administration was pushed into action and by February 1 resettlement checks was [sic] being received." The farmers had other complaints against the Shawnee County relief authorities, and sixty of them occupied the office overnight until they won their demand for the county to fill grocery orders for the needy. The farm rebellion also raised money to send delegates to participate in the demonstration in Washington DC to get the attention of Congress to their plight and increase WPA rolls. This successful uprising increased agrarian membership in KAW to about three hundred farmers.[50]

On March 1, 1937, following the initial WPA contractions, approximately fifty former WPA employees met in the KAW hall.

They decided to petition Governor Walter Huxman for a meeting with him, the Shawnee County commissioners, and the Shawnee delegates to the state legislature to discuss their situation, which had improved very little. At that point the legislature was dead-locked over how to finance the new Social Security pension plan. Governor Huxman had recommended a regressive one-cent sales tax increase to provide the money, which the lawmakers ultimately had to accept. The senate wanted the state to assume the entire burden, but the house insisted on the state providing $2 million, the federal $2 million, and the county units $4.5 million, disre-garding the burden under which the local governments already labored by providing relief for so-called unemployables and their families. Also at issue was the question of "beer or no beer." Law-makers finally accepted the sale of 3.2 malt beverages, shatter-ing their long-held intoxicating principles primarily because of the need for additional revenues from some source. The house version of the measure placated the traditional Prohibitionists by assuring them that 3.2 beer was nonintoxicating, and the bill passed as a revenue act because of the urgent need for money.[51]

The Shawnee County commissioners finally met with KAW leaders in what proved to be a stormy session. The unemploy-ables demanded, among other exactions, that the county pay their rent and/or taxes during the crisis and that their agency be rec-ognized as their collective bargaining unit. The commissioners remained adamant. They refused recognition, insisting that no one in the county was being denied assistance if they were eli-gible for relief, although the mere application did not guarantee they would receive it. Furthermore, the county could not assume any further financial burdens as their funds were almost depleted because of the increased financial strains of recent weeks, a sugges-tion that some might be denied assistance in the future. When the unemployed complained about the inefficiency of the poor relief program, a harbinger of future discord, the commissioners lamely responded that their relief provisions and procedures were the best they could possibly provide. Workers disgruntled over the admin-istration of their relief work in Wichita had created a serious riot in 1934 and thus set a precedent for the KAW workers to emulate.[52]

After two weeks of meetings, complaining, and occasionally impossible demands, the KAW people took direct action. Much to the surprise of county officials, approximately 150 men and women seized the relief headquarters on March 20 in an unusual sit-down strike, a month after the end of the action in Flint, Michigan, had gained widespread notoriety. The crowd, in good humor, spent the night at relief headquarters with a stringed orchestra. Those who did not want to dance played pitch or other card games. The reinstatement of WPA workers over age sixty-five who had been discharged proved to be their major demand. As a lesser grievance, they wanted the quotas of production terminated in the WPA sewing room that occupied the third floor of the relief offices, a new issue injected into the negotiations. With this show of support, 142 sewing room workers struck later that night, demanding the resignation of poor commissioner Lyle O. Armel and the appointment of an entirely new county relief staff. They further insisted on the county paying rent for the unemployables not on relief; a distribution of surplus commodities before they spoiled, not afterward; the right of an applicant for relief to choose someone to help present his case; and a 20 percent increase in the county relief budget. The sewing room people specifically wanted a halt to the termination of workers for insufficient production, a cessation of what they considered to be coercion and intimidation by supervisors; the removal of supervisory powers to determine standards of efficiency; and a clear understanding of the functions of their floor stewards. Sheriff Roy Boast and county attorney Paul Harvey, hearing of the strike, investigated and found no evidence of violence. For three days the strikers sat, arms folded, gossiping with neighbors and drawing their pay but with no production. WPA officials said that if the strike continued, their pay would be stopped. A deputy sheriff and a city policeman were "watching over them" until the issue was settled.[53]

After 119 of the women were dismissed, Sheriff Boast's forces finally evicted the 35 who remained, and they encamped in the WPA offices. Only two WPA people were present when the crowd appeared, but another happened to drive by, immediately sensed what was happening, and sent a colleague running to the door to intercept the strikers. The intruders arrived first, though, and held the doors open until their buddies could "squeeze in." Appeals to city officials brought the response that this was a federal affair now and they could not act. Officials were unable to remove them because Judge Richard J. Hopkins was in the nation's capital, and there were no other federal personnel with authority present to act. With great empathy, "just before midnight some WPA officials raised a small fund from their own pockets and sent out for some food for the hungry demonstrators."[54]

The forced occupancy of the first floor, and thus access to the remainder of the building, continued throughout the weekend. The strikers came in shifts, staying a few hours, then returning home to do chores or run necessary errands. Leo Palmer, the leader, threatened to call in two thousand KAW members from across the state to come to Topeka for a "hunger march." It was reported that other unemployed organizations across the Great Plains and the nation were watching with great interest the outcome of the Topeka strike. Lyle Armel responded to these developments with the wry observation that while the occupancy continued, it was causing additional suffering among the "legitimate needy" because relief personnel had no access to their offices to process claims and to carry on their work.[55]

The strikers continued to occupy the first floor, however, determined to stay until they received satisfaction on their grievances. Occasionally, farm groups came and pledged their support. Children joined their parents during the day and then went home at night to sleep. There was a noticeable increase in participants in the evenings and during the night. They stopped dancing for the Sabbath, and a couple of preachers, including C. L. Atkins of the First Congregational Church, delivered sermons. Supporters prepared meals in the KAW hall. Strikers settled their differences with the WPA "temporarily" with additional work relief funds to expand relief rolls but insisted they had "run after" the county commissioners for four years in pursuit of satisfaction and "now they can come to us." If their demands were not met by March 24, they promised to extend their sit-down to the courthouse and prevent transaction of county business, although this action did not materialize. It was reported that many "rubber neckers," as the strikers called spectators, came to view the protest. Finally, on March 27 the county commissioners agreed to meet with the strikers, Armel, and county attorney Harvey in the KERC office of Jerry Driscoll.[56]

Nothing came of this preliminary meeting, except additional mistrust, because the county commissioners insisted on the strikers vacating the building first and then presenting their "demands" later. The group refused to accept this obvious ploy and voted unanimously to continue the strike. They also began applying pressure on the Topeka Chamber of Commerce to support their cause or the KAW would campaign against the pending $850,000 bond issue for a new city hall, not because they opposed it but because they believed relief funding took precedence in this situation. One citizen complained to a newspaper at this point that he was indignant, as a taxpayer, because the county sheriff, the county attorney, and a candidate for mayor had made major contributions to these "irresponsible" strikers.[57]

A breakthrough came on March 28 with the announcement that "through the persistent and special efforts of Democratic Governor Huxman," additional funding had been acquired for WPA projects in Kansas, which resolved that issue momentarily. Federal officials authorized Clarence Nevins to rehire some of the terminated employables over sixty-five as a "temporary" solution until the new pension law went into effect. That day the strikers in Topeka voted to end their ten-day takeover on the promise by the commissioners to give them a hearing. The *Topeka Daily Capital* noted that the "novelty" of the occupancy had "apparently wore off." KAW acquired some three hundred new members during the lengthy conflict.[58]

This controversy took a slightly different twist in southeastern Kansas. A meeting of some 350 KAW members from Crawford, Cherokee, and Bourbon Counties was held in Pittsburg, where they planned a "move-in" of their courthouses on April 1, 1937. Leaders of the group said they were going to strike to protest removal of those over sixty-five from the work relief rolls. Area WPA workers promised a sympathy strike, and Bourbon County farmers Local 43 pledged its support, as did the two Townsend Clubs in Pittsburg. Working with representatives from these three counties posed a problem different from that of the Shawnee County strike. Some KAW leaders believed they should mail their demands to WPA officials as these officials would need time to reply before the three separate counties' commissioners met to consider their responses. All this, obviously, could not be accomplished in the one week remaining before the announced takeover. In addition, the three groups had slightly different agendas to pursue.[59]

The Bourbon County group met again in less than a week and decided on a courthouse occupancy on April 1 regardless of the decisions of the other two county delegations. The county relief problems were staggering, and the Bourbon County KAW members wanted to relieve the local government of some of this burden and place it on the shoulders of the WPA, where, they insisted, "it rightly belongs." In addition to the demands that the WPA rehire those over sixty-five who had been terminated, they wanted common labor wages to be increased to fifty cents an hour and to $40 minimum monthly. They demanded work assignment immediately for all eligible and certified county relief applicants. Finally, after employables were assigned to WPA jobs, they insisted that all direct relief payments be raised to $30 monthly until the Social Security pensions were available. The county commissioners expressed sympathy but declared they were unable financially to do more than what they were currently providing. Leaders set a strike for all three counties for April 1 despite Clarence Nevins's promise of extra WPA funding to rehire elderly workers temporarily.[60]

The KAW men and women in Pittsburg met and voted to proceed with their sit-down, but first they had to enjoy a hearty lunch scavenged by their local "mooching committee." "Enough food to cover the top of a large table and $10.40 was solicited." The money would be used to buy more food later. After the repast a caravan of 150 people drove to Girard, where they finally determined arbitration was the best route. They chose a committee that included John Babbitt, A. J. Fritter, Booker T. Cummins, and Bill Wiggins to accompany officials to Topeka to plead their case with WPA leaders. The WPA agreed to adjust unfair wage scales and quotas of workers and promised transportation of WPA workers for long distances to jobs or assign them work closer to home. Thus ended the uprising.[61]

A reversal of causes occurred on a paving job near Chanute with a dispute between workers and the private company employing them. Cherokee County, which had had a strike that brought about martial law over the shooting of nine men in 1935, saw another strike in 1937. Common laborers demanded their wages be raised from thirty-five cents to the fifty-cent level being paid on WPA jobs in the area. The superintendent informed the men their thirty-five-cent rate was set by the state Highway Department and ordered work resumed the next morning. The workers, represented by KAW, refused to return and blockaded the highway, preventing materials from reaching the project. The state president of KAW, Ralph Ridley of Columbus, received a telegram from Evan Griffith affirming what the superintendent had told the strikers, which did not satisfy the workers. Ridley responded that the Highway Commission had found ways in the past to increase workers' pay even after contracts had been let. Spring rains prevented a showdown on the construction job, though, but when the weather cleared, violence again threatened. Supply trucks appeared, and workers stopped them and told the drivers to return to town as there would be no work that day. The sheriff arrived and arrested four pickets. The remaining strikers voted forty to seven to return to work, the four pickets were not charged, and the strike ended.[62]

With these sit-downs drawing national attention and setting a bad precedent for WPA projects, the House of Representatives' Rules Committee voted to investigate. This decision came after committee chairman John O'Connor visited with President Roosevelt, and his committee had "a bitter and prolonged debate" over a resolution calling for an inquiry into the automobile industry, introduced by Texas Democrat Martin Dies. Senate leaders subsequently tried to slough off the issue to the Interstate Commerce Committee, but conservative southern Democrats defeated this move. President Roosevelt declined to express his opinion at a news conference.[63]

When Congress debated the $1.5 billion relief bill that May, members voted to cut Harry Hopkins's salary from $12,000 to $10,000, and an attempt was made to amend the measure to deny relief workers the right to strike. "This is the most ridiculous thing I ever heard of," thundered Democrat Maury Maverick of Texas. "Why we must be crazy even to listen to a thing like that." He added that the Democratic majority had resembled "a bunch of Chinese warlords fighting among themselves" over pork in the bill. "We've earmarked and earmarked," he shouted, "until the bill hasn't any earmarks left." "I know this is a very strong—almost radical—amendment," admitted Arkansas Democrat Claude A. Fuller, its sponsor, "but there is nothing un-American about it." He blamed the earmarks on the "animosity and rulings" of Harry Hopkins, saying the representatives were just trying to protect their projects.[64]

The next day angry southerners and northerners again agreed to cut Hopkins's salary and resumed their dispute over pork in the relief bill. They continued the bitter debate over setting aside one-third of the $1.5 billion for "PWA, flood control and highway projects." Democratic majority leader Sam Rayburn of Texas promised he would discuss the controversy with President Roosevelt over the weekend to work out some kind of compromise "fair to every section and every project." President Roosevelt was in a difficult situation at this time, though, with a current Supreme Court fight, but he put pressure on Congress for action. This, plus the Workers Alliance of America demonstration, resulted in a compromise with some WPA reductions. When the appropriations were completed after the WAA march, Roosevelt could assure Lasser in late August that "further dismissals" in WPA projects "will not be necessary."[65]

On March 31, 1937, the state legislature completed its marathon session, and Governor Huxman was reported to be "rushing" to set up the administration for the new social welfare programs in order for the state to qualify for federal financing. On April 3 the Shawnee County commissioners rejected all the strikers' demands, including the firing of Armel, although they failed to reappoint him on May 25 and appointed Frank Long as his replacement.

Armel had been in office for four years, and rumors had circulated the previous year that two of the three commissioners were unhappy with him. The state's leading newspaper believed that the sit-in had aroused the ire of the commissioners to the extent that they had delayed their vote to remove him from office. The commissioners received an unexpected shock, however, when M. T. Kelsey, "an efficient case worker," resigned in protest over the removal of his boss.[66]

At this point a major problem developed that John Stutz had raised before he resigned from the KERC, an issue that the Social Security Act of 1935 had created for elderly workers. Evan Griffith noted that as older persons assigned to WPA qualified for a pension, new replacements could then be made on WPA projects for their vacated jobs. In response to this development, Stutz declared incorrectly that "there is no provision in the Federal Social Security Program for giving pensions to the needy aged."[67]

Part 3 of the Social Security Act of August 14, 1935, provided for grants-in-aid up to $15 monthly to help states meet their cost of old-age pensions for people who would not come under the purview of Old Age and Survivors Insurance (OASI). This type of welfare had been previously handled in Kansas by the county poor commissioner through commodity distribution and by county poor farms but not through grants of money. State law now needed to be changed to establish a pension plan for participation in the national program in order to receive the federal matching funds. Difficulties arose when many legislators proved content with the current system. They also held little sympathy for helping the poor when relatives could do so but declined. Social Security was a whole new approach to relief for the elderly, so the lower house sent a copy of its proposal to Washington to verify that its plan would comply with federal law and thus qualify for the matching grants. After federal approval and extensive debate, the lower house passed its bill on March 13, 1937, by a vote of eighty-two to two. The upper house endorsed a different measure on March 18 with a thirty-seven to zero tally. The proposal then went to conference to iron out the differences between the two approaches, especially over prohibiting persons from receiving old-age assistance if any relative was financially capable of helping them. The conference committee finally omitted this objectionable requirement, and the lower house endorsed the compromise ninety-nine to zero on March 30; the senate gave its approval thirty-four to zero on the same day.[68]

Social welfare officials held a series of informative meetings across the state to explain the new program. Deputy assistant director of social welfare Lester Wickliffe observed that "in time it should reduce the relief rolls to a considerable extent and will place the counties on a more substantial financial structure." One should not confuse old-age assistance with old-age pensions, he reminded his listeners. Pensions were a part of the total picture, but they would not begin until 1942, when persons over sixty-five who had paid into the OASI system would qualify for retirement. The immediate need was to provide assistance for the needy over sixty-five who would never qualify for OASI. Governor Walter Huxman received notice at the end of August that the Kansas program qualified and he could begin to establish the new office. Financed by a sales tax, counties began assistance for the elderly, blind, and dependent children as soon as officials certified them. The federal government would match state funds up to $15 monthly.[69]

The Kansas statute established a state board of social welfare to administer the program, coordinating state funding with matching federal grants. It included this significant reactionary disclaimer: "It is not the policy of the state to discourage or interfere with the universally recognized moral obligation of kindred to provide when possible, for the support of dependent relatives, but rather it is the policy of the state to assist the needy and where necessary, the relatives in providing the necessary assistance for dependents."

Other rural states were even more demeaning by requiring recipients to sign a pauper's oath to qualify. The law provided assistance that would permit abolishing the archaic, degrading poor farm. Several criteria served as guidelines for the board in qualifying people for the assistance: insufficient income; being a Kansas residence for one continuous year; not being an inmate of a state institution; and no transfer of property to anyone by the applicant for two years prior to application.[70]

Meanwhile, the delay in enacting this Social Security program was proving critical to thousands of Kansans. Because of the availability of this assistance later and the need to spread meager relief funds as far as possible, in late January 1937 WPA officials announced that those eligible for old-age assistance (over sixty-five) would be discharged from their jobs gradually, beginning the following month. "If we do not take them off," Clarence Nevins correctly observed, "they would never be eligible for old age assistance." He explained that in addition to their advanced age (life expectancy in America then was sixty-seven, and many of the people he was describing were over sixty-five), their work was often dangerous, and they also needed to be protected from the inclement weather on the Great Plains. He noted that Kansas was the only state in the midwestern region that had been permitted to keep their elderly workers on the WPA rolls. The problem, though, was to resolve the question of what these people were to do for support between their WPA termination date and when the state would have the new system available.[71]

Washington DC officials announced a "springtime" cut in WPA rolls for Kansas from 41,500 to 30,200 by June 1, but the problem of older relief workers went beyond this cutback. This presented a real crisis because action by the state legislature at that point still was indefinite and certainly the timing was questionable as lawmakers had not yet begun even to consider proposals to provide matching relief funds. The day after the announcement by Nevins, state officials received notification that Kansas would receive just over $2.7 million, in matching funds for Social Security assistance, plus money to administer the program whenever the state established it. This heightened the pressure on the legislators because until they acted, those who had been laid off WPA jobs would have no income. Other states faced the same dilemma. The governors of Illinois, Massachusetts, Minnesota, New York, Rhode Island and Wisconsin, in officially protesting the rapid reduction in WPA payrolls, summed up the situation succinctly when they observed that the "costs of relief to the unemployables cannot be bourne [*sic*] by local units of government." Most important, these aged workers were reluctant to give up a WPA job paying a minimum of $30 monthly for a settlement of an unknown amount.[72]

The district supervisor of WPA in the Tri-State region announced that his rolls would be reduced by 10 percent for each of the coming five months, similar to other district cuts. He expressed the hope that the largest reductions would come in the "purely agricultural counties" so that he could take into account "the seasonal decrease" in the coal mining industry because the area would soon see "hundreds" of men unemployed. Fifty of these elderly unemployed met in the KAW hall in Topeka to protest being dropped from the WPA. They decided to petition Governor Huxman, the Shawnee County commissioners, and the county legislative delegation to resolve their problem. The following day they endorsed a resolution to present to the state legislature demanding an old-age "pension" of "not less than $30 monthly." They further went on record as supporting a sit-down strike if a resolution of the situation was not forthcoming.[73]

This pressure produced results. On March 13 Howard O. Hunter assured Senator Arthur Capper that Kansas would be assigned extra WPA funds to prevent further immediate WPA cuts. He emphasized that "no one now employed by the WPA who is still in need will be dismissed" and reminded listeners that when drought farmers had been taken off WPA rolls earlier, they "were not left high and dry but were accepted by the Resettlement Administration for grants and loans."[74]

Three hundred and fifty protesters from Crawford, Cherokee, and Bourbon Counties met in the local labor temple to declare their support for these threatened older workers. Leaders declared that the national relief officers had "proved to their satisfaction" that the difficulties lay in the local administration of relief funds, and they planned a move-in of county relief offices on April 1 if they were not satisfied with improvements. Fortunately, WPA officials resolved the crisis before that deadline.[75]

Dissension continued to simmer over WPA operations in the Tri-State region, however, and organized workers carried on an extensive, and eventually futile, feud with officials in Topeka. In April, while the Shawnee County sit-in was in full swing, Bourbon County KAW people planned a sit-down strike, then concluded it would be advantageous, instead, to arbitrate the issue of WPA removal of persons over sixty-five from work rolls. Clarence Nevins headed off this action by promising to put needy employables back on relief work. Then in early June, Farmer-Labor Union state president Joe Saia charged Crawford County WPA officials with "political corruption and graft." Some 750 persons from the Tri-State region leveled these charges against Crawford County Democratic chairman Dr. Allan W. Sandridge, who responded that Saia was leading the union "to work into a better job." Saia countercharged that WPA timekeepers and foremen were "friends of Dr. Sandridge" who "should be ineligible to be drawing money that was appropriated for you working needy people."[76]

The following month protesters at a mass meeting determined that Saia should lead them on a march to Chanute, where they would meet other dissidents from Baxter Springs and Bourbon County to make certain all certified persons be employed and to force an investigation of "corruption" in the local WPA. They planned to remain in the WPA offices in Chanute "until we get results." Saia again denounced Dr. Sandridge, charging that people who received state jobs "had paid for them" and that the money supported Sandridge's machine. The following week Ralph Ridley brought the KAW organization into the fracas. He had received a telegram from Clarence Nevins promising to "employ every possible certified person that we can get with funds made available" and that they had requested additional funding.[77]

A week later Ridley addressed a joint meeting of five hundred KAW workers and business and professional men that proved productive. They agreed on a joint committee of six businessmen and three workers to investigate charges that "some people are refused relief, while others with means of support are granted assistance." Clarence Nevins laid the blame at the feet of "the local relief office" and further declared that there were insufficient projects to employ all the needy. Ridley replied that there were projects shut down at that time in Cherokee County "because there are no men assigned to operate them." If the men remained united, Ridley declared, "the citizens of Columbus will see that justice is done." If there had not been injustice previously, he insisted, "there would not be a KAW organization with 57 units." Ray Phillips of Columbus said he worked on a WPA job for six months at $5 weekly and that when he was laid off, he applied for county relief. Officials there informed him he "should have saved enough to live a year" even though groceries consumed all his wages. When foremen were ordered to cut back on personnel, they gave no weight to need, and in reducing the number of workers, they "simply laid off those workers he [sic] did not want to work."[78]

Finally, two hundred men from Crawford and Cherokee Counties occupied WPA district headquarters. "We are prepared to stay this time till our demands are met," declared union president Saia. "We are not going to be satisfied with a bunch of promises this time." After occupying the building, the state secretary of KAW, McNutt, observed that "we are just a bunch of law abiding Americans and we have just as good a right in this federal building as anyone else. We intend to sleep and eat here until WPA meets our demands." They insisted that (1) all certified eligible workers be employed until funds were exhausted; (2) discharges be made on the basis of needs, not the whim of foremen; (3) employees be kept on projects until they are completed; (4) all workers be given "their full time"; (5) women be treated the same as men; and (6) three WPA supervisors be discharged as "they have been unfair to labor." Their major bone of contention, Saia declared, was point 3, in which men were discharged if they were not approved by Dr. Sandridge. Police said they had no intention of interfering with the KAW members as "they seem pretty peaceful." The men had money to buy food and were spending nights in the WPA building, with the overflow "in Chanute Park."[79]

Strikers took over the administrative offices after employees left for the day. They ate mulligan stew that evening and had oatmeal and milk the following morning. Trotlines failed to supply fresh fish. That morning they decided to vacate the WPA building after officials asked them to do so "peacefully." Saia, however, promised to return to the WPA offices "if our demands are not met." The strikers voted unanimously to remain in Chanute until they achieved their goals. The acting director of the WPA responded that if discrimination was found, it would be stopped. In case of terminations the WPA retained those "most needed for efficient project completion," and WPA policy treated women and men equally. He added that termination of officials had to be referred to "higher authorities." He made no reference to points 1, 3, and 4.[80]

Marchers soon began drifting home as their leaders were waiting for Clarence Nevins to return from Washington DC, and police reported the next day that only about half of the original 250 marchers remained. Saia, living in a city park, said they would await Nevins's return, and "if he doesn't meet our demands we will move back into WPA headquarters and nothing but a federal court order will get us out." Ridley promised to get as many officials as possible to meet with Nevins to stop "this buck passing." At home the KAWs were told that the district WPA officials were at fault. At the WPA headquarters they blamed the situation on county officials. "When we got to Topeka to see Nevins," Ridley complained, "he blames it on Congress."[81]

Speaking from Topeka, Nevins claimed he had authority to employ people who had been released from their jobs because they had become eligible for old-age assistance. Ridley caught Nevins's ploy that they would reemploy those over sixty-five who were "in need," not all those over sixty-five "who have not bettered their condition." This meant he was leaving it to the local relief offices to determine eligibility, another passing of the buck. Ridley further announced that the county poor fund would "be broke in the next thirty days." He then asked about what would become of the employables who would not be rehired. He promised that the KAW would proceed with its plans to confer with Nevins soon. After police removed Ridley and Saia from the WPA building, most of the remaining strikers "addressed a message of thanks" to Chanute officials for their "kindness and sympathy" and returned home. They had fought the good fight, and all that was left was for Saia and Ridley to meet Nevins in Topeka at his invitation and to hope that he could secure sufficient funding to employ those who needed income until the Social Security old-age plan was implemented.[82]

Communists certainly played a role in the Workers Alliance of America, but it is difficult to determine their influence in Kansas events. The Hesters, Jack Shaw, and William Brumley tried to shape unemployment demonstrations, and CPUSA records show that John Hester reported at a party meeting that "there were three party units in Kansas functioning very slightly, one in Pittsburg and one in Fort Scott and the third in Kansas City." But the CPUSA district that included the Sunflower State "had a relatively small membership throughout its existence." In 1948 Kansas had only six party members. It was former Socialists who provided the leadership for the unemployed organizations.[83]

Anti-Communists, however, managed to see "reds" everywhere. Victor F. Ridder, state chairman of the New York Board of Social Welfare and former director of the WPA in New York City, charged that Communists dominated relief work in that state. He insisted that the WAA controlled $900 million monthly in relief work in the Empire State. His accusations drew the attention of Texas Democrat Martin Dies, chairman of the House Un-American Activities Committee, which was busy investigating all sorts of American organizations for ties to reds. His committee heard a procession of witnesses, including Ridder, testifying as to the influence of Communists. The committee eventually concluded that not only the Boy Scouts but also the WAA was dominated by Communists, an attack that David Lasser hotly denied.[84]

The New Deal continued its WPA projects until 1943, well into World War II, but with constant periodic reductions by an antagonistic Congress from 1938 until its demise. Every congressional cut in appropriations was met with opposition by Kansas relief workers, with the one in 1939 producing a national strike. The workers learned well from the successes of their early demonstrations and managed to keep relief work alive until unemployment during the war effort made it unnecessary.

On the other hand, once Franklin D. Roosevelt and his New Deal statists co-opted the basic features of Socialist statism, the radicals had little else with which to appeal to the voters. While the CPUSA grew slightly during the New Deal and World War II, when the Soviet Union was an ally, the Socialists continued to shrink to oblivion.

Depression, poverty, and hard times are breeding grounds for dissent, agitation, and enlistment of new members into radical organizations. The Great Depression years of the 1930s were no different, as labor and employment issues became a major topic and concern. Millions across the United States were out of work, broke, hungry, and had families to provide for. The Midwest, including Kansas, was particularly hard-hit. The Dust Bowl affected Kansas agriculture, making the land unsuitable for farming, and many farmers had to abandon their farms. National and state relief programs helped, but in desperate times people turn to desperate measures, and socialism and communism seemed attractive answers to some. These organizations benefited from the times, not just in Kansas but in other places of the country. Dissent was also evident as government-funded relief measures only offered partial help to the unemployed.

CONCLUSION

E ducation was a dominant theme in socialism, and Kansas emerged as one center for its implementation. Leaders were determined that educating their followers was vital to the ultimate success of their cause. J. A. Wayland contributed greatly in this regard with his *Appeal to Reason*. The newspaper never served as an outlet for political philosophy, but its fantastic circulation promoted the cause more than any other media. In addition to its written message, the *Appeal* achieved much in advertising and coordinating Socialist speakers who were touring the hustings, spreading the message throughout the nation. The *Appeal*'s mailing list alone was priceless. In keeping with their pedagogic philosophy, Socialists successfully operated their People's College for several years, providing higher-level education for those unable to afford the traditional college route.

Socialism was a heterogeneous movement with a big umbrella to cover great variations in philosophy, goals, and achievements. All the movement's efforts at educating often had a divisive effect and tended to splinter the membership into factions and those into cliques, to accelerate these divisions rather than unify. While they could unite and support a great leader, such as Eugene V. Debs, they could sometimes come apart on the smallest issues, especially political philosophy or strategy. Even American Communists, the most regimented and centrally controlled Socialists, managed to split into groups throughout America, much to the dismay of Kremlin leaders.

Socialism generally did not attract American Catholics basically because the party leaders were anti-clerical. But in the Tri-State Mining Region, where there were numerous French and Italian immigrants who were nominally Catholic, socialism had appeal. Because many of these people lived in poverty, the Catholic clergy could not depend on them for financial support. In general the Catholic miners tended toward anti-clerical positions and were strongly Socialist, following their own leaders, such as Alexander Howat. The church, normally a social hub, was not always present, so the union hall provided the center for social activities and a staging area for marches.

Socialists were on the cutting edge of achieving equality of the sexes. While the Socialist Party was male dominated in the East, the western states accorded women much greater parity. Not only did they promote equality, but some of their finest and most successful members were women. Kate O'Hare was second only to Eugene Debs as a speaker, Annie Diggs was as effective as a political operator as any man, and Caroline Lowe was one of the most capable organizers and lawyers the party had in the Midwest.

Socialists were most successful in implementing their goals within smaller communities. They prevailed frequently on the local level and, when in positions of power, demonstrated they could administer government capably, without signs of radicalism. Their candidates often were farmers, laborers, or people interested in politics or the art of administering government, which made them more effective in promoting local issues. Their success was difficult for members of the dominant middle class to accept. Many believed Socialists were dangerous radicals, but as local leaders, their neighbors seemed so quietly effective in making city hall operate efficiently. Their greatest success came through "gas and water socialism," measures that demonstrated their philosophy was practical and showed taxpayers that taking the profit out of city services actually helped their pocketbooks, sometimes significantly. Gas and water socialism yielded long-lasting benefits; after a brief period needed to establish its efficacy and earn the appreciation of the community, it became a permanent part of American life, especially on the municipal level.

Conclusions can be drawn by comparing radical activities in other areas of the country. Political events in Canton, Illinois, followed a similar pattern to that in Crawford County, Kansas, in the Tri-State region. Canton was in a coal mining district, and Socialists were active there, led by Adolph Germer, a member of the Socialist National Committee and state UMW official. In the municipal election in 1911, Socialists gained a majority on the Canton City Council, with four of the six winners receiving over 60 percent of the vote. While the Socialists were jubilant and looked forward to the mayor's race the next year, the opposition was appalled and immediately organized a Combined, or Fusionist, ticket of "Democrats, Republicans, Law and Order Leaguers, Wide Open Town Advocates, Preachers, Saloon Keepers, Church Members, Gamblers, YMCA, Dive Keepers, Progressives, Mossbacks, Wets, Drys," similar to opposition actions in Crawford County. They made an issue of "Socialism against Capitalism . . . the red flag against the stars and stripes" and eventually managed to rescue their town from this "scourge," although they suffered through a term of a red mayor. As in so many other instances, World War I devastated the Socialists in Canton.[1]

The small town of Marion, Indiana, experienced many of the same tribulations that took place in Kansas. Some of the leading Socialists were businessmen and clergy. The factory areas provided the core strength of the party, but when Socialists gained control of a city government, they achieved "very little of a lasting nature." The main issue in the election of 1917 proved to be prohibition, not war. Superpatriotism dominated the town during and after World War I, and to be a "slacker" in refusing to buy bonds or give lip service to the war effort was considered on par with desecrating the flag. Socialist activities were mostly ignored in capitalist media. When strikers assaulted scabs, the local police judge treated them as "IWWS, anarchists, and every one of you ought to be in the penitentiary." A local Democratic leader asserted that anyone who voted the Socialist ticket was "voting to dishonor the memory of those who lie in Flanders field." Many residents of Marion "felt that Socialism, Bolshevism, and Anarchism were virtually identical." Apparently, the American

Legion in Great Bend, Kansas, was more aggressive in its opposition to Socialists than its comrades in Marion. Otherwise, the
litany sounds familiar.[2]

Elwood, Indiana, experienced a Socialist development similar to that of small-town Kansas. Socialist strength was strongest
in the ward where the Amalgamated Association of Iron, Steel,
and Tin Workers Union had its greatest membership, although
Socialists "showed gains in nearly all the city precincts." Prohibition also proved to be an issue here, taking precedence over
the question of patriotism during the war, along with the local
employer establishing an open shop. Socialists campaigned in
the municipal election of 1917 in support of the strikers fighting
their employer. Despite gaining almost total control of the city
administration, they were unable to institute a city waterworks
or purchase the street railway system. They did, however, bring
the city "honest government" and managed to have taxes raised
on the Tin Plate Company, which employed 68 percent of the
town's workforce. The end of the war and the beginning of the
Big Red Scare undermined both the Labor and Socialist movements in Elwood. While a strike was in progress, the labor local
announced that a nationally known Socialist would speak on the
topic of "Political Prisoners in America." The American Legion
post "curtly informed the Mayor" that the speech would not take
place, and it was canceled.[3]

Socialists failed to elect any congressmen or senators in Kansas for the national office and few to the state legislature. They
elected no candidate to the mayoralty of any major city. Again,
however, they enjoyed great success in some of the smaller communities, occasionally sweeping control in a local area. This was
especially true in the Tri-State region, where economic conditions were harsher than in most of the rest of the state. In any
case Socialists in Kansas never gained the predominance they did
in numerous farm belt areas of Oklahoma. In 1914 the Socialist
candidate for governor in Oklahoma carried three counties and
ran second in twenty-six others. But the Socialist vote in Oklahoma was concentrated in the southern agrarian counties, while
in Kansas its greatest strength was in the Tri-State region, and as

a group, agrarians were less attracted by Socialist thought than
urban workers.[4]

Kansas Socialists missed a possible opportunity to achieve some
of their goals when they refused to cooperate with the Nonpartisan League. Arthur Townley attracted farmers to his organization
by emphasizing agrarian issues, regardless of their commitment to
other Socialist policies, and in North Dakota leaders forced him
and his followers out of the party. The NPL went on to achieve
several Socialist goals in North Dakota. In Kansas the state's reactionary forces managed to take advantage of the postwar patriotism, and the members of the American Legion proved to be
powerful enough to repress the NPL. Repression can be a two-
edged sword, but in this case Kansans' commitment to middle-
class values was too powerful for the NPL to overcome.

In the Southwest the younger Depression agitators revived
socialism, but it came not in the old cotton counties of Oklahoma
but "in the newly settled region of the Arkansas delta." These
young men followed the organizing tactics of the old masters by
building "an interracial industrial union for desperate sharecrop-
pers." The Southern Tenant Farmers Union, James Green asserts,
"was a fitting tribute to . . . the interracial unionism of the IWW
and the Working Class Union." When it declined, in the later
1930s, there was nothing to replace it. In Kansas, Earl Browder
and James Cannon were unsuccessful in building a meaningful
socialism movement, and World War II ended unemployment,
the issue Ernest McNutt and the Kansas Workers Alliance might
have utilized to expand their protest movement. Prosperity and
a New Deal–rejuvenated capitalism left them with no economic
or political issues to belabor, although the nation continued its
New Deal statist philosophy through the Great Society and implemented some old Socialist programs.[5]

Roosevelt's overwhelming reelection in 1936 prompted the
Socialists to reevaluate their prospects. They were able to spend
less than $25,000 in that campaign, less than half what they had
spent four years earlier. Membership had "dropped precipitously,"
to fewer than 6,500 members. The Socialist Convention of 1937
banned factional publications, but Cannon's Trotskyites ignored

this mandate and were expelled. They established the Socialist Workers Party, and no one could quell the factionalism. After World War II the Socialist Party failed to revive. As David Shannon points out, American Socialists, unlike Socialists in other Western nations, never believed in the value of political organizing or of local issues. When they strove for homogeneity, they violated a basic principle of American political parties and, most important, failed to win organized labor to their cause. Finally, they discovered there was almost no class consciousness in America. All this was true of the movement in Kansas.

Socialists made a great contribution to the revolutionary philosophy of the New Deal in regard to the role of the central government in times of crisis. With desperate people watching their children starve, they proved willing and eager to look to Washington DC for relief because they found a president and first lady who were sincerely concerned about their well-being. As one voter expressed it, Roosevelt was the only president he had ever known who would understand that "my boss is a sonofabitch." It appeared strange, though, to New Dealers, who were dedicated to helping the needy, to see those workers express the typical anti-statism of Americans and demand something better than what hard-pressed taxpayers and zealous bureaucrats were providing from Washington. Workers found they could get attention, if not redress, by striking for better conditions, rather than the "no-brainer" alternative of quitting the job. Perhaps some Kansas farmers began to appreciate the plight of exploited laborers who used the weapons of strike, boycott, and picketing to achieve their goals. Anti-statism was strong in Kansas. It would be interesting to compare this protest experience with that in other states.

Historians have often been mystified in analyzing the Great Depression and the relatively peaceful revolution it brought to American society. Why did not the mass of workers rise up in revolt and overthrow their "masters"? How was American exceptionalism so pervasive? At the turn of the twentieth century, leading Socialist theorists were certain that America would lead the way to the creation of Socialist republics because it had the most advanced industrial system. Why did they allow Franklin Roosevelt and his New Dealers to prop up a sick capitalist system and make it function while other world leaders were taking their countries down the path to fascism, Nazism, and communism to revolutionize their economies? Seymour Martin Lipset and Gary Marks pondered this question in *It Didn't Happen Here: Why Socialism Failed in the United States.*

So many reasons must be factored in to make any answer plausible, especially in evaluating radicalism in Kansas. There were many, some overlapping, some contradictory. The American two-party system relegates third parties to the role of promoting their ideas until one of the major parties adopts part or all, and then it fades away. The success of the Populists in the early twentieth century indicated the two major political parties no longer enjoyed dominance, opening the way for third parties, especially Socialists, to emerge. Eugene Debs won almost one million votes, "and the party placed two members in Congress and countless others in local and state positions." Over the decades of the twentieth century the major parties adopted elements of Socialist ideas, especially "gas and water socialism," a process that greatly accelerated during and after the New Deal and World War II, so that the political system socialized much of the economic system. For those interested in abolishing capitalism, there was still much to be done. In the case of many third party concepts, especially if they appeared radical, they failed to appeal to Kansans because voters did not want to "throw away their vote." This proved true of socialism.[6]

The American cultural system played a significant role in retarding Kansas radicalism. Being a state, within a nation, of immigrants with relatively equal status, there was no residue of classes as existed in Europe, where the working class and the aristocracy were distinct and laborers accepted this classification and their role in it. In contrast, Kansans, like Americans, are wholly committed to the concept of middle-class values and have little tolerance for alternative viewpoints. Socialism is statist, and Americans are imbued with the Declaration of Independence's anti-statism. Americans find the declaration to be too radical for their taste but do find fulfillment in frequently expressing the concept that "all men are created equal," even though they unconsciously and emphatically repudiate its implementation. Doing so would require acceptance of Christ's concept of being your brother's keeper. The principle of socialism, "with its emphasis on . . . the means of production and distribution and equality through taxation," was at odds with the dominant values of American culture.[7]

Socialism failed nationally, especially in Kansas, in not establishing a permanent labor party. In other countries Socialists "tried to insulate themselves from the dominant" culture through labor parties and unions, although Kansans tried to do this through their publications and party schools. It was not until the New Deal that the Communist Party USA tried to influence and control CIO unions and gain a significant foothold in the trade union movement. The major parties, especially the dominant Republicans in Kansas, exploited the commitment to middle-class values and propagandized farmers into believing that they not only had nothing in common with the regimented laborers but actually should be antagonistic to union goals. Socialist leaders angered union leaders, but in Kansas, Agrarians were always opposed to union leadership. If the Populists, and later the Socialists, could have promoted their commonality more effectively, the political combination could have easily dominated the political arena and more successfully achieved Socialist goals.

NOTES

Introduction

Socialism in Kansas developed in two primary ways, and to represent its evolution, part of the book is presented as historical narrative, part as biography.

1. Whitehead, "Kansas Response to the Haymarket Affair," 72.

2. Johnson, *They Are All Red Out Here*, is a good introduction to this early movement.

3. Nugent, *Tolerant Populists*, 35–58.

4. Clanton, *Common Humanity*, 1–32.

5. See Lee, *Farmers vs. Wage Earners*, for the labor problem; and Clanton, *Common Humanity*, for this political movement in the Sunflower State.

6. For the movement of populism to socialism, see Lee, *Principle over Party*, chap. 11.

7. Grubbs, *Struggle for Labor Loyalty*, 4.

8. Shannon, *Socialist Party of America*, 3–4, 43–44.

9. Shannon, *Socialist Party of America*, 204.

10. Diggins, *American Left in the Twentieth Century*, 54–57.

11. Entz, *Llewellyn Castle*, 13–18.

12. Lee, "Ill-Fated Kansas Silk Industry," 241–43.

13. Miller, "Danish Socialism and the Kansas Prairie," 156–68.

14. Kansas Bureau of Labor and Industrial Statistics, *Report* (1885), 100.

15. Shannon, *Socialist Party of America*, 1–8.

16. Bissett, *Agrarian Socialism in America*, 6, 8.

17. Lee, *Publisher for the Masses*.

1. The Capitalistic Socialist

1. Jack London to Emanuel Julius, June 17, 1913, Haldeman-Julius Collection, Leonard H. Axe Library, Pittsburg (KS) State University; hereafter cited as Axe Library.

2. Le Sueur, *Crusaders*, 26; Wayland, from back cover of Graham, *Yours for the Revolution*.

3. Shore, *Talkin' Socialism*, 14–18.

4. Graham, *Yours for the Revolution*, 1–2.

5. Graham, *Yours for the Revolution*, 3. Ruskin's points are from *Wyandotte Herald*, August 23, 1900.

6. Graham, *Yours for the Revolution*, 2–3.

7. Graham, *Yours for the Revolution*, 75–76.

8. Shore, *Talkin' Socialism*, 55–75.

9. Laurence Gronlund to G. C. Clemens, November 13, 1893, Clemens Collection, Kansas State Historical Society, Topeka; hereafter cited as KSHS.

10. *Worker's Chronicle*, July 17, 1914.

11. Quint, "Julius A. Wayland," 596.

12. Graham, *Yours for the Revolution*, 12.

13. Graham, *Yours for the Revolution*, 8.

14. Graham, *Yours for the Revolution*, 30–32; *Appeal to Reason*, January 5, 1907, and October 15, 1910.

15. Ginger, *Bending Cross*, 201.

16. Ginger, *Bending Cross*, 197.

17. *Appeal to Reason*, October 24 and November 7, 1903.

18. *Appeal to Reason*, August 31, 1895.

19. *Appeal to Reason*, November 23, 1912; Shore, "Julius Augustus Wayland," 826–27.

20. Quint, "Wayland," 595–96.

21. William D. Vincent, quoted in Clanton, *Kansas Populism*, 68.

22. *Appeal to Reason*, June 27, 1903.

23. *Appeal to Reason*, May 1, 1909.

24. *Appeal to Reason*, May 16, 1896.

25. Graham, *Yours for the Revolution*, 184.

26. *Appeal to Reason*, November 18, 1899, and January 16, 1904.

27. Quoted in Winters, *Soul of the Wobblies*, 20.

28. Salvatore, *Eugene V. Debs*, 191.

29. *Appeal to Reason*, November 23, 1912, and August 31, 1901. "Best work" quotation from J. A. Wayland, *Coming Nation*, quoted in Shore, *Talkin' Socialism*, 55.

30. Shore, *Talkin' Socialism*, 204–6, 184–85; Piehler, "Henry Vincent," 25.

31. *Pittsburg Daily Headlight*, March 14 and April 11, 1907.

32. Graham, *Yours for the Revolution*, 11.

33. Graham, *Yours for the Revolution*, 177.

34. *Worker's Chronicle*, February 13, 1914.

35. Nord, "*Appeal to Reason* and American Socialism," 78.

36. Nord, "*Appeal to Reason* and American Socialism," 84.

37. Nord, "*Appeal to Reason* and American Socialism," 78.

38. Nord, "*Appeal to Reason* and American Socialism," 80–81.

39. Nord, "*Appeal to Reason* and American Socialism," 182–84.

40. *Girard Press*, January 26, 1911; "greedy capitalist" quotation from *Girard Press*, June 26, 1913.

41. Sterling, "Federal Government, v. the Appeal to Reason," 33–37.

42. For this trial, see Lukas, *Big Trouble*, chap. 11.

43. Ginger, *Bending Cross*, 305–6.

44. Graham, *Yours for the Revolution*, 14–15.

45. *Worker's Chronicle*, March 6, 1914; *Appeal to Reason*, April 13, 1913.

46. *Appeal to Reason*, November 22, 1912.

47. Lee, "Isms in Ahs," 9–10.

48. Lee, "Isms in Ahs," 9.

49. Clippings, Henry Laurens Call Collection, Axe Library; Marcet Haldeman to Anna Haldeman, September 15, 1912, Haldeman-Julius Collection, Axe Library.

50. Thiessen, "Henry Laurens Call's Aviation Attempts," 1.

51. Henry Laurens Call Collection, no. 26, Axe Library.

52. *Girard News*, December 3, 1908, Henry Laurens Call Collection, Axe Library.

53. Flint, "Flint Reviews Airplane Venture."

54. *Kanhistique*, February 6, 1981.

55. *Kanhistique*, March 6, 1981.

56. Michaelis, "C. B. Hoffman," 68.

57. *Topeka Daily Capital*, April 11, 1886.

58. *Kanhistique*, February 1981.

59. Michaelis, "C. B. Hoffman," 169–70.

60. Michaelis, "C. B. Hoffman," 171.

61. Michaelis, "C. B. Hoffman," 170; for the Gulf & Interstate, see Lee, "Populist Dream of a 'Wrong Way' Transcontinental."

62. Quotations from Michaelis, "C. B. Hoffman," 173.

63. *Topeka Daily Capital*, November 17, 1900.

64. Clippings, dated June 1 and July 15, 1910, from Kansas City newspapers, KSHS. The clippings fail to specify which journals.

65. Michaelis, "C. B. Hoffman," 176–77; *Kanhistique*, February 6, 1981, 5.

66. Quoted in Michaelis, "C. B. Hoffman," 177.

67. Michaelis, "C. B. Hoffman," 174.

68. *Gunn Powder* (Kansas City), March 13, 1914.

69. *Appeal to Reason*, July 31, 1915.

2. The Empathetic Socialist

1. Bar Association of Kansas, *Minutes*, 1907, KSHS; King, "Gaspar Christopher Clemens," 626–27.

2. Brodhead and Clanton, "G. C. Clemens."

3. Bar Association of Kansas, *Minutes*, 1907, KSHS.

4. "About Mr. Clemens, the Topeka Anarchist," an admiring story in the *Topeka Mail and Breeze*, July 9, 1897.

5. Kansas Bureau of Labor and Industrial Statistics, *Report* (1885), 72, vii.

6. Quoted in Brodhead and Clanton, "G. C. Clemens," 477.

7. Quoted in Brodhead and Clanton, "G. C. Clemens," 482.

8. Shawnee County clippings, 25, 626, KSHS.

9. Brodhead and Clanton, "G. C. Clemens," 490–91; for the Kansas City police story, see *Western Socialist News*, May 1900.

10. Lee, *Farmers vs. Wage-Earners*, 2.

11. For the use of railroad employees as militia and officers in the strike of 1878, see Lee, *Farmers vs. Wage-Earners*, 28–33; G. C. Clemens, *Kansas Law Journal*, May 12, 1885.

12. Novak, "G. C. Clemens," 26.

13. Green, *Death in the Haymarket*, 2–23, 26.

14. Green, *Death in the Haymarket*, 169–70.

15. Green, *Death in the Haymarket*, 182–88.

16. Green, *Death in the Haymarket*, 184–89.

17. Green, *Death in the Haymarket*, 292–94.

18. Lee, *Farmers vs. Wage-Earners*, 70.

19. Parsons, *Life of Albert R. Parsons*, 26–27.

20. Parsons, *Life of Albert R. Parsons*, 30–31.

21. *Daily Citizen*, July 10, 1885; *Kansas Sun and Globe*, July 9, 1885.

22. Clemens, "Industrial Arbitration," 3.

23. Clemens, "Industrial Arbitration," 3.

24. Whitehead, "Kansas Response," 75.

25. Novak, "G. C. Clemens."

26. West, "Moses Harman Story," 51–54.

27. Lee, *Farmers vs. Wage-Earners*, 46–53.

28. Clemens, *Ultimate Aim of Trades-Unions*.

29. Clemens, *Ultimate Aim of Trades-Unions*.

30. Clemens, *Labor Problem*.

31. Clemens, *Points for Populists*.

32. Clanton, *Common Humanity*, 129–36.

33. Brodhead and Clanton, "G. C. Clemens," 489.

34. Bar Association of Kansas, *Minutes*, 1907, 27, KSHS.

35. Clemens, "Appeal."

36. G. C. Clemens, Notebooks, KSHS.

37. Clemens, Notebooks.

38. Clemens, Notebooks.

39. Grondlund to Clemens, November 13, 1893, Clemens Collection, KSHS.

40. Clemens, Notebooks.

41. *Pittsburg Daily Tribune*, March 14, 1898.

42. *Topeka Daily Capital*, March 20, 1898.

43. *Topeka Daily Capital*, June 29, 1898.

44. Clemens, *Primer on Socialism*.

45. Proceedings of the Second Annual Convention, 1899, State Society of Labor and Industry, KSHS.

46. Proceedings of the Second Annual Convention.

47. Proceedings of the Second Annual Convention.

48. *Topeka Daily Capital*, March 15, 1899.

49. *Topeka Daily Capital*, March 15, 1899.

50. *Topeka Daily Capital*, March 15, 1899.

51. *Topeka Daily Capital*, April 11, 1899.

52. *Topeka Daily Capital*, August 2, 1899.

53. *Topeka Daily Capital*, August 27, 1899.

54. Clemens, Notebooks.

55. *Appeal to Reason*, August 12, 1900.

56. *Topeka Daily Capital*, August 12, 1900. See also the July–August 1900 issue of *Western Socialist News*.

57. Brodhead and Clanton, "G. C. Clemens," 498–99.

58. Paulson, *Radicalism and Reform*, 129–34. See also Gibson, "Effect of the Populist Movement."

59. *Topeka Daily Capital*, April 22, October 22, and November 11, 1899.

60. Brodhead and Clanton, "G. C. Clemens," 500.

61. *Western Socialist News*, April 1900. For another Socialist appeal to Populists, see "Radicalism in Kansas," *Appeal to Reason*, August 15, 1908.

62. *Western Socialist News*, April 1900.

63. *Western Socialist News*, June 1900.

64. *Western Socialist News*, June 1900.

65. Clemens, Notebooks.

66. Kansas Bureau of Labor and Industrial Statistics, *Report* (1885), 72, viii.

3. The Female Socialists

1. Buhle, *Women*, chap. 2; Basen, "Kate Richards O'Hare," 166.

2. *Appeal to Reason*, August 11, 1899. Willard expanded on her Christian socialism concept in *Appeal to Reason*, September 21, 1901.

3. Levinson, "Petticoat Politics," 20.

4. Levinson, "Petticoat Politics," 21.

5. Diggs, "Study of Mrs. Nation."

6. *Transactions of the Kansas State Historical Society*, 6:233–34.

7. Levinson, "Petticoat Politics," 21.

8. News clipping, Kansas Biographical Scrapbook, D, II, KSHS.

9. Weisgerber, "Kansas Spellbinders," 37.

10. Levinson, "Petticoat Politics," 21; Clanton, "Annie L. Diggs," 303.

11. Roberts, "Women in Populism."

12. Diggs, *Speech on Women's Suffrage*.

13. Quoted in Clanton, *Common Humanity*, 160–62.

14. *Topeka Daily Capital*, November 11, 1899.

15. Levinson, "Petticoat Politics," 22.

16. Levinson, "Petticoat Politics," 22–23.

17. *Kansas City Star*, August 19, 1900.

18. Diggs, "English Garden City."

19. Diggs, "Captains of Industry."

20. Diggs, *Story of Jerry Simpson*; Diggs, *Bedrock*.

21. *Notable American Women*, 1:482. Clanton, *Kansas Populism*, 226, has a different version: in this work she described herself as "an opportunist Socialist," meaning she "would apply socialistic principles to everyday conditions as fast as the conditions would warrant; taking a little today, adding a little tomorrow and so on."

22. Buhle, *Women*, 114; *Appeal to Reason*, May 25 and June 29, 1901.

23. Buhle, *Women*, 115, 117. Graham, *Yours for the Revolution*, 76–77, 228, reprints some of her poetry. For her "Emancipation of Women" clipping, see *Appeal to Reason*, May 2, 1903; for the piano, see *Appeal to Reason*, July 25, 1903.

24. Buhle, *Women*, 148–49.

25. Buhle, *Women*, 306–7.

26. Shore, *Talkin' Socialism*, 156.

27. Shore, *Talkin' Socialism*, 166.

28. *Appeal to Reason*, December 13, 1902.

29. Shore, *Talkin' Socialism*, 167.

30. *Appeal to Reason*, January 4, 1905.

31. *Girard Press*, June 26, 1913.

32. Buhle, *Women*, 307–8, 319.

33. Buhle, *Women*, 154.

34. Buhle, *Women*, 151.

35. Burbank, *When Farmers Voted Red*, 10.

36. *Appeal to Reason*, September 25, 1909.

37. Buhle, *Women*, 155–56.

38. Buhle, *Women*, 326n2.

39. White, "Wichita Indictments and Trial," 69–70, 180–81, 250–51, 265, 283; see also the editorial on the press in *People's Weekly Forum* (Lawrence), May 20, 1919.

40. Ray, "Katherine 'Red Kate' O'Hare," 33; Miller, *From Prairie to Prison*, 4–10; Foner and Miller, *Kate Richards O'Hare*, 35.

41. Basen, "Kate Richards O'Hare," 170–71.

42. Miller, *From Prairie to Prison*, 16–17; Foner and Miller, *Kate Richards O'Hare*, 42.

43. *Shawnee County Socialist* (Topeka), August 3, 1913.

44. Basen, "Kate Richards O'Hare," 172; Foner and Miller, *Kate Richards O'Hare*, 38.

45. Basen, "Kate Richards O'Hare," 173.

46. Shore, *Talkin' Socialism*, 149.

47. Shore, *Talkin' Socialism*, 174.

48. *Girard Press*, June 30, 1910; Miller, *From Prairie to Prison*, 48–49.

49. Brommel, "Kate Richards O'Hare," 8–9. According to Shore, *Talkin' Socialism*, 196, when Debs turned over his scheduling to the O'Hares, it resulted in "a dismal nightmare."

50. Brommel, "Kate Richards O'Hare," 9; Shannon, *Socialist Party of America*, 25–26.

51. Basen, "Kate Richards O'Hare," 176–83.

52. Miller, "Kate Richards O'Hare," 267–68.

53. Miller, "Kate Richards O'Hare," 268–69.

54. Foner and Miller, *Kate Richards O'Hare*, 56, 98–99.

55. Miller, "Kate Richards O'Hare," 109–10.

56. Buhle, *Women*, 248, 272; Miller, *From Prairie to Prison*, 68–69.

57. Miller, *From Prairie to Prison*, 86; *Appeal to Reason*, December 11, 1909.

58. Miller, *From Prairie to Prison*, 130–39.

59. Brommel, "Kate Richards O'Hare," 10.

60. Brommel, "Kate Richards O'Hare," 10.

61. Miller, *From Prairie to Prison*, 144–46; Brommel, "Kate Richards O'Hare," 10–11.

62. Brommel, "Kate Richards O'Hare," 14–16.

63. Foner and Miller, *Kate Richards O'Hare*, 173–74; Brommel, "Kate Richards O'Hare," 17–19.

64. Miller, *From Prairie to Prison*, 160–66.

65. Miller, *From Prairie to Prison*, 187–91. For protest meetings supporting Debs and O'Hare, see *Weekly People's Forum* (Lawrence), May 1, 1919.

66. Lovin, "Banishment of Kate Richards O'Hare."

67. Mallach, "Red Kate O'Hare Comes to Madison."

68. Miller, *From Prairie to Prison*, 205–6; Bronco, "Family Album."

69. Miller, *From Prairie to Prison*, 200–202.

70. Miller, *From Prairie to Prison*, 220–23.

71. Miller, *From Prairie to Prison*, 223–26.

72. Miller, *From Prairie to Prison*, 226–28.

4. The Mining Socialists

1. Lee, *Farmers vs. Wage-Earners*, 12–13, 104.

2. Wood-Simons, "Mining Coal and Maiming Men."

3. Lee, "Apogee of Labor Legislation," 3.

4. Lee, *Farmers vs. Wage-Earners*, 82.

5. Vining, "Men and Coal," 32.

6. "Alexander Howat," 558–60.

7. Vining, "Men and Coal," 27–28.

8. Mary Ross, fax to a friend, January 6, 2000, Alexander Howat clipping file, Special Collections, Axe Library.

9. Vining, "Men and Coal," 125.

10. *Girard Press*, January 13 and 27, 1910.

11. *Girard Press*, November 30, 1911.

12. Vining, "Men and Coal," 190–91.

13. Vining, "Men and Coal," 177–78, 183.

14. *Western Socialist News*, April 1900.

15. News clippings, Henry and Ida Hayman Callery Collection, Axe Library.

16. News clippings, Callery Collection.

17. News clippings, Callery Collection.

18. News clippings, Callery Collection.

19. *Worker's Chronicle*, April 20, 1917.

20. Karson, *History of Trade Unions in Kansas*, 11.

21. For details of Howat's crusade, see Lee, *Farmers vs. Wage Earners*, chap. 5.

22. Wolff Packing v. Court of Industrial Relations, 262 US 522 (1923).

23. *Weir City Journal*, March 30, 1900.

24. Vining, "Men and Coal," 192–97.

25. *Girard Press*, July 22 and December 9, 1897.

26. *Girard Press*, July 7, 1898.

27. *Girard Press*, May 25, 1899.

28. *Girard Press*, January 2, 1899.

29. *Girard Press*, February 19, 1903; *Pittsburg Headlight*, October 11, 1902, for Socialist candidates.

30. *Girard Press*, December 1, 1904.

31. *Girard Press*, August 27, 1903.

32. *Pittsburg Headlight*, October 27, 1902.

33. *Girard Press*, April 7 and December 1 and 5, 1904.

34. *Weir City Journal*, April 13, 1906.

35. *Girard Press*, July 9, 1908.

36. *Girard Press*, July 16, 1908.

37. *Worker's Chronicle*, April 2, 1915.

38. *Pittsburg Tribune*, November 10, 1898; *Girard Press*, November 19, 1900.

39. *Girard Press*, November 8, 1904, November 2, 1908; *Pittsburg Headlight*, November 1, 1904.

40. *Girard Press*, June 10, 1909.

41. *Girard Press*, September 2 and 30, 1909.

42. *Girard Press*, November 17, 1910.

43. *Girard Press*, November 14, 1912.

44. *Girard Press*, February 6, 1913; "steal" quotation from *Girard Press*, February 1, 1913; "dirty, uncouth" quotation from Vining, "Men and Coal," 193.

45. *Topeka Daily Capital*, November 14, 1912.

46. *Girard Press*, March 13, 1913.

47. *Labor Herald*, August 16, 1912, November 28, 1913.

48. *Labor Herald*, September 27, 1912.

49. *Pittsburg Daily Headlight*, November 6, 1912.

50. *Pittsburg Daily Headlight*, November 6, 1912.

51. *Pittsburg Daily Headlight*, January 2, 1913.

52. *Girard Press*, April 2, 1914.

53. *Labor Herald*, November 28, 1913.

54. *Labor Herald*, March 6, 1914.

55. *Worker's Chronicle*, February 6, 1914.

56. *Worker's Chronicle*, February 20, 1914.

57. *Worker's Chronicle*, February 27, 1914.

58. *Worker's Chronicle*, March 28, 1914.

59. *Kansas City Star*, November 1, 1914.

60. *Kansas City Star*, March 2, 1914.

61. *Kansas City Star*, February 6, 1914.

62. *Kansas City Star*, March 20, 1915.

63. *Kansas City Star*, June 12, 1914.

64. *Kansas City Star*, August 2, 1914.

65. *Kansas City Star*, October 9, 1914.

66. *Kansas City Star*, September 11, 1914.

67. *Kansas City Star*, August 21, 1914.

68. *Kansas City Star*, October 2, 1914.

69. *Kansas City Star*, October 23, 1914.

70. *Girard Press*, October 29, 1914; *Pittsburg Daily Headlight*, October 19, 1914.

71. *Pittsburg Daily Headlight*, October 20, 1914.

72. *Pittsburg Daily Headlight*, October 22, 1914.

73. *Pittsburg Daily Headlight*, November 4, 1914.

74. *Pittsburg Daily Headlight*, October 23, 1914.

75. *Fort Scott Republican*, November 6, 1914, April 4, 1915.

76. *Fort Scott Republican*, April 5, 1915.

77. *Worker's Chronicle*, November 6 and 13, 1914; Burbank, *When Farmers Voted Red*, 91; *Girard Press*, November 14, 1914.

78. *Worker's Chronicle*, February 27, 1914.

79. *Worker's Chronicle*, November 13, 1913.

80. *Worker's Chronicle*, November 27, 1914.

81. *Worker's Chronicle*, December 18, 1914.

82. *Worker's Chronicle*, January 29, 1915.

83. *Worker's Chronicle*, February 5, 1915.

84. *Appeal to Reason*, February 6, 1915.

85. *Worker's Chronicle*, February 12, 1915.

86. *Worker's Chronicle*, March 26, 1915.

87. *Worker's Chronicle*, February 9, 1915; *Pittsburg Daily Headlight*, February 11, 1915.

88. *Worker's Chronicle*, February 19, 1915; *Pittsburg Daily Headlight*, February 17, 1915.

89. *Worker's Chronicle*, February 19, 1915; *House Journal*, 1915; *Senate Journal*, 1915.

90. *Worker's Chronicle*, January 28, 1916.

91. *Worker's Chronicle*, October 20, 1916.

92. *Worker's Chronicle*, November 10, 1916.

93. *Worker's Chronicle*, November 17 and December 8, 1916.

94. *Worker's Chronicle*, December 29, 1916.

95. *Worker's Chronicle*, December 14, 1915, January 12, 1917.

96. *Worker's Chronicle*, March 30 and April 13, 1917.

97. *Worker's Chronicle*, August 3 and 17, October 12, December 14, 1917, and January 4, 1918.

98. Vincent, "History of Salt Discovery and Production in Kansas," 358.

5. The Successful Socialists

1. *Appeal to Reason*, November 16, 1912. His explanation of the decline in 1908 from *Kansas City Times*, November 6, 1908.

2. *Western Socialist News*, April 1900.

3. Clanton, *Kansas Populism*, 225–27.

4. *Western Socialist News*, August 1900.

5. *Western Socialist News*, April 1900.

6. *Western Socialist News*, August 1900.

7. *Western Socialist News*, September 1900, July–August 1900.

8. Secretary of State, Thirteenth Biennial Report; *Appeal to Reason*, November 22, 1902.

9. *White City Register*, January 20, 1900; *Abilene Daily Chronicle*, March 12, 1903; *Appeal to Reason*, April 18, 1903.

10. Nye, *Midwestern Progressive Politics*, 234.

11. *Decatur County Socialist*, October 26, 1906.

12. *Appeal to Reason*, July 4, 1903.

13. *Appeal to Reason*, May 26, 1906.

14. *Prolocutor* (Garden City), May 19 and June 16, 1910.

15. Graham, *Yours for the Revolution*, 174.

16. *Decatur County Socialist*, October 19, 1906.

17. Fink, *Workingmen's Democracy*, 5.

18. *Kansas City Star*, November 3, 1900.

19. *Kansas City Times*, January 22, 1902.

20. *Kansas City Star*, December 8, 1903.

21. *Kansas City Star*, July 3, 1904.

22. *Line-Up* (Kansas City KS), May 5, 1905.

23. *Appeal to Reason*, September 5, 1905.

24. *Western Socialist News*, April 1900, June 1900.

25. *Topeka Daily Capital*, n.d., clippings, KSHS.

26. *Topeka Daily Capital*, n.d., clippings, KSHS. The item had to be dated sometime in 1902 because it included a story and picture of A. S. McAlister, candidate for governor that year.

27. *Kansas City Post*, October 22, 1911.

28. *Topeka State Journal*, March 21, 1913; April 23, 1913, for the story of the "fallen women."

29. *Topeka Daily Capital*, November 6, 1908; the Debs vote in Kansas comes from *Appeal to Reason*, October 16, 1912, with that year estimated. The Socialist tallies come from Kansas Secretary of State, *Biennial Reports*.

30. The assessment of Populist strength is difficult because the authority on Kansas populism, Clanton, *Kansas Populism*, has no maps to show Populist strength in the state. His narrative forces one to speculate on their strength for Governors Lewelling and Leedy, although on p. 168 he asserts that Crawford, Cherokee, and Osage Counties were "strong Populist counties." My speculation here is based largely on Lee, *Bizarre Careers of John R. Brinkley*, 5, which covers Brinkley's campaigns for the governorship in 1930 and 1932. "Brinkleyism" contained features rather similar to populism, and he drew considerable strength from those former Populist counties.

31. Quoted in Richmond, *Kansas*, 211–12.

32. *Appeal to Reason*, August 17, 1901.

33. *Fort Scott Republican*, June 20, 1914.

34. *Fort Scott Republican*, June 21, 1914.

35. *Fort Scott Republican*, June 21, 1914.

36. *Fort Scott Republican*, June 21, 1914.

37. *Fort Scott Republican*, July 2, 1914.

38. *Fort Scott Republican*, July 7, 1914.

39. *Fort Scott Republican*, July 14, 1914.

40. *Fort Scott Republican*, July 17, 1914.

41. *Fort Scott Republican*, July 18, 1914

42. *Fort Scott Republican*, July 26, 1914.

43. *Fort Scott Republican*, August 16, 1914.

44. *Fort Scott Republican*, August 29 and October 4, 1914.

45. *Fort Scott Republican*, October 24, 1914.

46. *Fort Scott Republican*, November 12, 1914.

47. *Fort Scott Republican*, December 16, 1914, January 24, 1915.

48. *People's College News*, November 1916.

49. *Fort Scott Republican*, July 10, 1915.

50. *Fort Scott Republican*, July 27, 1915.

51. *People's College News*, November 1918.

52. *People's College News*, April 1917.

53. *People's College News*, July 1917.

54. *People's College News*, December 1918.

55. *People's College News*, October 1917.

56. *People's College News*, November 1918.

57. *People's College News*, July 1918.

58. *Fort Scott Tribune*, January 15, 1919.

59. *Fort Scott Tribune*, February 2, 1902.

60. Lee, *Snake Oil*, 2.

61. Lee, *Snake Oil*, 63–64.

62. *Topeka Daily Capital*, November 8, 1904; *Pittsburg Daily Headlight*, April 27, 1907; *Labor Herald* (Pittsburg), August 4, 1911.

63. *Iola Cooperator*, July 13, 1912, July 5, 1913; *Shawnee County Socialist*, November 22, 1913.

64. *Kansas Government Journal*, May 1951; *Wyandotte Herald*, September 1, 1904, August 6, 1908, March 17, 1910.

65. *Herington Sun*, April 23 and August 20, 1908.

66. *Herington Sun*, October 30, 1906.

67. *Labor Herald*, August 4, 1911.

68. *Coffeyville Daily News*, April 13, 1901.

69. *Kansas Government Journal*, May 1941; *Topeka State Journal*, May 17, 1947.

70. Bickers, "Oasis in the Short Grass," 23–25.

71. *Kansas Leader*, September 24, 1925.

72. Lee, *T-Town*, 124–29.

73. Sanders, *Roots of Reform*, 149–52; Tucker, "Populism Up-to-Date," 198–201.

74. Kansas State Board of Agriculture, *44th Annual Report*, 120; *Hutchinson Daily News*, May 21, 1907.

75. Evans, "From Kanasin to Kansas," 282.

76. *Emporia Gazette*, February 16, 1910.

77. Connelly, "Farmers Union in Kansas," 2175–76. The *Topeka Daily Capital*, March 14, 1919, presented the brokerage story.

78. 262 US 522.

6. The Wobblies

1. Tyler, *Rebels of the Woods*.

2. Preston, *Aliens and Dissenters*, 39–41; transient quotation from Pratt, "Historians and the Lost World," 284.

3. Preston, *Aliens and Dissenters*, 39–41, 47.

4. Haywood, testimony before Committee on Industrial Relations, in Walsh and Manly, *Industrial Relations*, 10575.

5. Dubofsky, *We Shall Be All*, 76, 78, 81.

6. Quoted in Winters, *Soul of the Wobblies*, 20.

7. Winters, *Soul of the Wobblies*, 20; newspaper quotation from Townsend, *Running the Gauntlet*, 1.

8. Cortner, "Wobblies and Fiske," 32–33.

9. Renshaw, *Wobblies*, 237.

10. Preston, *Aliens and Dissenters*, 247–49.

11. Pankratz, "Suppression of Alleged Disloyalty," 289; Peterson and Fite, *Opponents of War*, 19.

12. Page, "Industrial Workers," 4.

13. Page, "Industrial Workers," 12–18.

14. Vincent, *History of Organized Labor*, 95; Pankratz, "Suppression of Alleged Disloyalty," 289.

15. Preston, *Aliens and Dissenters*, 48–50.

16. This migrant labor system and harvesting is detailed in Lee, *Farmers vs. Wage Earners*, 5.

17. White, "Wichita Indictment," 43, 46–47.

18. Applen, "Migratory Harvest Labor," 159–60.

19. Grossardt, "Harvest(ing) Hoboes," 294.

20. Page, "Industrial Workers," 23.

21. Sellars, *Oil, Wheat, and Wobblies*, 35.

22. Page, "Industrial Workers," 25–26.

23. Wheat clippings, no. 157, KSHS.

24. *Topeka State Journal*, June 17, 1915.

25. *Topeka State Journal*, June 22, 1914.

26. *Topeka State Journal*, June 11, 1915.

27. *Salina Evening Journal*, April 9, 1917.

28. *Salina Evening Journal*, April 16, 1917.

29. *Salina Evening Journal*, June 9, 1917.

30. *Salina Evening Journal*, June 29 and 30, 1917.

31. *Salina Evening Journal*, July 21, 1917.

32. *Topeka Daily Capital*, July 28, 1917, June 22 and August 9, 1918.

33. *Topeka Daily Capital*, April 9, 1918.

34. *Topeka Daily Capital*, July 13, 1916.

35. *Topeka Daily Capital*, July 13, 1916.

36. *Topeka Daily Capital*, June 18, 1916.

37. Page, "Industrial Workers," 26.

38. Dowell, *History of Criminal Syndicalism Legislation*, 17–18.

39. Governors Correspondence, Arthur Capper, July 8, 1916, box 27-08-02-04, KSHS.

40. Page, "Industrial Workers," 30–31.

41. *Topeka Daily Capital*, July 17, 1917.

42. *Topeka Daily Capital*, August 4, 1917.

43. Committee on Industrial Relations (CIR), report, serial set no. 69391, 10570.

44. *Topeka Daily Capital*, November 21, 1917.

45. These conditions are explored in Lee, *Farmers vs. Wage Earners*, 5.

46. *Topeka State Journal*, April 17, 1919.

47. These delays were reported in *Topeka Daily Capital*, June 2, 11, and 12, 1919.

48. *Topeka Daily Capital*, July 1, 1920.

49. White, "Wichita Indictment," 214–17, 222–24.

50. *Topeka Daily Capital*, June 19, 1918.

51. *Topeka Daily Capital*, June 8 and November 16 and 21, 1919, and June 16, 1918.

52. Preston, *Aliens and Dissenters*, 259–67; White, "Wichita Indictment," 236–47. *Kansas City Times*, March 13, 1919, for the NPL quotation.

53. *Topeka Daily Capital*, December 19 and 20, 1919.

54. Cortner, "Wobblies," 33.

55. 274 US 562.

56. *Topeka Daily Capital*, March 19, 1919.

57. *Topeka Daily Capital*, June 28, 1919.

58. *Topeka Daily Capital*, July 6, 1919.

59. *Topeka Daily Capital*, July 6, 1919.

60. *Topeka Daily Capital*, July 8, 1919.

61. *Topeka Daily Capital*, September 6, 1919.

62. Page, "Industrial Workers," 7; Hall, *Harvest Wobblies*, 208.

63. Hall, *Harvest Wobblies*, 179–83.

64. Hall, *Harvest Wobblies*, 193–95.

65. Page, "Industrial Workers," 39.

66. *Topeka Daily Capital*, June 22, 1920.

67. *Topeka Daily Capital*, June 30, 1920.

68. *Topeka Daily Capital*, July 8, 1920.

69. *Topeka Daily Capital*, July 9, 1920.

70. Page, "Industrial Workers," 40–41.

71. *Topeka Daily Capital*, June 14, 21, and 29, 1921.

72. *Topeka Daily Capital*, June 27, 1922. "Beatings" quotation from Page, "Industrial Workers," 43.

73. *Topeka Daily Capital*, May 16, 1923.

74. Page, "Industrial Workers," 41–42.

75. *Topeka Daily Capital*, July 6, 1923.

76. *Topeka Daily Capital*, June 21 and 28, 1923.

77. Page, "Industrial Workers," 43–44.

78. Cortner, "Wobblies," 37–38.

79. Peterson and Fite, *Opponents of War*, vii.

7. The Losing Socialists

1. MacKay, *Progressive Movement*, 50.

2. Morlan, *Prairie Fire*, 22–23.

3. Nye, *Midwestern Progressive Politics*, 291.

4. Huntington, "Election Tactics," 613.

5. Morlan, *Prairie Fire*, 23–25.

6. Morlan, *Prairie Fire*, 30–32, 208.

7. Morlan, *Prairie Fire*, 30–31.

8. Morlan, *Prairie Fire*, 47–51, quotation on 29.

9. Morlan, *Prairie Fire*, 52–54.

10. Morlan, *Prairie Fire*, 60, 67, 211.

11. Morlan, *Prairie Fire*, 230–33.

12. Fite, *Peter Norbeck*, 8, 69.

13. *Kansas City Star*, November 25, 1920.

14. Peterson, *I.W.W. and the Nonpartisan League*; fight over the Industrial Commission from Morlan, *Prairie Fire*, 230, 304.

15. Saloutos, "Expansion and Decline," 237.

16. Page, "Industrial Workers," 32–33; *Kansas City Star*, December 23, 1919; *Ellsworth County Leader*, January 1, 1920.

17. *Kansas City Star*, September 7, 1917; *Emporia Gazette*, November 8, 1917.

18. Morlan, *Prairie Fire*, 123; *Kansas City Star*, September 7, 1917.

19. *Topeka Daily Capital*, January 15, 1918.

20. *Topeka State Journal*, January 9, 1918.

21. *Kansas City Star*, April 7, 1918.

22. *Kansas City Star*, April 7, 1918.

23. *Kansas City Star*, April 7, 1918

24. *Topeka Daily Capital*, April 30, 1918.

25. *Kansas City Star*, May 1, 1918.

26. *Kansas City Star*, May 8, 1918; *Topeka State Journal*, May 9, 1918.

27. *Topeka State Journal*, June 20, 1918.

28. *Topeka State Journal*, May 12, 1919.

29. *Ellsworth County Leader*, May 1, 1919.

30. *Ellsworth County Leader*, October 23, 1919.

31. *Ellsworth County Leader*, November 13, 1919.

32. *Ellsworth County Leader*, January 17, 1920.

33. Larson, "Kansas Newspaper."

34. *Ellsworth County Leader*, November 4, 1920.

35. *Topeka State Journal*, June 2, 1920; *Topeka Daily Capital*, June 19, 1920.

36. *Hutchinson News*, June 8, 1920.

37. Larson, "Kansas Newspaper," 103.

38. *Topeka State Journal*, June 2, 1920; *Ellsworth County Leader*, June 10, 1920.

39. *Topeka Daily Capital*, June 19, 1920.

40. *Topeka State Journal*, October 12, 1920.

41. *Ellsworth County Leader*, June 17, 1920.

42. *Kansas Leader*, December 30, 1920.

43. "Townley in Kansas," *Literary Digest*, March 12, 1921.

44. Larson, "Kansas Newspaper," 104.

45. "Townley in Kansas."

46. Lee, "Early History," 473–74.

47. *New York Times*, January 7, 1921.

48. Lee, "Early History," 475–76.

49. *New York Times*, January 8, 1921.

50. *New York Times*, January 9, 1921.

51. *Topeka Daily Capital*, January 5 and 6, 1921.

52. *Topeka Daily Capital*, January 8, 1921.

53. *Topeka Daily Capital*, January 8, 1921.

54. *Topeka Daily Capital*, February 1, 1921.

55. *Topeka Daily Capital*, January 7, 1921.

56. *Topeka State Journal*, March 4, 1921.

57. Larson, "Kansas and the Nonpartisan League," 53.

58. Lee, "Early History," 474. See Lee, "Joseph Ralph Burton," for Burton's troubles with the Roosevelt administration.

59. *New York Times*, March 14, 1921.

60. *New York Times*, March 26, 1921.

61. *Topeka State Journal*, March 17, 1921.

62. *Topeka State Journal*, March 18, 1921; *Topeka Daily Capital*, March 19, 1921.

63. *Topeka State Journal*, March 16, 1921.

64. *Topeka State Journal*, March 22, 1921.

65. *Topeka State Journal*, April 11, 1921.

66. *Topeka State Journal*, April 11, 1921.

67. *Kansas Leader*, April 21, 1921.

68. *Topeka Daily Capital*, September 8, 1921.

69. Larson, "Kansas and the Nonpartisan League," 54.

70. Larson, "Kansas and the Nonpartisan League," 55–56.

71. Larson, "Kansas and the Nonpartisan League," 56–57.

72. Larson, "Kansas and the Nonpartisan League," 63; *Ellsworth County Leader*, February 17, 1921.

73. *Kansas Leader*, August 18, 1921.

74. Larson, "Kansas and the Nonpartisan League," 64.

75. Larson, "Kansas and the Nonpartisan League," 64.

76. Larson, "Kansas and the Nonpartisan League," 64–65.

77. Larson, "Kansas and the Nonpartisan League," 66–67.

78. *Topeka Daily Capital*, January 20, 1921.

79. *Topeka Daily Capital*, January 20, 1921.

80. *Topeka Daily Capital*, August 25, 1921.

81. *Topeka Daily Capital*, May 26, 1921.

82. *Topeka Daily Capital*, January 29 and July 24, 1924.

83. Morlan, *Prairie Fire*, 344.

84. *Kansas Leader*, May 15 and August 21, 1924.

85. Nye, *Midwestern Progressive Politics*, 305–14; Pratt, "Lost World," 287, quoting MacKay, *Progressive Movement*.

8. The Depression Radicals

1. *Appeal to Reason*, May 6, 1926.

2. Warren, *Alternative Vision*, 3–5.

3. *American Freeman*, August 1936; Lee, "Isms in Ahs," 11.

4. Palmer, *James P. Cannon*, 34–45.

5. Palmer, *James P. Cannon*, 52–56.

6. Palmer, *James P. Cannon*, 94–98.

7. Ryan, *Earl Browder*, 4–10.

8. Ryan, *Earl Browder*, 10–14.

9. Ryan, *Earl Browder*, 15–20.

10. Ryan, *Earl Browder*, 21–27.

11. Ryan, *Earl Browder*, 8–33, 37–38.

12. Fearon, *Kansas in the Great Depression*, is an excellent economic account of this relief experience in the Sunflower State.

13. Copy of "John Stutz Hurdled Schools in Record Time," *Kansas Business*, April 1934, in FERA records, RG 69, entry 10, National Archives; hereafter cited as NA.

14. Sherrard Ewing to Harry Hopkins, October 6, 1933; Harry Hopkins to Harlee Branch, October 9, 1933, FERA records, RG 69, entry 10, NA. A copy of an undated memo in Governor Alf Landon's papers signed by T. J. Edmonds is even more effusive, saying that Stutz's work was "unexcelled in any other state." Governor's Correspondence, Alf M. Landon, 27-11-04-03, folder 3, KSHS.

15. Schuyler, *Dread of Plenty*, 64, 75, 89. See Svobida, *Farming in the Dust Bowl*, for the story of a wheat farmer during the Great Depression.

16. *Topeka Daily Capital*, July 18 and 19 and August 1, 1934, discusses the slaughter program. Svobida, *Farming in the Dust Bowl*, 17, lists the 107,000 figure.

17. Governor's Correspondence, Alf M. Landon, 27-06-04-03, box 12, folder 6, KSHS; KERC Report, November 9, 1939, KSHS. See also Schuyler, "Federal Drought Relief Activities in Kansas," 412–16.

18. Fearon, *Kansas*, 102–12.

19. Schruben, *Kansas in Turmoil*, 160–61. The "life itself" quotation is from Riney-Kehrberg, "Hard Times–Hungry Years," 167.

20. Schuyler, *Dread of Plenty*, 133. For the evolving concepts of relief stipends during this period, see Burns and Kerr, "Survey of Work-Relief Wage Policies."

21. Comer, *Tale of a Fox*, 11, for the fox story; Hopkins, *Spending to Save*, 98–99; KERC, "Public Welfare Spending in Kansas."

22. Lee, "[Not] a Thin Dime," 475–76.

23. *Topeka Daily Capital*, December 10, 1933; Harris, director of the Social Science Research Council, to Hopkins, November 5, 1935, WPA records, RG 69, entry 10, NA. Harris volunteered this information on the court decision to Hopkins, who penciled in a notation at the top of the letter that read, "Wish I had known it at the time." The court delivered its opinion in 138 *Kansas Reports* 913 (1934), quotation on 914.

24. L. L. Exker to Aubrey Williams, November 2, 1935, FERA records, RG 73, entry 10, NA; *Topeka Daily Capital*, February 28, 1935.

25. Exker to Williams, November 2, 1935.

26. Landon to Hopkins, January 21, 1935, Governor's Correspondence, 27-11-04-03, box 12, folder 3, KSHS; budget figures from *Topeka Daily Capital*, June 20, 1936; Schlesinger, *Politics of Upheaval*, 352; *New York Times*, November 2, 6, and 8, 1935. For the cash-basis law, see Fearon, "Alfred M. Landon," 210.

27. *American Freeman*, December 1936.

28. McJimsey, *Harry Hopkin*, 89; *Topeka Daily Capital*, May 25 and 28, June 28, July 23, and December 16, 1935; *Topeka State Journal*, November 1, 1935.

29. McNutt, *Kansas Unemployed Organizations*, 3–4.

30. Fearon, *Kansas*, 99–100.

31. McNutt, *Kansas Unemployed Organizations*, 68; *New York Times*, July 7, 1935.

32. *New York Times*, August 26, 1936.

33. WAA proceedings of their second and third conventions, copies in KSHS. *Topeka Daily Capital*, June 26, 1938, on McNutt; *Topeka State Journal*, February 15, 1937. For the Lundeen Bill, see Casebeer, "Workers Unemployment Insurance Bill."

34. McNutt, *Kansas Unemployed*, 72–75.

35. *KAW Bulletin*, June 12, 1936, KSHS.

36. *Pittsburg Headlight*, April 26, 1934.

37. *Pittsburg Headlight*, May 1 and 2, 1934.

38. *Pittsburg Headlight*, May 3, 8, 9, 11, 15, and 17, 1934.

39. *Emporia Gazette*, June 7, 1935.

40. McNutt, *Kansas Unemployed*, 65–66.

41. *Emporia Gazette*, June 8, 1935.

42. *Emporia Gazette*, June 10, 1935.

43. *Emporia Gazette*, June 10, 1935.

44. *Emporia Gazette*, June 12, 13, 14, and 15, 1935.

45. *Kansas City Kansan*, August 6, 1935.

46. *Kansas City Kansan*, August 8, 1935.

47. *Kansas City Kansan*, August 11 and 12, 1935.

48. "For the most part" quotation from Hazelton, "Work Relief," 85.

49. *New York Times*, March 12, 1937.

50. McNutt, *Kansas Unemployed*, 75–80.

51. *Topeka Daily Capital*, March 1, 1937.

52. *Topeka Daily Capital*, March 6, 1937; Fearon, "Riot in Wichita," 264–79.

53. *Topeka Daily Capital*, March 20 and 23, 1937.

54. *Topeka Daily Capital*, July 24, 1937.

55. *Topeka State Journal*, March 22, 1937.

56. *Topeka Daily Capital*, March 22 and 24, 1937.

57. *Topeka Daily Capital*, March 24, 1937.

58. *Topeka Daily Capital*, March 25, 1937.

59. *Pittsburg Headlight*, March 22, 1937; *Fort Scott Tribune*, March 23, 1937.

60. *Fort Scott Tribune*, March 27 and 30, 1937; *Pittsburg Headlight*, April 1, 1937.

61. *Pittsburg Headlight*, April 1, 1937.

62. *Columbus Daily Advocate*, May 21, 24, 25, 27, and 28, 1937.

63. *Topeka Daily Capital*, April 2, 1937.

64. *Topeka Daily Capital*, May 7, 1937.

65. *Topeka Daily Capital*, May 28, 1937; *Chanute Daily Tribune*, August 24, 1937.

66. *Topeka Daily Capital*, April 3, 1937.

67. John Stutz to Evan L. Griffith, December 21, 1935, Stutz Papers, RH MS 327, box 1, folder 5, Spencer Library, University of Kansas.

68. *House Journal*, 1937, 854; *Senate Journal*, 1937, 677, 726; *Topeka Daily Capital*, March 11 and 31, 1937.

69. *Columbus Daily Advocate*, July 23, 1937; *Topeka Daily Capital*, July 31, 1937.

70. Kansas, *Laws*, 1937, chap. 327.

71. *Topeka Daily Capital*, January 28, 1937.

72. *Columbus Daily Advocate*, January 30, 1937; *Topeka Daily Capital*, January 29 and March 1, 1937.

73. *Topeka Daily Capital*, February 17 and March 1 and 5, 1937.

74. *Topeka Daily Capital*, March 13, 1937; *Topeka State Journal*, March 13, 1937.

75. *Pittsburg Headlight*, March 22, 1937.

76. *Topeka State Journal*, April 1, 1937; *Pittsburg Headlight*, June 7, 1937.

77. *Pittsburg Headlight*, July 5, 1937; *Columbus Daily Advocate*, July 13, 1937.

78. *Columbus Daily Advocate*, July 22 and 24, 1937.

79. *Chanute Tribune*, July 26, 1937.

80. *Chanute Tribune*, July 27, 1937.

81. *Chanute Tribune*, July 28, 1937.

82. *Chanute Tribune*, July 29 and 30, 1937.

83. Pratt, "Lost World," 290.

84. *New York Times*, April 18, 1937; September 16 and 18, 1938; and February 21, 1939.

Conclusion

1. Stevens, "Socialist Party."

2. Stevens, "Main Street Socialism," 68–89.

3. Stevens, "Labor and Socialism."

4. See election maps in Burbank, *When Farmers Voted Red*.

5. Green, *Grass-Roots Socialism*, 397.

6. Johnson, *They Are All Red Out Here*, 4.

7. Lipset and Marks, *It Didn't Happen Here*, 22, 266.

BIBLIOGRAPHY

Socialist Newspapers Published in Kansas

Advance (Dodge City), May 24, 1900–February 28, 1901.

American Freeman (Girard), April 13, 1929–November 1951.

American Non-Conformist (Girard), October 7, 1886–September 3, 1891.

Appeal to Reason (Girard), August 31, 1895–November 4, 1922.

Coming Nation (Girard), September 10, 1910–April 15, 1913.

Crusader (Iola), March 1914–October 1915.

Decatur County Socialist (Oberlin), October 19, 1906–November 1, 1896.

Emporia Convincer (Emporia), March 3, 1912–November 2, 1912.

Freedom's Banner (Iola), August 8, 1913.

Gaa Paa! (Girard), December 15, 1903–November 19, 1904.

Girard News (Girard), December 13, 1878–April 3, 1879.

Graham Gem (Hill City), August 6, 1897–April 5, 1901.

Gunn Powder (Pittsburg), November 20, 1913–January 22, 1914.

Haldeman-Julius Weekly (Girard), November 11, 1922–April 6, 1929.

Independent News (Girard), May 14, 1896–August 14, 1899.

Iola Cooperator (Iola), May 11, 1912–July 26, 1913.

Labor Herald (Pittsburg), March 3, 1911–November 28, 1913.

Line-Up (Kansas City), November 15, 1904–August 5, 1905.

Long Island Leader (Long Island), July 29, 1886–May 27, 1905.

Moreland Independent (Moreland), March 21, 1901–February 6, 1902.

National Socialist (Girard), April 1914–November 1914.

People's Advocate (Munden), May 4, 1912–March 29, 1913.

Progressive Herald (Lawrence), August 17, 1913–December 31, 1915.

Prolocutor (Syracuse), May 21, 1909–August 17, 1911.

Shawnee County Socialist (Topeka), August 9, 1913–June 27, 1914.

Social Ethics (Wichita), June 1904–April 1905.

Weekly People's Forum (Lawrence), March 6, 1919–May 1, 1919.

Worker's Call (Wichita), April 13, 1912–April 20, 1912.

Worker's Chronicle (Pittsburg), February 6, 1914–August 31, 1923.

"Alexander Howat." In *Illustriana Kansas*. Hebron NE: Illustriana, 1933.

Applen, Allan G. "Migratory Harvest Labor in the Midwestern Wheat Belt, 1870–1940." PhD diss., Kansas State University, 1974.

Avrich, Paul. *The Haymarket Tragedy*. Princeton NJ: Princeton University Press, 1984.

Basen, Neil K. "Kate Richards O'Hare: The 'First Lady' of American Socialism, 1904–1917." *Labor History* 21, no. 2 (1980): 165–99.

Bickers, Margaret A. "Oasis in the Short Grass: Geography, Politics, and Urban Water Supply in Garden City, Kansas, 1925–1960." *Kansas History* 30, no. 1 (Spring 2007): 20–35.

Bissett, Jim. *Agrarian Socialism in America: Marx, Jefferson, and Jesus in the Oklahoma Countryside, 1904–1920*. Norman: University of Oklahoma Press, 1999.

Brodhead, Michael, and O. Gene Clanton. "G. C. Clemens: The Sociable Socialist." *Kansas Historical Quarterly* 40, no. 4 (Winter 1974): 475–502.

Brommel, Bernard J. "Kate Richards O'Hare: A Midwestern Pacifist's Fight for Free Speech." *North Dakota Quarterly* 44 (Winter 1976): 5–19.

Bronco, Harold. "The Family Album: Kate Richards O'Hare." *World Tomorrow*, February 9, 1926.

Buhle, Mari Jo. *Women and American Socialism, 1870–1920*. Urbana: University of Illinois Press, 1981.

Burbank, Garin. *When Farmers Voted Red: The Gospel of Socialism in the Oklahoma Countryside, 1910–1924*. Westport CT: Greenwood Press, 1976.

Burns, Arthur, and Peyton Kerr, "Survey of Work-Relief Wage Policies." *American Economic Review* 27, no. 4 (December 1937): 711–24.

Casebeer, Kenneth. "The Workers Unemployment Insurance Bill: American Social Wage, Labor Organization, and Legal Ideology." In *Labor Law in America*, edited by Christopher L. Tomlins and Andrew J. King. Baltimore: Johns Hopkins University Press, 1992.

Clanton, O. Gene. *A Common Humanity: Kansas Populism and the Battle for Justice and Equality, 1854–1903*. Manhattan KS: Sunflower University Press, 2004.

———. "Annie L. Diggs." In *Reader's Encyclopedia of the American West*, edited by Howard R. Lamar. New York: Crowell, 1977.

———. *Kansas Populism: Ideas and Men*. Lawrence: University Press of Kansas, 1969.

Clemens, G. C. "An Appeal to True Populists." In *People's Party Pamphlets*, vol. 6. Copy in Kansas State Historical Society, Topeka.

———. "Industrial Arbitration." *Kansas Law Journal*, April 3, 1886.

———. *The Labor Problem*. Pamphlet, 1887. Copy in Kansas State Historical Society, Topeka.

———. *Points for Populists as to Organizing the House of Representatives*. Pamphlet, 1897. Copy in Kansas State Historical Society, Topeka.

———. *A Primer on Socialism*. Terra Haute IN: Debs Publishing Co., 1900. Copy in Kansas State Historical Society, Topeka.

———. *The Ultimate Aim of Trades-Unions*. Pamphlet, 1889. Copy in Kansas State Historical Society, Topeka.

Comer, Bert. *Tale of a Fox: As Kansans Know Alfred M. Landon*. Wichita KS: Bert Comer, 1936.

Connelley, William E. "Farmers Union in Kansas." In *Standard History of Kansas and Kansans*, vol. 4. Chicago: Lewis Publishing, 1918.

Cortner, Richard C. "The Wobblies and Fiske v. Kansas: Victory amid Disintegration." *Kansas History* 4, no. 1 (Spring 1981): 30–38.

Currie, Harold W. *Eugene V. Debs*. Boston: Twayne Publishers, 1976.

Diggins, John P. *The American Left in the Twentieth Century*. New York: Harcourt Brace Jovanovich, 1973.

Diggs, Annie L. *Bedrock: Education and Employment, the Foundation of the Republic*. Detroit: Social Center Publishing, 1912.

———. "Captain of Industry." *Cosmopolitan*, February 1904.

———. "An English Garden City." *Cosmopolitan*, June 1903.

———. "Relation of the Traveling Library to the Farm Home." *Kansas State Bulletin of Agriculture*, March 1901.

———. *Speech on Women's Suffrage*. Pamphlet, February 2, 1894. Copy in Kansas State Historical Society, Topeka.

———. *Story of Jerry Simpson*. Wichita KS: Jane Simpson, 1908.

———. "A Study of Mrs. Nation: The Responsibility of Topeka Women." *New Republic*, March 1901.

Dowell, Eldridge Foster. *A History of Criminal Syndicalism Legislation in the United States*. Baltimore: Johns Hopkins Press, 1939.

Dubofsky, Melvyn. *We Shall Be All: A History of the Industrial Workers of the World*. Chicago: Quadrangle, 1969.

Entz, Gary R. *Llewellyn Castle: A Workers Cooperative on the Great Plains*. Lincoln: University of Nebraska Press, 2013.

Evans, Sterling. *Bound in Twine: The History and Ecology of the Henequen-Wheat Complex for Mexico and the American and Canadian Plains, 1890–1950*. College Station: Texas A&M Press, 2007.

———. "From Kanasin to Kansas: Mexican Sisal, Binder Twine, and the State Penitentiary Twine Factory, 1890–1940." *Kansas History* 24, no. 4 (Winter 2001–2): 276–99.

Fearon, Peter. "Alfred M. Landon: Budget Balancer." In *John Brown to Bob Dole: Movers and Shakers in Kansas History*, edited by Virgil W. Dean. Lawrence: University Press of Kansas, 2006.

———. "From Self-Help to Federal Aid: Unemployment and Relief in Kansas, 1929–1932." *Kansas History* 13, no. 2 (Summer 1900): 107–25.

———. *Kansas in the Great Depression: Work Relief, the Dole, and Rehabilitation*. Columbia: University of Missouri Press, 2007.

———. "Kansas Poor Relief: The Influence of the Great Depression." *Mid-America: An Historical Review* 78 (Summer 1996): 157–59.

———. "Relief for Wanderers: The Transient Service in Kansas, 1933–1935." *Great Plains Quarterly* 26, no. 4 (Fall 2006): 245–64.

———. "Riot in Wichita, 1934." *Kansas History* 15, no. 4 (Winter 1992–93): 264–79.

———. "Taxation, Spending, and Budgets: Public Finance in Kansas during the Great Depression." *Kansas History* 28, no. 4 (Winter 2005–6): 230–43.

Fink, Leon. *Workingmen's Democracy: The Knights of Labor and American Politics.* Urbana: University of Illinois Press, 1985.

Fite, Gilbert C. *Peter Norbeck: Prairie Statesman.* Pierre: South Dakota State Historical Society Press, 2005.

Flint, Porter. "Flint Reviews Airplane Venture in Girard." *Petroleum Press*, May 26, 1941. Reprinted in *Library Bulletin*, Kansas State College of Pittsburg, 8 (1974): 11.

Foner, Philip S., and Sally M. Miller, eds. *Kate Richards O'Hare: Selected Writings and Speeches.* Baton Rouge: Louisiana State University Press, 1982.

Frank, Thomas. *What's the Matter with Kansas? How Conservatives Won the Heart of America.* New York: Metropolitan Books, 2004.

Gibson, Virginia Noah. "The Effect of the Populist Movement on Kansas State Agricultural College." Master's thesis, Kansas College of Agriculture and Applied Sciences, 1932.

Ginger, Ray. *The Bending Cross: A Biography of Eugene V. Debs.* New Brunswick NJ: Rutgers University Press, 1949.

Graham, John, ed. *Yours for the Revolution: The Appeal to Reason, 1895–1922.* Lincoln: University of Nebraska Press, 1990.

Green, James R. *Death in the Haymarket: A Story of Chicago, the First Labor Movement, and the Bombing That Divided Gilded Age America.* New York: Anchor Books, 2007.

———. *Grass-Roots Socialism: Radical Movements in the Southwest, 1895–1943.* Baton Rouge: Louisiana State University Press, 1978.

Grossardt, Ted. "Harvest(ing) Hoboes: The Production of Labor Organization through the Wheat Harvest." *Agricultural History* 70, no. 2 (Spring 1996): 283–301.

Grubbs, Frank L., Jr. *The Struggle for Labor Loyalty: Gompers, the A. F. of L., and the Pacifists, 1917–1920.* Durham NC: Duke University Press, 1968.

Hall, Greg. *Harvest Wobblies: The Industrial Workers of the World and Agricultural Laborers in the American West, 1905–1930.* Corvallis: Oregon State University Press, 2001.

Hazelton, Victoria. "Work Relief." *Saturday Evening Post*, March 2, 1935.

Hillquit, Morris. *History of Socialism in the United States.* New York: Funk & Wagnalls, 1910.

Hopkins, Harry. *Spending to Save: The Complete Story of Relief.* Seattle: University of Washington Press, 1972.

Huntington, Samuel P. "The Election Tactics of the Nonpartisan League." *Mississippi Valley Historical Review* 36, no. 4 (March 1950): 613–32.

Johnson, Jeffrie A. *They Are All Red Out Here: Socialist Politics in the Pacific Northwest, 1895–1925.* Norman: University of Oklahoma Press, 2008.

Karson, Marc. *A History of Trade Unions in Kansas, Prepared for the Kansas State Federation of Labor.* 1956. Copy in Kansas State Historical Society, Topeka.

King, J. L. "Gaspar Christopher Clemens." In *History of Shawnee County, Kansas and Representative Citizens*, edited by James L. King. Chicago: Richmond & Arnold, 1905.

Larson, Bruce L. "Kansas and the Nonpartisan League: The Response to the Affair at Great Bend, 1921." *Kansas Historical Quarterly* 34, no. 1 (Spring 1968): 51–71.

———. "A Kansas Newspaper and the Nonpartisan League, 1919–1920." *Journalism Quarterly* 49 (Spring 1972): 98–106.

Lee, R. Alton. *The Bizarre Careers of John R. Brinkley.* Lexington: University of Kentucky Press, 2002.

———. *Farmers vs. Wage Earners: Organized Labor in Kansas, 1860–1960.* Lincoln: University of Nebraska Press, 2005.

———. *From Snake Oil to Medicine: Pioneering Public Health.* Westport CT: Praeger Publishers, 2007.

———. "The Ill-Fated Kansas Silk Industry." *Kansas History* 23, no. 4 (Winter 2000–2001): 240–55.

———. "Isms in Ahs: Radical Politics in Depression Kansas." *Journal of the West* 41, no. 4 (Fall 2002): 6–12.

———. "Joseph Ralph Burton and the 'Ill-Fated' Senate Seat of Kansas." *Kansas History* 32, no. 4 (Winter 2009–10): 245–65.

———. "[Not] a Thin Dime: Kansas Relief Politics in the Campaign of 1936." *Historian* 67, no. 3 (Fall 2005): 474–88.

———. "The Populist Dream of a 'Wrong Way' Transcontinental." *Kansas History* 35, no. 2 (Summer 2012): 74–89.

———. *Principle over Party: The Farmers' Alliance and Populism in South Dakota, 1880–1900.* Pierre: South Dakota State Historical Society Press, 2009.

———. *Publisher for the Masses, Emanuel Haldeman-Julius.* Lincoln: University of Nebraska Press, 2018.

———. *T-Town on the Plains.* Manhattan KS: Sunflower University Press, 1999.

Lee, Thomas A. "Early History of the Kansas Department, American Legion." In *Collections of the Kansas State Historical Society, 1919–1922*, edited by William E. Connelley. Topeka: Kansas State Printing Plant, 1922.

Le Sueur, Meridel. *Crusaders: The Radical Legacy of Marian and Arthur Le Sueur.* St. Paul: Minnesota Historical Society Press, 1984.

Levinson, Harry. "Petticoat Politics." *Kansas Magazine*, 1949.

Lipset, Seymour Martin, and Gary Marks. *It Didn't Happen Here: Why Socialism Failed in the United States.* New York: W. W. Norton, 2000.

Lovin, Hugh T. "The Banishment of Kate Richards O'Hare." *Idaho Yesterdays* 22 (Spring 1978): 20–25.

MacKay, Kenneth Campbell. *The Progressive Movement of 1924.* New York: Octagon Books, 1966.

Mallach, Stanley. "Red Kate O'Hare Comes to Madison: The Politics of Free Speech." *Wisconsin Magazine of History* 53, no. 3 (Spring 1970): 204–22.

McJimsey, George. *Harry Hopkins: Ally of the Poor and Defender of Democracy.* Cambridge: Harvard University Press, 1987.

McNutt, Ernest F. *Kansas Unemployed Organizations.* wpa Writers Project, Topeka ks, 1940. Copy in Kansas State Historical Society, Topeka.

Michaelis, Patricia. "C. B. Hoffman: Kansas Socialist." *Kansas Historical Quarterly* 42, no. 2 (Summer 1975): 166–82.

Miller, Kenneth E. "Danish Socialism and the Kansas Prairie." *Kansas Historical Quarterly* 38, no. 2 (Summer 1972): 156–68.

Miller, Sally M. *From Prairie to Prison: The Life of Social Activist Kate Richards O'Hare.* Columbia: University of Missouri Press, 1993.

———. "Kate Richards O'Hare: Progression towards Feminism." *Kansas History* 7, no. 4 (Winter 1984–85): 263–79.

Morlan, Robert L. *Political Prairie Fire: The Nonpartisan League, 1915–1922.* St. Paul: Minnesota Historical Society Press, 1985.

Nord, David Paul. "The *Appeal to Reason* and American Socialism, 1901–1920." *Kansas History* 1, no. 2 (Summer 1978): 75–89.

Novak, Susan S. "Come Take a Trip in My Airship." *Kansas Heritage* 11, no. 3 (Winter 2003): 14–18.

Nugent, Walter T. K. *The Tolerant Populists: Kansas. Populism and Nativism.* Chicago: University of Chicago Press, 1963.

Nye, Russel B. *Midwestern Progressive Politics: A Historical Study of Its Origins and Development, 1870–1950.* New York: Harper & Row, 1965.

Page, Thomas R. "The Industrial Workers of the World in Kansas, 1904–1927." Lawrence: University of Kansas, Department of History, 1973. Copy in Kansas State Historical Society, Topeka.

Palmer, Brian D. *James P. Cannon and the Origins of the American Revolutionary Left, 1890–1928.* Urbana: University of Illinois Press, 2010.

Pankratz, Herbert. "The Suppression of Alleged Disloyalty in Kansas during World War I." *Kansas Historical Quarterly* 42, no. 3 (Fall 1976): 277–307.

Parsons, Lucy. *The Life of Albert R. Parsons, with Brief History of the Labor Movement in America.* Boston: Elibron Classics Reprint, 2005.

Paulson, Ross. *Radicalism and Reform: The Vrooman Family and American Social Thought, 1837–1937.* Lexington: University of Kentucky Press, 1968.

Peterson, Elmer T. *The I.W.W. and the Nonpartisan League.* Pamphlet. Copy in Kansas State Historical Society, Topeka.

Peterson, Horace, and Gilbert C. Fite. *Opponents of War: 1917–1918.* Seattle: University of Washington Press, 1968.

Piehler, Harold. "Henry Vincent: Kansas Populist and Radical-Reform Journalist." *Kansas History* 2, no. 1 (Spring 1972): 14–25.

Powell, William E. "Former Coal Mining Communities of the Cherokee-Crawford Field of Southeastern Kansas." *Kansas Historical Quarterly* 38, no. 2 (Summer 1972): 187–99.

Pratt, William C. "Historians and the Lost World of Kansas Radicalism." *Kansas History* 30, no. 4 (Winter 2007–8): 270–91.

———. "Socialism on the Northern Plains, 1900–1924." *South Dakota History* 18, no. 1 (Spring–Summer 1988): 1–35.

Preston, William, Jr. *Aliens and Dissenters: Federal Suppression of Radicals, 1903–1933*. Cambridge: Harvard University Press, 1963.

Quint, Howard H. "Julius A. Wayland: Pioneer Socialist Propagandist." *Mississippi Valley Historical Review* 35, no. 4 (March 1949): 585–606.

Ray, J. Karen. "Katherine 'Red Kate' O'Hare." In *Kansas Chautauqua*. Emporia KS: Center for Great Plains Studies, Emporia State University, 1989.

Renshaw, Patrick. *The Wobblies: The Story of Syndicalism in the United States*. Garden City NJ: Doubleday & Co., 1967.

Richmond, Robert W. *Kansas: A Land of Contrasts*. Wheeling IL: Forum Press, 1989.

Riney-Kehrberg, Pamela. "Hard Times–Hungry Years: Failure of the Poor Relief in Southwestern Kansas 1930–1933." *Kansas History* 15, no. 3 (Fall 1992): 154–67.

Roberts, Lawrence E. "Women in Populism, 1888–1892." *Heritage of the Great Plains* 23, no. 3 (Summer 1990): 15–27.

Ryan, James G. *Earl Browder: The Failure of American Communism*. Tuscaloosa: University of Alabama Press, 1997.

Saloutos, Theodore. "The Expansion and Decline of the Nonpartisan League in the Western Middle West, 1917–1921." *Agricultural History* 20, no. 4 (October 1946): 235–52.

Salvatore, Nick. *Eugene V. Debs: Citizen and Socialist*. Urbana: University of Illinois Press, 1982.

Sanders, Elizabeth. *Roots of Reform: Farmers, Workers, and the American State, 1877–1917*. Chicago: University of Chicago Press, 1999.

Schlesinger, Arthur M., Jr. *The Politics of Upheaval, 1935–1936*. Boston: Houghton Mifflin, 1960.

Schruben, Francis W. *Kansas in Turmoil, 1930–1936*. Columbia: University of Missouri Press, 1969.

Schuyler, Michael W. *The Dread of Plenty: Agricultural Relief Activities of the Federal Government in the Middle West, 1933–1939*. Manhattan KS: Sunflower University Press, 1989.

———. "Federal Drought Relief Activities in Kansas, 1934." *Kansas Historical Quarterly* 42, no. 4 (Winter 1976): 403–24.

Sellars, Nigel Anthony. *Oil, Wheat, and Wobblies: The Industrial Workers of the World in Oklahoma, 1905–1930*. Norman: University of Oklahoma Press, 1998.

Shannon, David A. *The Socialist Party of America: A History*. Chicago: Quadrangle Books, 1967.

Shore, Elliott. "Julius Augustus Wayland." In *American National Biography*, edited by John A. Garraty and Mark C. Karnes. New York: Oxford University Press, 1999.

———. *Talkin' Socialism: J. A. Wayland and the Radical Press*. Lawrence: University Press of Kansas, 1988.

Sterling, David L. "The Federal Government v. the Appeal to Reason." *Kansas History* 9, no. 1 (Spring 1986): 31–42.

Stevens, Errol Wayne. "Labor and Socialism in an Indiana Mill Town, 1905–1921." *Labor History* 26, no. 3 (Summer 1985): 353–83.

———. "Main Street Socialism: The Socialist Party of America in Marion, Indiana, 1900–1921." In *Socialism in the Heartland*, edited by Donald T. Critchlow. University of Notre Dame Press, 1986.

———. "The Socialist Party of America in Municipal Politics: Canton, Illinois, 1911–1920." *Journal of the Illinois State Historical Society* 72, no. 4 (November 1979): 257–72.

Svobida, Lawrence. *Farming in the Dust Bowl: A First-Hand Account from Kansas*. Lawrence: University Press of Kansas, 1986.

Thiessen, Duane D. "Henry Laurens Call's Aviation Attempts in Girard, Kansas." *Library Bulletin*, Kansas State College of Pittsburg, 8, nos. 3–4 (Spring–Summer 1974): 1–5.

Townsend, John Clendenin. *Running the Gauntlet: Cultural Sources of Violence against the IWW*. New York: Garland, 1986.

Tucker, William P. "Populism Up-to-Date: The Story of the Farmers' Union." *Agricultural History* 21, no. 4 (October 1947): 198–208.

Tyler, Robert L. *Rebels of the Woods: The IWW in the Pacific Northwest*. Eugene: University of Oregon Press, 1967.

Vincent, Frank. "History of Salt Discovery and Production in Kansas, 1887–1915." In *Collections of the Kansas State Historical Society, 1915–1918*, edited by William E. Connelley. Topeka: Kansas State Printing Plant, 1918.

Vincent, Stillman P. *A History of Organized Labor in Kansas*. Topeka: Kansas Federation of Labor, March 30, 1951. Copy in Kansas State Historical Society, Topeka.

Vining, Stanley A. "Men and Coal in Kansas: Their History and Politics." Master's thesis, University of Kansas, 1957.

Walsh, Frank P., and Basil Maxwell Manly. *Industrial Relations: Final Report and Testimony, Submitted to Congress by the Commission on Industrial Relations*. Washington DC: GPO, 1912.

Warren, Frank A. *An Alternative Vision: The Socialist Party in the 1930s*. Bloomington: Indiana University Press, 1974.

Weisgerber, Virginia E. "The Kansas Spellbinders in the Populist Party Campaign of 1890." Master's thesis, University of Wisconsin, 1942.

West, William Lemore. "The Moses Harman Story." *Kansas History* 37, no. 1 (Spring 1971): 41–63.

White, Earl Bruce. "The Wichita Indictments and Trial of the Industrial Workers of the World, 1917–1919, and the Aftermath." PhD diss., University of Colorado, 1980.

Whitehead, Fred. "The Kansas Response to the Haymarket Affair." *Kansas History* 9, no. 2 (Summer 1986): 72–82.

Winters, Donald E., Jr. *The Soul of the Wobblies: The I.W.W., Religion, and American Culture in the Progressive Era, 1905–1917.* Westport CT: Greenwood Press, 1985.

Wood-Simons, May. "Mining Coal and Maiming Men." *Coming Nation*, November 11, 1911.

INDEX